STRATEGIC DIMENSIONS OF ECONOMIC BEHAVIOR

Foreign Policy Issues
A Foreign Policy Research Institute Series

Series Editor
NILS H. WESSELL

STRATEGIC DIMENSIONS OF ECONOMIC BEHAVIOR

Edited by

Gordon H. McCormick and
Richard E. Bissell

PRAEGER

PRAEGER SPECIAL STUDIES • PRAEGER SCIENTIFIC

New York • Philadelphia • Eastbourne, UK
Toronto • Hong Kong • Tokyo • Sydney

Library of Congress Cataloging in Publication Data
Main entry under title:

Strategic dimensions of economic behavior.

(Foreign policy issues)
Includes index.
1. War—Economic aspects—Addresses, essays, lectures.
2. International economic relations—Addresses, essays, lectures. I. McCormick, Gordon H. II. Bissell, Richard E. III. Series.
HC79.D4S77 1984 337 84-13292
ISBN 0-03-070548-7 (alk. paper)

Published in 1984 by Praeger Publishers
CBS Educational and Professional Publishing
a Division of CBS Inc.
521 Fifth Avenue, New York, NY 10175 USA

456789 052 987654321

Printed in the United States of America
on acid-free paper

Foreword

This volume is another in the Foreign Policy Research Institute's book series, *Foreign Policy Issues*. Established in cooperation with Praeger Publishers, the series includes both collectively and individually authored works on contemporary international affairs. The series provides a publications outlet for work by the staff of the Foreign Policy Research Institute and by other authors in the academic and policy communities.

In this collective work, the authors examine a wide range of subjects that have long been neglected in this country by the excessively compartmentalized communities of strategists and economists, who, as the editors point out, only infrequently talk to each other.

As several of the volume's authors observe, the history of nations using economic instruments to project power abroad has been one chiefly of failure. The United States in recent years has been particularly tempted to resort to economic sanctions as a substitute for political and military measures seen as either unfeasible or unable to sustain popular support. But top leaders here and abroad tend not to understand fully the interaction of economic and political factors in foreign policy. Moreover, as Klaus Knorr observes, in modern governments "political and economic expertise tend to be dispersed over separate bureaucracies" without any integrative mechanism. Staff are trained along narrow disciplinary lines without the multidisciplinary background needed to offer policy-making generalists the analytic insights without which policy will founder. Perhaps the strongest justification for production of this volume is Knorr's conclusion that the "performance of statecraft in attempts at using things of economic value for projecting international power will not improve unless these weaknesses are remedied."

The following chapters were originally prepared as papers for delivery to the conference on Strategic Dimensions of Economic Behavior, sponsored by the Foreign Policy Research Institute in Washington, D.C., in February 1982. Messrs. McCormick and Bissell conceptualized the project, and Mr. McCormick stimulated the extensive revisions to many of the original manuscripts, rendering them more timely, and complementary. Elizabeth D. Dunlap capably oversaw production of the resulting volume.

Nils H. Wessell
Series Editor
Foreign Policy Issues
A Foreign Policy Research Institute Series

Preface

Since the end of World War II, the economies of the advanced industrialized world have come to experience an unparalleled degree of economic interdependence. While the benefits of economic interpenetration have been widely discussed, many of its attendant problems are only now being recognized. Most importantly for our purposes here, growing economic integration and the associated loss of national control over domestic economic activity lend an important strategic dimension to foreign economic relations. To the degree that the economic well-being of a state is in the hands of foreign powers, its security position can be jeopardized. Alternatively, the security of a state is enhanced to the degree it controls economic forces in other countries while maintaining control over its own economic future. Although the strategic application of economic power has occurred infrequently in the postwar period, as interpenetration advances, attempts to use economic ties in this manner will undoubtedly increase.

Despite the growing importance of economic factors to U.S. national security, our understanding of the strategic dimensions of economic behavior remains limited. The subject has been clearly neglected in the fields of both economics and strategic studies. With certain notable exceptions, economists have tended to be professionally uninterested in national security questions. When they have contributed to the field of security studies their work has usually been quite narrowly defined, focusing on such issues as procurement, budgeting questions, or comparative defense spending. There have been few attempts among economists to examine the larger relationship between economic, political, and military power. While sensitive to the strategic importance of economic behavior, the defense community has also failed to explore this subject in the detail it requires. The field of strategic studies is dominated by individuals whose primary academic background is in the areas of political science and regional affairs. More often than not, they have come to the field with little or no formal training in economics. The result is a dearth of analysis on strategic-economic issues.

The present volume has brought together an interdisciplinary group of scholars to explore some important strategic dimensions of economic behavior. In recognition of the fact that this issue is not new to the late twentieth century, the first set of papers examines some of the ways in which nations have historically exploited economic variables in peace and war. This is followed by a second set of papers focusing on how national economic requirements and organization affect the vulnerability of modern economies, and constrain the degree to which economic factors can be manipulated for strategic purposes. The third set of papers explores the various ways in which economic factors, in combination with other instruments of national power, might be usefully employed for military and political ends.

January 1984
Philadelphia, Pennsylvania

Contents

I

The Tradition of Strategy and Economics

1

Strategic Considerations in the Development of Economic Thought

Gordon H. McCormick

Concern for the relationship between strategy and economic behavior can be traced to the earliest development of economics as a separate field of inquiry during the late sixteenth century. Although speculations on the nature of economic activity were certainly evident long before this time, such inquiries were infrequent, unsystematic, and, more often than not, subordinate to questions of ethics, philosophy, or political theory. Even within the advanced economies of the ancient world, independent, analytical investigation into the character of economic life was conspicuous for its absence. The Assyrians, Hittites, Egyptians, and Chinese provided us with some of the earliest examples of planned economies, based on autocratic-administrative systems of control, monetary institutions, and a primitive system of banking and credit. Nowhere in the evidence that has survived these civilizations, however, is there any indication of serious economic inquiry. The same can be said for the Greco-Roman world which, despite major contributions in such fields as mathematics, astronomy, mechanics, and law, never rose above the rudimentary study of economic behavior. This trend continued through the period of the Middle Ages where, in the West, the dominance of scholasticism and the localized character of economic activity served as major barriers to the exploration of economic processes.

It was not until the late Renaissance that economic inquiry began in earnest. As this occurred, it is evident that the first concerns of early economic thinkers were as much strategical as they were economical in nature. With the decline of the manorial system, and the gradual development of interregional and international commerce, the stage had been set for the rise of economics as a separate discipline. With the consolidation of state power under the monarchy, and the subsequent need for large standing military forces, it was equally certain that these initial investigations into the nature of economic life would be pursued not first for the purpose of advancing humanity's knowledge of its environment, or even for the purpose of bettering its condition, but for the object of enhancing the position of the state, and discovering the means to finance its defense and further expansion.

These views were first evident in mercantilist economic writings, which constitute the first important stage in the development of modern economic thought. The second phase of development began in reaction to mercantilist concepts and is manifest in the early writings of the physiocrats and the development of economic liberalism. Liberalism, in turn, elicited its own reaction which developed in response to its attempt to depoliticize economic theory, and led to a revival of economic protectionism in the late nineteenth century.

MERCANTILISM, POWER POLITICS, AND THE STATE

Eli Heckscher once observed that "mercantilism never existed in the sense that Colbert and Cromwell existed."[1] Mercantilism was never more than a loose collection of concepts concerning the nature and purpose of economic activity. The mercantilists had neither an agreed set of principles nor a common analytical method. It has even been argued that mercantilism as a school of thought did not actually exist until Adam Smith, in reaction to its methods, defined it as such in *The Wealth of Nations*. However, while it is true that mercantilist writings between the late sixteenth and middle eighteenth centuries may not be classified as a disciplined school of opinion, they did share certain clear doctrinal similarities which allow us to approach these writings as a separate and distinct body of economic thought. Principal among these are mercantilist views on the purpose of economic activity and the proper relationship between the national economy and the state.

Mercantilist economic theory forwarded two primary objectives: one, the political and commercial unification of the state and, two, the maximization of external state power. Mercantilism as a system of unification was best explained by Gustav Schmoller in his work *The Mercantile System and its Historical Significance*, first published in 1884. Schmoller wrote that mercantilism at its very core was nothing other than *Staatsbildung*—not state building in the narrow sense, but in the sense of the simultaneous formation of the state and the national political economy into a unified whole. What was at stake was "the creation of real *political* economies." This could only be achieved by "the total reorganization of society as well as of the state and its institutions, by substituting for the local and provincial economic policy that of the state and the nation." For Schmoller, as for earlier mercantilist writers concerned with the problem of economic unity, the larger object of this policy was not first to eliminate the natural inefficiencies of intranational barriers to economic exchange, but to realize the social and political benefits associated with the consolidation of the economy and the state.[2]

The second and more important objective of mercantilist policy was to support and enhance the power of the state through economic means. While economic unification was perhaps the necessary condition for achieving this goal, the essence of mercantilism was statecraft. The governing objective of economic activity was to advance the military and political position of the state in relation to other powers. This concept found it fullest expression under the pure *Staatsmerkantilismus* of early Prussia and France where the economic policies of the monarchy were generally uncorrupted by the private interests of the commercial classes. In England, for example, where by the late eighteenth and early nineteenth centuries the influence of the private sector was much stronger than on the continent, we see a greater concern for the welfare implications of mercantilist economic activity; the power of the state was not the only objective worthy of being pursued through mercantilist methods. Even here, however, the early priorities had been clear ones. Where individual economic interests came into conflict with the concerns of statecraft, they tended to give way to the good of the nation. As noted by the English economic historian, William Cunningham, "the politicians of the sixteenth, seventeenth, and greater part of the eighteenth centuries were agreed in trying to regulate all commerce and industry, so that the power of England relating to other nations might be promoted.... On every hand private tastes and personal convenience had to give way to the patriotic duty of strengthening the nation."[3]

The question of "power vs. plenty" has long been a source of controversy among modern interpreters of mercantile theory. Jacob Viner, in response to Heckscher's apparent exaggeration of the power factor in mercantilist writing, argued that economic advancement was as much a goal of this body of thought as was the advancement of the state. It was not always evident to Viner that state power was the sole, or even always the primary, objective of mercantilist policy.[4] Even considering these objections, however, it seems difficult to argue that, as a general rule, "national position" was not the driving force behind the development and execution of mercantilist policies at the state level. The question is one of priorities. While economic strength was an essential determinant of state power, and was thus actively sought as an important *intermediate* objective, it was seldom an end in itself. For the clear majority of mercantilist countries, national wealth was rather a means to the end of state power. While admitting that both power and opulence "have been, and must be, of importance to economic policy of every description," Heckscher illustrated this difference in priorities by pointing out "that these two aims changed places in the transition of mercantilism to *laissez-faire*. All countries in the nineteenth century made the creation of wealth their lode-star, with small regard to its effect upon the power of the State, while the opposite had been the case previously."[5]

In the end, however, it is important that we do not carry the distinction between wealth and power too far. In the view of most mercantilist writers the two were inextricably bound. As noted earlier, with the consolidation of the state and the development of national armies, economic considerations became increasingly important in determining a government's ability to finance a standing military force. Without a constant source of bullion, the costs of maintaining a standing army or navy, and, in the case of the maritime empires in particular, of frequently employing these forces in the numerous foreign campaigns of the mercantile era, would have quickly outrun the ability of the government to support it. At the same time, military power was also a means of securing national wealth. As Viner admits, "colonial and other overseas markets, the fisheries, the carrying trade, the slave trade, and open trade routes over the high seas, were all regarded, and rightly so, as important sources of national wealth." These assets were only available, however, "to countries with the ability to acquire or retain them by means of the possession and readiness to use military strength." In the absence of such strength, a nation's overseas economic interests would soon fall prey to those of its political rivals. This dual emphasis on wealth and power is pervasive throughout mercantilist writings, and is continually reflected in the economic policies of the great mercantilist states.[6]

The clearest expression of the interrelationship between economic power and the power of the state in mercantilist theory remains Schmoller's discussion of the concept of unified political economy. As Schmoller's writings exemplify, ideally there was to be no separation between the national economy and the nation-state. The two were to operate "hand in hand" as a "unified organism" bringing the goals of wealth and power into harmony. This policy implied the integration of the economic, foreign, and military instruments of national power in a manner not always immediately apparent to modern commentators. The pure mercantilist system sought to establish a "national agriculture, national industry, national shipping and fisheries, a national currency and banking system, a national division of labour, and a national trade." The domestic economy would ideally be mobilized under state control, becoming a *political* economy in the fullest sense of the term. As a practical measure this would allow the state to channel "economic activity directly towards the particular ends demanded by political, and more especially military, power," as well as create "a reservoir of economic resources generally, from which the policy of power could draw what it required." By the same token, the "nationalization" of economic activity would also permit the state to better employ military and political measures in support of commercial ends. Together these measures would work to maximize the external position of the mercantilist state.[7]

Mercantilist writers quite accurately observed that power is a relational rather than an objective phenomenon. The object of mercantilism was not to enhance the power of the state per se, but to maximize the nation's position in relation to other states. It was not enough that the state be strong, it sought dominance, which meant that it must be powerful over its military and political competitors. This view was clearly expressed by the German mercantilist von Hornigk, who observed in 1684 that "whether a nation be today mighty and rich or not depends not on the abundance or security of its power or riches, but principally on whether its neighbors possess more or less than it." With the power of the state defined in terms of its relative position to other international actors, a nation might grow more powerful not only by augmenting its own strength, but by engineering the decline of its adversaries. Either action would serve to enhance its own relative strategic position. Because the power of the nation was thought ultimately to rest on the strength of its economy, this meant in practice that the mercantilist state pursued an aggressive and predatory foreign economic policy, designed not only to reinforce its own economic base, but to undercut the economic and commercial activities of its opponents.

Mercantilist writers took this concept a step further with the view that the world's economic resources were virtually finite, and that the advancement of one's own economic position required, in almost every case, seizure of the economic assets or commercial ties of other states. This notion of the static nature of economic life was rooted in the early scholastic view "that the profit of one man is the damage of another." As Viner points out, this concept was assumed by mercantilist theory, and applied to national and international economic activity at large. While this view is to be found commonly throughout mercantilist literature, Colbert provides us with a particularly good illustration of the perceived natural limits of economic growth in a discussion of the growing English/Dutch rivalry for commercial shipping in 1669. Colbert begins his assessment with the assumption that "the trade of all Europe is carried out in about 20,000 ships of all sizes," and that "this number cannot be increased so long as the populations in all countries and consumption is always equal." Noting that England "seeks primarily to increase her trade," he observes that "this cannot come about execpt either through the discovery of new, hitherto unknown, trade or through the decrease in the number of ships of one or the other nations." In Colbert's view, "the discovery of new trade is very uncertain" and if it were to occur would be an "accident," leading him to conclude "that England cannot increase the scope of employment for the ships of her subjects or increase their number other than by a diminution of those of the Dutch."[8]

This static view of economic activity was clearly evident in mercantilist financial policy. As we have seen, the accumulation of precious metals was considered to be a critical means of reinforcing a nation's economic base and, indirectly, of improving its larger strategic position. As with other economic values, however, the world supply of precious metals was thought to be effectively limited to stocks already held by the international community. States subscribing to this view were thus left with no alternative but to forgo the strategical benefits of expanding their own stocks of bullion, or acquiring, through commerce or war, some portion of the supply of precious metals held by their neighbors. The clearest expression of this view is again provided by Colbert who argued that "as there is only a fixed quantity of silver circulating in the whole of Europe . . . it is not possible to increase [the stock of one country] by 20, 30, or 50 million without at the same time taking the same quantity from neighboring states." In view of the static character of economic activity, the nation capable of increasing its stocks of precious metals could look forward to a twofold adjustment in its relative economic-strategic position. An inflow of bullion would not only contribute to the "power and greatness" of the state by bolstering its own economic base, it would do so also by contributing to the decline of the economic power of its "enemies and ill wishers."[9]

The implications of this view for trade policy were evident. The principal object of commercial intercourse was to augment the monetary stocks of the national treasury. Accordingly, all efforts were geared toward establishing and maintaining a favorable balance of trade. Any difference between exports and imports would be made up with monetary transfers; and by maximizing this differential, the nation with a trade surplus could, in turn, maximize the inflow of precious metals. To achieve this objective, mercantilist states sought to establish a high degree of control over international commerce. Such control manifested itself in a variety of ways, including the extensive use of import barriers such as duty charges, licenses, and quotas, designed to regulate and usually minimize imports, and the widespread use of subsidies and rebates designed to stimulate the volume of exports. Common also were the use of trading companies established under government charter. These organizations consisted of collections of merchants who were encouraged to combine their resources under official sponsorship and engage in long-term commercial ventures overseas. Examples of such organizations included the Dutch and British East India Companies, the Hudson Bay Company, and John Law's ill-fated South Seas Company. In each case, the trading company served as an extension of the domestic economy, and sought to aid in the accumulation of precious metals. By concentrating the state's international commercial activity, the trading company also served as an effective instrument of trade regulation.

PHYSIOCRACY, ECONOMIC LIBERALISM, AND THE DECLINE OF NATIONAL ECONOMICS

Well before the end of the mercantile era, a reaction had already begun against mercantilist policies. This reaction began as a move away from excessive government control over economic life, toward the liberalization of domestic and foreign economic activity. The earliest evidence of this was to be found in

France, where little had been gained by the aggressive commercial policies of the *ancien régime*. By the time of the war of the Grand Alliance and the following war of the Spanish Succession, the policies of Colbert and Louis XIV were "turning impoverishment into nationwide misery." Two of the earliest writers associated with this reaction were Pierre Boisguillert and Sebastien de Vauban, the latter being best known for his work on military fortifications. The primary concern of each of these writers was the numerous "obstructions to prosperity" which had been imposed as wartime measures over the French economy, and which they perceived as standing in the way of economic recovery. For both Boisguillert and Vauban, national wealth would only come with the elimination of all barriers to commerce, such as quotas, custom duties, excessive taxation, or guilds, which interrupted the "natural harmony" of economic life. In sharp contrast to prevailing mercantile views, less not more government interference was the key to economic power.[10]

While these views had little impact on prevailing French commercial policy, they contributed to the movement for economic reform through their influence on early physiocratic thought. As with the concepts of Boisguillert and Vauban, physiocracy, or literally, the "rule of nature" developed in response to dissatisfaction with the mercantilist policies of the monarchy. Physiocratic thought, which is perhaps most commonly associated with the work of François Quesnay and his disciples, maintained that there was a predetermined or natural harmony inherent in economic life which, if allowed to fulfill itself, would end in national property. The policy prescription associated with this view of economic behavior was simplicity itself. All that was required to achieve natural balance was to refrain from interfering in the economic process. If permitted to evolve naturally, the economic forces at work in society would find their own equilibrium, resulting in maximum social welfare. The physiocrats further distanced themselves from prevailing mercantilist policies by attacking the notion that trade was the primary source of national wealth. For Quesnay and his followers trade was an unproductive activity, for it merely involved the exchange of equal values, whether defined in monetary terms or in terms of real goods. While advocating free trade, the purpose of international commerce in physiocratic thought was not to increase the wealth or relative "position" of the state by expanding its stocks of precious metals, but to acquire a higher quality and selection of goods and services than could otherwise be available to consumers under a system of autarky.[11]

In the end, the views of the physiocrats belonged as much to the realm of philosophy as to economic science. While the work of Quesnay, Rivière, and Baudeau did indeed make a number of important methodological contributions to modern economics, many of the assumptions underlying their analysis, most importantly their views on the natural harmony of economic life, were not established analytically but were considered to be self-evident truths. Nevertheless, the physiocrats stood as the forerunners to the early doctrine of laissez-faire. Their uncompromising hostility to mercantilist policies had led them to the other extreme of advocating a policy of noninterference, which was to become the foundation of nineteenth-century liberal thought.

Economic liberalism was most firmly established in England, where a growing middle class had gradually come to dominate industry and trade. As in France, the English liberal movement was stimulated by dissatisfaction over the restrictive economic policies of mercantilism, which, rather than contributing to the economic advance of the state, were believed to stand as barriers to economic progress. Commonly associated with these views were such diverse individuals as Bernard de Mandeville, Dudley North, Nicoholas Baubon, David Hume, and Adam Smith. While often in sharp disagreement over various other aspects of social and economic policy, these early theorists of laissez-faire were in close agreement over the evils of state involvement in economic life, and the need to liberalize prevailing economic institutions to permit the unfettered progress of commercial forces. In an opinion reminiscent of physiocratic views on "the rule of nature," Adam Smith spoke of an "invisible hand" which operated throughout the economy, and through which individuals pursuing their own economic interests would indirectly serve the commonweal. Smith argued that "no regulation of commerce can increase the quantity of industry in any society beyond what its capital can maintain. It can only divert a part of it into a direction into which it might not otherwise have gone; and it is by no means certain that this artificial direction is likely to be more advantageous to the society than that into which it would have gone of its own accord." Though foreign trade is something which can be profitably pursued, it will prove valuable only if allowed to develop spontaneously, on the basis of the special commercial advantages of participating countries. Any attempt to interfere with this process, according to Smith, would prove to be detrimental to the general welfare.[12]

Smith directed his strongest attack against mercantilist views on the relationship between precious metals and national wealth. According to Smith there was little relationship to be found between the size of the national treasury and the economic power of the state. Economic power was much more a function of the productive capacity of the economy than it was of the government's financial position vis-à-vis its neighbors. A shortage of precious metals would, in the end, cause less disruption in the economy than a shortage of almost any other commodity. The same held true for the relationship between the stock of precious metals and the capacity of the state to go to war. While sympathetic to the need to maintain an active military and naval establishment, it was his view that "fleets and armies are maintained not with gold and silver, but with consumable goods." The government which, "from the annual produce of its domestic industry, from the annual revenue arising out of its lands, labor, and consumable stocks, has the wherewithal to purchase those consumable goods in distant countries, can maintain foreign wars there."

Even the problem of financing foreign military operations could be better handled by forsaking large "war chests" and public debts, for a war tax imposed on the population for the duration of the conflict. In agreement with the earlier views of Malachy Postlethwayt and the later writings of David Ricardo, Smith argued that such a policy could not only prove to be economically attractive, but would have the additional benefit of deterring unnecessary involvement in unwanted conflicts. "The heavy and unavoidable burdens of war would hinder the people from wantonly calling for it when there was no real or solid interest to fight for."[13]

Adam Smith broke with the mercantilists further in disputing the static, or zero-sum character of international trade. For Smith, as for other English liberals, international trade was not a conflictual but a cooperative endeavor, based on the particular economic advantages of participating states. The value of international trade was that it permitted specialization on the basis of absolute labor costs. With trade, nations would concentrate their productive efforts on those commodities they were capable of producing most inexpensively, and exchange these products abroad for goods that were either impossible or expensive to acquire at home. While these views would later be refined by Ricardo's theory of comparative advantage, the underlying principle of commercial exchange remained unchanged. A nation's gains from trade were not to be had by "beggaring its neighbors," but by purchasing commodities abroad at a cheaper rate than might be had domestically. In this respect, although the purpose "of the political economy of every country is to increase the riches and power of that country," it was not true that one nation's gains from trade necessitated the loss by another. While military or political power might be usefully described in relational terms, economic welfare could not. "The wealth of a neighboring nation, however dangerous in war and politics," Smith argued, "is certainly advantageous in trade."[14]

It has been frequently assumed that, in repudiating mercantilist economic doctrine, Adam Smith also rejected the importance of economic factors for the security of the state. In fact, Smith ignored neither the demands of economic power, nor the close relationship between the economic base and national defense. "The first duty of the sovereign," he argued, was "that of protecting the society from the violence and invasion of other independent societies." This could "be performed only by means of military force" and thus necessitated a large standing military presence. The financial and production demands associated with such an establishment, in turn, required a viable economic base of support. "In modern war the great expense of firearms gives an evident advantage to the nation which can best afford this expense and consequently to an opulent and a civilized over a poor and barbarous state."[15]

While in general sympathy with mercantilist views concerning the relationship between economic and military power, disagreement arose over the question of methods. As noted, far from encouraging growth, Smith viewed a policy of commercial restriction to be a major impediment to economic development. If wealth was the prerequisite to power, the position of the state would thus be improved *not* by regulating international economic activity, but by stimulating commercial intercourse by withdrawing artifical restrictions on trade. In Smith's view, the goals of "defense" and "opulence" need not always be in conflict.

Even with regard to methods, Adam Smith recognized the need for selective restrictions on international trade where such measures were clearly required for purposes of national security. It was his view "that the kingdom depend as little as possible upon its neighbors for the manufactures necessary for its defense." With this in mind, he thought it "advantageous to lay some burden upon foreign, for the encouragement of domestic industry, when some particular industry is necessary for the defense of the country." In the event these industries "cannot be maintained at home," he thought it "reasonable that all other branches of industry be taxed in order to support them." A clear example of these views in practice was Smith's position on the navigation acts, which he thought to be "perhaps the wisest of all commercial regulations of England." Smith was fully aware of the degree to which Britain was dependent upon the free use of the seas for both her prosperity and defense. British industry required ready access to materials and markets located abroad, while as an insular nation, England required control of the sea approaches to the British Isles for her continued security. The navigation acts, which were designed to maintain a large merchant marine and a ready supply of trained seamen, both to guarantee trade and for use in the fleet in times of war, thus received his full support. "The defense of Great Britain," he argued, "depends very much upon the number of its sailors and shipping. The act of navigation, therefore, very properly endeavors to give the sailors and shipping of Great Britain the monopoly of trade of their own country.[16]

If, in the interests of national defense, Adam Smith was willing to make exceptions to a policy of free trade, the same cannot always be said for those economists in the English liberal tradition that came after him. In general, the English liberals either did not address the problem of strategic economics or were overtly hostile to the notion that considerations of economic welfare should, under any conditions, be subordinated to the needs of national security. One exception to this rule was Thomas Malthus who, although an ardent free trader, called for regulatory measures to be employed to protect England's agricultural base from foreign competition. His principal argument for instituting such measures was the danger that agricultural dependency might be turned against England in times of war. While noting that it may serve the economic interests of a belligerent to continue to supply Britain with foodstuffs, even under conditions of conflict, agricultural dependency would prove to be a valuable source of political leverage, which a state must be expected to employ even at some economic cost to itself. For strategic reasons then, Malthus argued that England "maintain a more equal balance between the agricultural and commercial classes by restricting the importation of foreign corn, and making agriculture keep pace with manufactures." This would be accomplished by placing a duty on imported cereals in an effort to raise their price and stimulate further domestic production. While commercially inefficient, an agricultural tariff was expected to eliminate an important point of vulnerability in the British economy, and was deemed to be justified on the grounds of national security.[17]

A second exception to this rule was John Stuart Mill. Like Smith and Malthus before him, Mill was sensitive to the possibility that an undisciplined policy of free trade would have a damaging effect on Britain's political future. Although a general advocate of laissez-faire, Mill followed his predecessors in arguing that restrictive economic measures were sometimes required for purposes of national security. As in the case of Smith, his position on this matter is best illustrated by his support for the navigation acts. While expressing some doubt concerning the need to continue the policy of protecting the British merchant trade, Mill was clearly in sympathy with the objectives for which it was originally established. "A country exposed to invasion by sea," he argued, "if it cannot otherwise have sufficient ships and sailors of its own to secure the means of manning in an emergency an adequate fleet, is quite right in obtaining those means, even at an economical sacrifice in point of cheapness of transport." At the time the navigation acts were passed, England was engaged in a major rivalry with the Dutch empire on the high seas. As an established maritime power, the Dutch found if far easier to maintain a large carrying trade, and thereby furnish the experienced seamen necessary to man her fleets than did England, which was in the position of challenging Dutch supremacy. "The Navigation Laws, by which this deficiency was remedied," were thus considered by Mill to be "economically disadvantageous" but nevertheless "expedient" on military and political grounds.[18]

While not in principle opposed to a policy of economic restriction for purposes of state security, Mill was decidedly against the program of agricultural protection forwarded by Malthus. In this he was supported by the liberal opinion of his day, which either did not consider agricultural dependency to be a serious security problem, or which saw in these proposals an invidious attempt to subvert the principles of free trade. Mill fell into the former category, arguing that "it is ridiculous to found a general system of policy on so improbable a danger as that of being at war with all nations of the world at once; or to suppose that, even if inferior at sea, a whole country could be blockaded like a town, or that the growers of food in other countries would not be as anxious not to lose an advantageous market, as we should be not to be deprived of their corn." These views were held similarly by David Ricardo, who found nothing unusual in the notion that belligerents would continue to trade in essential commodities under conditions of war. In an interesting twist of logic, Ricardo argued that the sheer size of the English market for wheat and corn ensured that the trade in foodstuffs would never be manipulated for political purposes. Any nation controlling this market, he argued, could never sever the flow of agricultural commodities without bringing on its own ruin. In the end, however, Ricardo fell into the second category of those who saw every exception to open markets as a threat to the general policy of free trade. Ricardo, like almost every other economist in the liberal tradition, was intolerant of the possibility of ever having to selectively regulate commerce, whether this be for economic or political purposes.[19]

Other outspoken opponents of regulating trade for purposes of national security included John Cairnes, Henry Fawcett, and John MacCulluch. One of the clearest expressions of this view can be found in the writings of MacCulluch, widely recognized in his day as a popularizer of Ricardo, if not as a seminal thinker in his own right. Building on Ricardo, MacCulluch devoted close attention to what he believed to be the indisputable benefits of free trade, and the economic and political costs associated with policies of commercial restriction. While certainly mindful of the need for a strong defense, nothing in his view justified interfering with the natural process of the market. National independence and strength, he argued, rested on far more than "the miserable machinery of custom-house regulations. . . . The possession of wealth was the best security; and as the freedom of commerce is, of all others, the most efficacious means of increasing wealth," it followed in his view that "those who are exerting themselves to give every facility to commerce, are, at the same time, exerting themselves in the most effectual manner to add to the power and independence of the country."[20]

MacCulluch directed his strongest attack against those who sought independence through autarky. Only the state that "should prefer poverty and barbarism to wealth and refinement," he argued, could afford to withdraw from the international marketplace. "To be truly independent," which in his view was "to have the greatest command of necessaries and conveniences, a nation must avail itself of the productive energies of every other people, and deal with all the world on [i.e. on the basis of] fair and liberal principles." For a state to desire "to be wholly unconnected with foreigners, and at the same time to continue as rich and prosperous as ever," was to desire something that "is contradictory and inconsistent with the nature of things." Given the close relationship between economic power and political position, MacCulluch concluded that those who in the name of national security defended a restrictive foreign economic policy were, without knowing it, "laboring to sap the foundations of (national) power, and to cast Great Britain down from its "high place amongst the nations of the earth."[21]

Building on the tradition of the physiocrats, the principles of liberal economics also found expression among a large number of French writers. Prominent among these were Jean-Baptiste Say, Frédéric Bastiat, Michel Chevalier, Frédéric Passy, and Gustave de Molinari. As their English contemporaries, the economists of the French liberal school spoke out actively against those who sought to impose restrictions on economic activities for purposes of national security. Such restrictions were not only viewed as counterproductive, but were themselves considered to be an important source of international conflict. If nations, Say argued, had not been "obsessed with trade balances and with the opinion that a state cannot prosper except at the detriment of another, one would have avoided fifty years of war in the course of the last two centuries." The establishment of a restrictive economic regime can only end in "rendering the evil which one claims to guard against, more imminent." Free trade, was, by contrast, thought to be a means bringing nations closer together. "By showing that the interests of men and nations are not opposed to one another, the theory of markets will necessarily scatter seeds of concord and peace, which will germinate as time goes on." This, in the view of the more optimistic, "would not be one of the least blessings of the truer opinion that will have been formed on the economy of societies."[22]

THE REVIVAL OF ECONOMIC PROTECTIONISM

While firmly established in England, liberal economic thought elicited a strong reaction on the continent. This reaction was particularly evident in Germany, where Bismarck declared free trade to be "the weapon of the strongest," clearly advantageous to the established power, but certainly not a recipe for achieving national greatness. In the view of their continental critics, the British empire had risen to a position of international prominence in large measure due to a policy of economic protection. Having gained a high level of control over international commerce, British industry no longer required such protective measures and now was the principal beneficiary of a policy of open markets. This view was clearly articulated by Friedrich List, who argued that "any nation which by means of protective duties and restrictions on navigation has raised her manufacturing power and her navigation to such a degree of development that no other nation can sustain free competition with her, can do nothing wiser than to throw away these ladders of her greatness, to preach to other nations the benefit of free trade, and to declare in pertinent tones that she has hitherto wandered in the paths of error, and has now for the first time succeeded in discovering the truth."[23]

The protectionist or neomercantilist school was based on the writings of such men as Charles Dupont-White, Charles Dupin, and Gottlieb Fichte. It was the view of these and other protectionists that *national* economies must evolve independently along their own individual paths to development. The economy of every country was believed to be subject to its own social, political, and commercial forces which, if allowed to evolve without foreign interference, would permit economic growth to proceed in a manner most suitable to the needs of the state. To achieve this goal, neomercantilism sought to impose restrictions on international commerce in an effort to discourage trade and turn the forces of economic activity inward. The basis of this policy lay with the notion that economies, like nations, required their own natural frontiers. Certain geographic areas were considered to be natural and even predestined political-economic units. Every state must expand to the limits of its natural frontiers if it was to realize its full political and economic potential. This concept was clearly expressed in the writings of Fichte, who in his study *The Closed Commercial State* argued that "one must not only think of frontiers militarily well covered and solid, but far more still, of a certain productive autonomy or self-sufficiency." According to Fichte, a primary goal of the government must be to guide the expansion of the economy, and by extension the state, to its natural limits. Having realized this goal, the nation would no longer require economic contact with the outside world, and would complete its turn inward by becoming a "closed" or autarkic economic unit.[24]

These views on the utility of economic independence and the need for a protective commercial policy were also reflected in the writings of such American neomercantilists as Raymond Duncan, Simon Patten, and Alexander Hamilton. For American protectionists, as for their colleagues on the continent, the overriding objective of restrictions on commerce was to enhance the international position of the state through economic means. According to Patten, for example, economic power would allow the United States "to exert a commanding influence upon the development of other nations." Similarly, Hamilton observed that through purposeful economic development, the United States "may hope, ere long, to become the arbiter of Europe in America, and to be able to incline the balance of power in this part of the world as our interests may dictate." It was argued that if the nation was to achieve this position, it must guard against the economic encroachment of other powers. This, it was believed, could only be achieved through a policy of economic protection, designed to allow the country to establish a diversified and independent industrial base. "Every nation," wrote Hamilton, "ought to endeavor to possess within itself all the essentials of national supply," comprising the means of "subsistence, habitation, clothing and defence." Self-sufficiency in these areas was considered to be "necessary to the perfection of the body politic (and) to the safety as well as to the welfare of the society." Any failure to achieve this position would mean "the want of an important organ of political life and motion; and in the various crises that await a state, it must surely feel the effects of any such deficiency."[25]

In principle, Alexander Hamilton was a proponent of free trade. Like Friedrich List years later, Hamilton viewed the policy of commerical protection to be a stage in the economic evolution of a developing nation. This stage was required, however, by the aggressive economic policies of established powers. As Hamilton argued in his *Report on Manufacturers* written in 1791, "if a system of industrial and commercial liberty had governed the conduct of nations more generally than it has done, there is room to suppose that it might have carried them faster to prosperity and greatness than they have attained by the pursuit of maxims too widely opposite." Despite the potential advantages of open markets, however, the established economies had consciously abandoned the principles of free trade "to the vain project of selling everything and buying nothing." In view of this fact, Hamilton argued that economic competition upon equal terms was not yet practical for the United States, and that it was therefore necessary to shield the young economy through its initial period of development. This was particularly important in the case of manufactures, which Hamilton thought to be critical for ensuring that America remain "independent of foreign nations for military and other essential supplies." The "independence and security of a country," he wrote, "appear to be materially connected with the prosperity of manufactures." With this in mind, Hamilton advocated the protection and selective "nationalization" of defense-related industries, considering it to be improvident to leave "these essential implements of national defense to the casual speculations of individual adventure."[26]

As with classical mercantilist doctrine, Hamilton sought to achieve his objective of industrial and political independence through economic unification. Hamilton observed that an economy as structurally diverse as that of the United States, need never be dependent for critical resources or commodities on outside sources of supply. National autonomy could be achieved by the close integration of each regional sector of the economy into a single, self-contained economic unit. "Where every part finds a particular interest in the Union, all parts of our Country will find greater independence" from the economic and political intrigues of other states. Beyond its commercial and political benefits, Hamilton argued that a concerted policy of national economic integration would also have certain direct military advantages. These he found to be particularly evident in the area of naval shipbuilding. In contrast to even the British, who throughout the age of sail remained critically dependent on North American and Baltic timber, the United States possessed a sufficiently broad resource base to support all the requirements of an indigenous shipbuilding industry. "The more southern states," Hamilton wrote, "furnish in greater abundance certain kinds of naval stores—tar, pitch, and turpentine. Their wood for the construction of ships is also of a more solid and lasting texture." At the same time, "some of the southern and middle states yield a greater plenty of iron ore, and of better quality." Because of its already large carrying trade, the seamen to man a fleet might "chiefly be drawn from the northern hive." In conclusion, Hamilton observed "that different portions of confederated America possess each some peculiar advantage" which if combined in a program of naval construction, would produce a fleet capable of defying "the little arts of the little politicians to control or vary the irresistible and unchangeable course of nature."[27]

Building on such views as those of Fichte and Hamilton, in 1841 Friedrich List published his *National System of Political Economy*, a study destined to become one of the most influential works of the neomercantilist school. As Fichte and Hamilton before him, List advanced the established view that each nation-state must pursue its own individual course of economic development, and that during the initial stages of the development process, would require the economic support provided by a system of commercial and industrial protection. In pursuing this argument, List makes a clear distinction between the "economy of nations" and the "political economy" of the state. Where the former seeks to discover "how the entire human race might attain prosperity," the latter "limits its teaching to the inquiry of how a given nation can obtain prosperity, civilization and power, by means of agriculture, industry and commerce." While not without merit in principle, List argued that the cosmopolitan or liberal approach to economic behavior is, as yet, an impractical ideal, because it fails to account for the nature of nationality and the existence of the state. In ignoring these factors, it effectively "assumes the existence of a universal union and a state of perpetual peace, and deduces therefrom the great benefits of free trade."[28]

Given the character of interstate relations, the nation has no alternative but to pursue a policy of political economy. The object of this policy "is not only wealth as in individual and cosmopolitical economy, but power and wealth, because national wealth is increased and secured by national power." The political economy of power and wealth is founded on a policy of economic protection, combining regulatory and military measures. The government, List argued, must bear the responsibility of promoting "every thing which may increase the wealth and power of the nation if this object cannot be effected by individuals." In this regard, "it is its duty to guard commerce by a navy, because the merchants cannot protect themselves; so it is its duty to protect the carrying trade by navigation laws, because the carrying trade supports naval power, as naval power protects the carrying trade; so the shipping interest and commerce must be supported by breakwaters—agriculture and every other industry by turnpike, bridges, canals and railroads—[and] new inventions by patent laws." In short, government must involve itself in every aspect of national economic development. In turn, economic growth will support the state, and appreciably enhance its position in international affairs.[29]

The immediate goal of economic protection is to expand the "productive powers" of the state. National wealth, and by extension national power, is not considered by List to be a function of the nation's store of exchangeable value, but of the national capacity to produce the goods required for internal consumption and international exchange. "The power to create wealth is . . . infinitely more important than wealth itself [for] it ensures not only the possession and the increase of what has been gained, but also the replacement of what has been lost." In pursuing this goal the state must seek to strike a balance between the industrial and agricultural sectors of the economy. "Just as power secures wealth, and wealth increases power, so are power and wealth, in equal parts, benefited by a harmonious state of agriculture, commerce and manufacturers. . . . Nothing contributes more strenuously to defense," List wrote, "than an evenly developed and equally vigorous agricultural and industrial force combined within the state."[30] In the absence of such a balance, the national economy would remain dependent on imports for essential products, and would always be vulnerable to having these imports severed in wartime. In view of the close relationship between wealth and power, this would not only be disruptive economically, it could also serve to threaten the political and military position of the state.

For Germany, the problem of balance was not agricultural but industrial. Although Germany possessed a well developed agricultural base, the productive capacity of German industry remained quite limited. Thus, like Hamilton, List argued that a policy of economic protection give particular attention to encouraging the growth of manufactures. A viable manufacturing sector would be directly beneficial to the economy by relieving it of the burden of industrial imports, and indirectly valuable by naturally complementing German agriculture and stimulating the construction of a supporting infrastructure of railroads and canals. In the end, however, the principal benefits of industrialization were strategical. "War or the very possibility of war," wrote List, "makes the establishment of a manufacturing power an indispensable requirement for any nation of first rank. . . . At a time when technical and mechanical science exerts such an immense influence on the methods of warfare (and) when all warlike operations depend so much on the condition of national revenue . . . at such a time, more than ever before, the value of manufactures must be estimated from a political point of view." The nation possessing a developed industrial base would, in turn, possess the means of building a modern army and navy capable of matching those of any established power. Without such a capacity, Germany would remain forever subject to the superior military power of other states.[31]

In the end, List saw the economics of protection to be only a stage on the way to a global policy of open markets. Unlike Fichte, who believed the "closed commercial state" to be the high point of economic development, List appreciated the economic benefits theoretically associated with free trade, and looked forward to the day when a *cosmopolitical* economy might develop. That day, however, was thought to be a long way off. The "previous progress made by other nations, foreign tariff systems, and war," List argued, "have compelled less advanced nations to look to themselves for the means of effecting a transition from the agricultural to the manufacturing stage." The developing state which failed to employ a system of economic restrictions in an effort to achieve this transfer, would never succeed in uplifting itself in the community of nations. Protective economics can be traced either to the effort "to obtain prosperity, independence, and power, or in consequence of wars and of the hostile trade policies" of the established manufacturing states. A policy of economic restriction is thus not "an invention of speculative minds" but rather is the natural consequence of a diversity of interests between nation-states. This system will cease, List argued "with the cessation of this conflict of national interests" and "the union of all nations under one and the same system of law."[32]

Similar views on the value of a protective foreign economic policy were advanced by the German Historical School, which arose during the late 19th century in response to the increasing abstraction of economic analysis. While economics, even as practiced by the English liberals, was not the ahistorical field of inquiry it was later to become, no group of economic thinkers had yet "deliberately sought in history and observation a means of reconstructing political economy as a whole." According to proponents of this school, investigations into the nature of economic life could not be usefully divorced from the social and political context of economic development. Economies, as nation states, were the products of a unique series of historical circumstances. The analysis of economic activity must consequently attempt to capture the color and spirit of the times, and should not proceed from the assumption that it is possible to reduce economic analysis to a common set of behavioral principles. As noted by Bruno Hildebrand, one of the founders of the historical school, "One should not forget that man as a social being is always a child of civilization and a product of history, and his needs, his education, and his relations to both material goods and to men never remain the same but differ geographically and constantly change historically, advancing with the entire culture of the human species."[33]

While practiced throughout the continent and in Great Britain, the historical method proved to be particularly important in Germany, where yielding to "either temptation or the call of duty," it became closely involved in nationalist politics.[34] While its nationalist overtones moved it out of the mainstream of economic theory, the German historical school nevertheless stands out as an important chapter in the history of strategic-economic thought. There was general agreement among the German historians concerning the need for close state control over the direction of national economic activity. As List had argued, the economic policy of the state must be a specifically national policy, tailored to the peculiar conditions and requirements of national economic and political life. Though historical economics did not arise with the expressed purpose of examining the economic basis of state power, it is not surprising that individual proponents of the historical method, most notably Rosher, von Stein, Schaffle, and Schmoller, gave close attention to the relationship between strategy and economics, and the manner in which Germany might improve its position in the international system through economic means.[35]

A recurring theme throughout the writings of the historical school was the problem of war. War according to most of these writers was a pervasive, if sometimes necessary evil. While recognizing that "a short war was sometimes the basis of a long peace" and was thus not to be condemned, it was generally believed that, even when successful, it could usually be conducted only to the detriment of the national economy. Even when initiated for economic reasons, the material benefits of conquest would seldom outweigh the economic costs that must inevitably be incurred. War, however, was recognized to be an aspect of the human condition. Nothing as a consequence could be more illusory than the promise of lasting social peace.

While impossible to avoid, war might be forestalled by the deterrent of a standing military presence. In distinction to such individuals as Say, Bastiat, Arnd, and Rotteck who argued that the creation of a national militia was a militarily suitable, and financially wiser alternative to a standing army, the members of the German historical school were united in their belief that the security of the state could only be had at the price of building and maintaining a professional military establishment. Any other course of action was subject to false economies and could serve only to invite a conflict that might otherwise be avoided. The time had passed when a nation might safely begin preparing for war with the advent of hostilities. The increasing industrialization of warfare, and the attendant lead times associated with equipping a modern military force, demanded that preparations for war be conducted on a continuing basis, long before the first shot was fired.

Not only might a state hope to forestall the advent of war by means of a large standing army, but the development and maintenance of a standing force was thought to carry with it a number of social and economic benefits. If carried on in a sensible manner, the preparation for war, as distinct from the actual conduct of war, was thought to be a productive enterprise, instilling in the nation the discipline and skills required for further economic advance. Quoting the elder Moltke, Wilhelm Rosher argued that war "fosters the nobelest virtues of man: courage and self-denial, obedience to duty and the spirit of sacrifice;" virtues essential to national greatness.[36] This view was shared by Gustav Schmoller, who considered a "military spirit" to be a prerequisite to national development. According to Schmoller, the individualism that is characteristic of a nonmilitant society "dissolves and weakens the state and permits its citizens to decay in their egoism." The individual in such a society exists to satisfy his own needs, rather than the needs of the state. If national development is to proceed, the state must be capable of harnessing the spirit of its citizens. The army in Schmoller's view is an ideal mechanism for doing this, imbuing the population with the direction and unity of purpose required for social and economic progress.[37]

The strategic and political views of the German historical school were held by few practitioners of the historical method outside of Germany. Among such non-German historical economists as Levasseur, Rogers, Leslie, and Laveleye, war as well as the preparation for war were socially and economically destructive and could not be justified. Nothing, according to Laveleye, was "more distressing and more calculated to confound reason" than the contrast between what he perceived to be the "advance of international solidarity and the revival of bellicose ideas."[38] An important manifestation of this revival was thought to be the renewed interest being shown in protectionist economic policies. Such policies, it was argued, were both economically detrimental and politically destabilizing. As evolutionists, uninspired by the "fever of nationalism," most historical economists outside of Germany believed "universal peace" to be an achievable goal. War, in their view, was becoming more and more disastrous, and nations it was argued, must finally understand "that it is to their advantage to avoid them by submitting to certain rules of law and equity." "The unity of the species" was the design of providence, and free trade, which was thought to be a means of achieving this unity, was a "providential act."[39]

CONCLUSIONS

In a forum as brief as this one it has not been possible to examine closely even the most important movements in the development of strategic-economic thought. The subject is well developed in the annals of economic theory, much more so than is commonly assumed. In addressing the subject, I have attempted to provide an overview of the most prominent personalities and ideas on the subject during the formative years of economics as a discipline of study. Throughout, I have focused on mainstream theorists, or in the case of some of the later protectionists, individuals who in their writings set out to examine directly the relationship between economics, strategy, and war. Even in this I have had to be selective. A large number of commentators, some of them quite important to the subject, have either been given only passing reference or have been left unmentioned.

Despite the brevity of this overview, it is clear that the problems of war and peace were widely discussed by the classical economists. Indeed as noted at the beginning of this essay, it is not difficult to argue that economics as a field of inquiry owes its existence, in large measure, to the need to better manage the relationship between economic means and strategic ends. This is evident in the writings of the early mercantilists, who dominated economic thinking from the late sixteenth until the middle eighteenth century. Mercantilism was first and foremost a system of power, with the balance of trade having a close relationship to diplomatic position and the balance of military strength. In the mercantilist view, there was a direct link between wealth and power. Each was an essential prerequisite for the other, and both were considered to be the legitimate ends of national policy.

As we have seen, the mercantilist consensus had begun to break down by the end of the eighteenth century. This was due initially to the influence of the physiocrats, and later to the rapid rise of economic liberalism. According to these contending schools of thought, the interests of the state would be best served, not by means of a protective foreign economic policy, but by an officially sanctioned policy of laissez faire. The imputed benefits of such a policy were twofold. First, free trade was economically advantageous. As demonstrated by the theory of absolute and later comparative advantage, international specialization and open commercial exchange could do no other than redound to the interests of each participating economy. Second, free trade was widely believed to be a force for peace. Among members of the French liberal school in particular, international conflict was thought to be the product, not of irreconcilable national interests, but of widespread misunderstanding concerning the benefits of international cooperation. By highlighting the value of collaboration and the costs of discord, free trade would assist in stabilizing interstate relations and reduce the risk of war. Evolution toward an increasingly peaceful international regime would occur gradually but persistently over time.

The principles and policy implications of economic liberalism elicited a strong reaction. This reaction was particularly evident on the continent, where it was argued that unrestrained commercial freedom could be beneficial only to the preponderant economy, and was destructive to the state entering the initial stages of economic unification and development. Free trade was an instrument of the strong against the weak, a thinly veiled attempt on the part of Great Britain to retain its supremacy over the industrializing economies of continental Europe. The "young" economy, it was argued, required the protection of a restrictive economic regime. In the absence of such a policy "there would be in Europe only one manufacturing people. All other nations would depend on it. Their means of exchange would be reduced to the produce of their soil. They would thus lose both their industry and their fleet. They would become subject."

While a policy of economic restriction was seen by many as a temporary expedient, others argued that the aggressive nature of international economic relations required that such measures be instituted on a permanent basis. In sharp contrast to the liberal school, proponents of economic protection tended to view interstate relations in exclusively competitive terms. With the exception of List, who believed in the eventual, if distant, triumph of a cosmopolitical economy, the protectionist school assumed war to be a permanent feature of international life. The inherently conflictual character of international relations made it essential that the beleaguered state move to shield its economy from the control or influence of the enemy. As the mercantilists before them, the later protectionists were sensitive to the close relationship between economic and political power. This relationship could only be defended, in their view, by abandoning any hope of "internationalism" for an economic policy designed to accommodate the specific commercial and political interests of the state.

In the end, the economists of the seventeenth, eighteenth, and nineteenth centuries must be considered within the context of their times. With certain notable exceptions, the ideas and policy recommendations advanced by these writers have either failed to survive our growing understanding of economic behavior, or have simply been overtaken by events. This has been particularly true of the literature on economics and strategy. Changes in the international system and the mechanics of war since the 19th century have ensured that these writings are of greater interest to the historian of economic thought than they are of direct use to the contemporary strategist. There is, nevertheless, a common assumption running through most of these writings that deserves our continuing attention. The issues of economy and war, we are told, are intimately related. While presented as a simple truth, this notion can only come as a revelation to those today who believe that each of these subjects can only be studied profitably in isolation from the other.

NOTES

1. Eli F. Heckscher, *Mercantilism*, translated by Mendel Shapiro, vol. 1, (New York: Macmillen, 1955), p. 21. For an overview of mercantilist thought, see P.W. Buck, *The Politics of Mercantilism* (New York: Holt, 1942) and J.W. Horrocks, *A Short History of Mercantilism* (London: Brentano, 1925).

2. Gustav Schmoller, *The Mercantile System and its Historical Significance* (New York: A.M. Kelley, 1967), p. 50.

3. See William Cunningham, *The Case Against Free Trade*, (London, 1911). See also Jacob Viner, "English Theories of Foreign Trade Before Adam Smith," *Journal of Political Economy*, vol. 37, (1930), 249-301, 404-457.

4. Jacob Viner, "Power versus Plenty as Objectives of Foreign Policy in the Seventeenth and Eighteenth Centuries," *World Politics*, vol. 1, (1948-49).

5. Eli F. Heckscher, "Revisions in Economic History, V. Mercantilism," *The Economic History Review*, vol. 7, 1936, p. 48.

6. Viner, "Power versus Plenty," p. 6. See also Walter E. Minchinton, *Mercantilism: System or Expediency* (New York: D.C. Heath, 1969).

7. Schmoller, *Mercantilism*, pp. 50-78. See also, Edmund Silberner, *La guerre dans la pensée economique du xvi au xviii siecle* (Paris: Recueil Sirey 1939). For an English translation of the preface and conclusions, see the *Annals of Collective Economy*, January-April, 1940, pp. 21-30.

8. Cited in Heckscher, *Mercantilism*, p. 26.

9. Ibid., p. 27.

10. For an elaboration on physiocratic thought, see Joseph A. Schumpeter, *History of Economic Analysis* (New York: Oxford Univ. Press, 1976), pp. 223-243. See also Ronald L. Meek, *The Economics of Physiocracy*, (Cambridge, England: Cambridge Univ. Press, 1963).

11. Physiocratic views on the proper relationship between the economy and the state are discussed in Schumpeter, *History*, p. 229.

12. Andrew S. Skinner, *A System of Social Science: Papers Relating to Adam Smith* (Oxford Univ. Press, 1979).

13. Adam Smith, *An Inquiry into the Nature and Causes of the Wealth of Nations*, (London: G. Bell and Sons, 1908), pp. 398-415, 679. Also interesting is Charles J. Bullock, "Adam Smith's View Upon National Defense," *Military Historian and Economist*, vol. 1 (1917), p. 2.

14. Smith, *Wealth of Nations*, pp. 460-461.

15. Smith, *Wealth of Nations*, p. 693.

16. Smith, *Wealth of Nations*, 430-431.

17. Thomas Robert Malthus, *An Essay on the Principle of Population*, (London: Murray, 1826) p. 191. These views are further developed in his *Observations on the Effects of the Corn Laws*, (London: Johnson, 1814).

18. John Stuart Mill, *Principles of Political Economy*, (New York: D. Appleton, 1929) p. 920.

19. Mill, *Principles*, pp. 920-921. See also "A Few Words on Non-Intervention" in *Dissertations and Discussions* (London, 1867); David Ricardo, *Principles of Political Economy* (London, 1817) and *On Protection to Agriculture* (London, 1822).

20. John Ramsay MacCulluch, *Principles of Political Economy* (London, 1825) pp. 159, 165.

21. Ibid., pp. 160, 165.

22. Jean-Baptiste Say, *Cours complet d'economie politique pratique*, cited in Edmund Silberner, *The Problem of War in Nineteenth Century Economic Thought* (Princeton: Princeton Univ. Press, 1946), p. 83.

23. Friedrich List, *The National System of Political Economy*, cited in Edward Mead Earle "Adam Smith, Alexander Hamilton, Friedrich List: The Economic Foundations of Military Power," Edward Mead Earle (ed.), *Makers of Modern Strategy* (Princeton: Princeton Univ. Press, 1971), p. 124.

24. Gottlieb Fichte, *Der geschlossene Handelsstaat* (Berlin: Brockhans, 1800) p. 480.

25. Simon N. Patten, *The Economic Basis of Protection*, (Philadelphia: R. Welsh & Co., 1890) p. 141. Henry Cabot Lodge (ed.), *Works of Alexander Hamilton*, vol. IV (New York, 1904) p. 135.

26. Hamilton, *Works*, vol. IV, p. 70, 167-168.

27. Alexander Hamilton, *The Federalist*, no. 11 (Washington, 1937). Also recommended is the introduction in this edition by Edward Mead Earle.

28. Friedrich List, *National System of Political Economy* (New York: A.M. Kelley, 1977), pp. 119-132.

29. List, "Outlines of American Political Economy," in his *Werke: Schriften, Reden, Briefe*, vol. II (Berlin: R. Hobbing, 1927-1935), p. 105.

30. List, *National System*, pp. 133-148.

31. List, *National System*, pp. 139, 197-210.

32. List, *National System*, 201-204, and Friedrich List, *Le system naturel d'economie politique*, cited in Silberner, *The Problem of War*, p. 148.

33. For a detailed accounting of the German historical school see Schumpeter, *History*, pp. 807-824. Bruno Hildebrand, *Die Nationalökonomie der Gegenwart und der Zukunft*, vol. 1 (Frankfort: Rütten, 1848).

34. See Schumpeter, *History*, p. 801.

35. See, for example, Lorenz von Stein, *System der Staatswissenschaft* (Stuttgart: J.G. Cotta, 1852), and E.F. Schaeffle, *Das gesellschaftliche System der menschlichen Wirtschaft* (Tübingen: Laupp, 1873).

36. Cited in Silberner, *The Problem of War*, p. 176n.

37. Gustav Schmoller, *Grundriss der allgemeinen Volkswirtschaftslehre* (Leipzig, 1923), p. 1337.

38. Emile Laveleye, *Des causes actuelles de guerre en Europe et de l'arbitrage* (Paris, Baillère, 1873), p. 9.

39. Silberner, *The Problem of War*, p. 186.

2

The Origins and Development of Mobilization Warfare

Martin van Creveld

The purpose of the present paper is to trace, briefly, the rise and development of mobilization warfare from its origins during World War I to its demise—in the West, at any rate—during the years after 1945. The discussion will focus on the divorce of war from industry, economy, and society during the early years of the twentieth century; on the factors that gave birth to mobilization warfare during the First World War; on the various schools of thought that sought to contend with the new phenomenon in the interwar period, and the extent to which they were proved right or wrong by World War II; and, finally, on U.S. and Soviet views concerning the role that economic mobilization plays, or should play, in a world dominated by nuclear arms.

By mobilization warfare, we mean that kind of war which requires the total commitment for war, not merely of a country's armed forces but of its entire socioeconomic infrastructure as well. We do not mean war based on the calling to the colors of a pool of trained manpower—the kind of detailed arrangements that had been perfected by every major power before 1914, and which today allow Israel, for example, to "mobilize" its forces within 48 hours. Mobilization warfare is a system of war based upon the total mobilization of a country's social and economic resources in addition to its purely military ones. Such a system is often referred to under the title "total war", but since this term also carries a variety of other meanings[1] we have decided to avoid its use in the present context.

INDUSTRIALIZATION AND STRATEGY BEFORE THE FIRST WORLD WAR

Between 1871 and 1914 a vast revolution swept over Europe and permanently altered the face of the Continent. Everywhere factories were erected, towns expanded, and millions of workers streamed from the countryside into the cities; come the beginning of the twentieth century and this process was virtually complete in many countries, and what had for millenia been essentially agricultural societies had been metamorphosed into industrial ones. To quote a few figures only,[2] the combined population of 38 major European cities had risen from 19,230,000 to 35,240,000, an 83 percent increase that took place in a period when the population as a whole only rose by 51 percent. Measured in terms of value, industrial production rose 155 percent in Austria-Hungary, 70 percent in France, 200 percent in Germany, 100 percent in Italy, 330 percent in Russia and as much as 900 percent in Sweden; even Britain, the only major country that was already industrialized in 1870 and whose economy was relatively stagnant, registered a 60 percent increase. The growth in the production of some key commodities was even larger than these figures indicate: mining for coal and lignite, for example, rose from 205.5 to 669.5 million tons annually, and the output of pig iron from 11,035 to 38,550 thousand tons. To adduce similar figures from other fields would be easy enough, but would only serve to prove what is already obvious.

As industrialization metamorphosed the countryside and shifted entire populations, one aspect could be identified in the national lives of most countries that remained curiously exempt from the changes taking place: the armed forces, or more particularly the land forces. While armies in this period were based upon universal male conscription and incorporated many technological innovations, from the telegraph and smokeless powder to the machine gun and recoilless artillery, the outlook of what a later generation would call "the managers of violence" remained curiously unaffected thereby; indeed they did not regard themselves as managers at all, but rather as leaders whose selection, training, and promotion systems were everywhere governed by social and political considerations more appropriate to a feudal age than to the scientific requirements essential in a technological one. The aristocratic origins and outlook of the various officer corps; the fact that what wars did occur took place mostly on remote continents against primitive peoples; and the fact that the wars of 1866 and 1870-71 had not, once the railroads had been left behind, involved either a terribly sophisticated use of technology or very much of it[3]—all these factors contributed to make the military into the closest thing to a refuge from the grime and soot of modern industrial cities.

Coupled with the horse-riding, field-maneuvering (the very term is indicative, as is the fact that to launch a war was to go "on campaign") life led by most officers went a profound ignorance of what modern war really meant; or indeed that it could mean anything much besides fun and games marred, occasionally, by a regrettable but heroic death. As a famous German soldier and military author of the time once put it, war would lead to a return "to the simpler circumstances of our ancestors,"[4] by no means an undesirable development. Encouraged by popular and indeed professional military books which depicted imaginary war—never as popular a literary theme as during precisely these years[5]—in terms of armies marching and fighting, millions thought of war not as an extension of industrial society but as a liberation from it, and enthusiastically welcomed it as such in 1914.[6] War was thought of as a kind of international football match *cum* national holiday, with the newspapers acting as cheerleaders and the entire nation as cheering spectators. Having had their fun, the competing teams—red, grey, or khaki—would pack up and return home by the time the leaves fell from the trees, and save for a province ceded, an indemnity extracted and paid, everything would go on as before.

Since war was regarded as not merely different from, but actually as opposed to, the normal pursuits of peace, for a civilian to claim a right to interfere in the way it should be conducted bordered on the preposterous; as Moltke once put it, war having broken out, the civilian rulers were to take a back seat until the warlord (German *Feldherr*, or Lord of the Field, another significant term) returned to the capital and, presumably clicking his heels, announced that the mission had been accomplished (or that defeat was staring him in the face). The Kaiser put it even more succinctly when he said that, once war broke out, "the idiotic civilians" would have to fall silent. The belief that civilian officials need know nothing of war, nor officers of peace, was carried to the point that the German Chancellor was left uninformed of some crucial aspects of the Schlieffen Plan, whereas that Plan in turn did not even envisage the employment of civilian engineering firms to repair damaged railways in Belgium, much less any possibility of industrial or economic mobilization.[7] When Hans Delbrück in the 1890s tried to teach the German General Staff something about the conduct of strategy—if only that of Frederick the Great 100 years previously—he was met first with *ad hominem* attacks and then by an outraged silence.[8] Better aware of his proper place, the German secretary of finance when asked to buy up stocks of grain at Rotterdam at the outbreak of war in 1914 replied that "civilians have no title to interference in a situation that might arise through war, which was a military matter."[9] While it would be easy to adduce further examples of blindness on both sides, it is the origins of this blindness that we wish to emphasize here: namely the perceived—and often jealously guarded—divorce between the industrial civilization of peace on the one hand and the still largely feudal culture of war on the other.

THE ORIGINS OF MOBILIZATION WARFARE DURING THE FIRST WORLD WAR

By a curious quirk of fortune, World War I did in fact begin much as had been expected by the generals on both sides. Spearheaded by cavalry corps whose regimental histories show them sharpening their lances each evening, the Schlieffen Plan went off as scheduled, launching 35 German corps on a sweeping movement into Belgium and France. On the French side Joffre's Plan XVII sent a slightly smaller force rushing first into Alsace and then the Ardennes, only to meet with bloody defeat in both theaters. The Russian Plan 19 hurled—literally so, since the Russian General Staff considered the men too stupid to learn any but two maneuvers, forward and back[10] —two armies into East Prussia and four more into Galicia, whereas the Austrians in turn attacked in both Serbia and Russia. Wherever one looked in September of 1914 armies marched, engaged on maneuvers, clashed and occasionally defeated each other; battles such as Mons, the Marne, Tannenberg, and the Masurian Lakes were fought in the best nineteenth century tradition, complete with envelopments, breakthroughs, glorious cavalry charges, and even—in at least one case—white gloves and pompoms.

Contrary to what had been expected, however, these early clashes did not lead to any rapid end to the war—and this for three basic reasons. One was the extraordinary increases in the power of the tactical defense brought about since 1870 by the perfection of smokeless powder, quick-firing (later also automatic) weapons, and barbed wire. The second was the fact that, between 1870 and 1914, the size of armies and their logistic requirements had increased out of all proportion to their mobility in the field, which left them no longer capable of marching sufficiently far, or fast, to force a strategic decision.[11] Third, there were the almost inexhaustible resources which the modern industrialized state, following great improvements in administrative efficiency and managerial techniques, was able to mobilize, so that even battles costing a few hundreds of thousands of men and leading to the loss of entire provinces no longer necessarily signaled defeat. Taken together, these three factors meant that the destructive abilities of armies had come to lag behind the productive forces of national economies, with the result that most armies—the British, for example, during the five-month Somme offensive—continued to wax and grow, especially in terms of equipment, even as they were being ground to pieces.

The first of the above factors, namely the tactical immobility enforced by the trenches, made mobilization warfare possible; the second, that is the logistic requirements of modern war, made it necessary. To quote a few figures only, the Russian armies in 1914 went to war with 420 rounds per gun in their caissons, a figure that was sometimes exceeded by the *daily* expenditure of French guns four years later. The German Army in 1914 was as well prepared as any, but it only had available a strategic reserve of 1,000 rounds per artillery barrel—enough, as it turned out, to last no more than five or six weeks. Yet the Germans in 1870 had gone to war with 150 rounds in their caissons and ended up expending no more than 199 per gun during a five-month campaign, so that to have 1,000 shells in strategic reserve and 420 immediately at hand should be (and was) considered not a sign of penury but, on the contrary, proof of very thorough preparation indeed. To illustrate the matter in a different way, some 90 percent of the German logistic requirements in 1870 had consisted of food and fodder. By 1916, these requirements had certainly not diminished—they were, if anything, more difficult to meet, since the stationary nature of trench warfare meant that only an insignificant fraction of either commodity could be locally procured—but it had been dwarfed by the demand for ammunition, engineering materials, and equipment of all kinds, which by that time made up approximately two-thirds of all supplies consumed. As a simple calculation shows, the weight of supplies required per man and per horse in the army had almost tripled in 45 years, and even this understates the problem confronted by the economies of the belligerent countries since the number of men under arms as a fraction of the population had increased—to illustrate, from 1:34 to 1:13 in Germany and from 1:74 to 1:10 in France. Using these figures as a very rough basis for calculation, it might perhaps be concluded that the logistic burden of waging war (as measured in tons) had increased nine- to fifteen-fold in the period in question. The rise in costs must have been much greater still, since the newly added logistic requirements consisted almost entirely of expensive industrial products as opposed to cheap agricultural ones.

Looking back with the benefit of hindsight, the fact that these developments were not anticipated by any of the belligerents cannot really be called surprising; there was, after all, nothing in historical experience (except for the American Civil War, which most European generals chose to disregard) to prepare people for the completely novel phenomenon that was industrial warfare. Thus it was possible for Britain to enter the war under the flag of free trade and with business as usual (the phrase, significantly, was coined by Winston Churchill with his extensive experience in colonial warfare) whereas the German chief of staff thought that the most important function of economic policy in wartime would be to relieve unemployment and thus prevent hunger. Italy, to take another example, made her entry into the conflict conditional upon receiving a 50 million pound loan from its allies; already in 1916 Britain was spending 10 percent of that sum every day, and by 1918 the cost exceeded that figure several times over.

As might be expected from the fact that all sides were now engaged in essentially the same type of industrial warfare, the course of economic mobilization followed a broadly similar pattern in every country.[12] The first call—after the facilities of the state-controlled factories proved hopelessly inadequate to meet the soaring demand—inevitably went out to the metal and chemical industries which were asked to provide what were by contemporary standards fantastic quantities of ammunition and equipment. There followed a gradual extension of controls over the commodities that were needed to produce that equipment and that ammunition—factory space, raw materials, transport, and last, but not least, manpower, which in most countries was tied to its workplaces, denied the right to strike, and confronted by frequently ineffective restraints on wages that were designed to "equalize the burden" and prevent the cost of the war from rising even higher than it did. It soon transpired, however, that the mobilization of the arms-producing industries alone was insufficient; what was needed was centralized control over all national resources, in order to harness them to the war-making effort. This extension of control, one of the most important if least understood revolutions of the twentieth century, was carried out in fits and starts in the various countries from the end of 1914 on; Walther Rathenau in Germany, Lloyd George in Britain, Clemenceau in France, and Bernard Baruch in the United States were some of the men with whose names this revolution will forever be associated.[13] Those countries, notably Russia, where the military-industrial base and the civilian establishment were too weak to carry out this revolution paid the price in the form of national collapse. Where efficiently carried out, however, economic mobilization made possible increases in production that would have appeared wholly preposterous before the war, and this in spite of the fact that up to 10 percent of the population—and those its most productive segments—were away in the field. To prove that there are no real limits to the productive forces that it is within the power of modern industrialized economies to unleash—that was the most important single economic lesson of the First World War, as it was of the Second.[14]

Too much has been written concerning the effect of industrial mobilization on the conduct of tactics and strategy to require repetition here.[15] It is worth pointing out, however, that war itself—traditionally regarded as the province of moral forces and therefore as an "art" —was now turned into an industrial exercise. As the conduct of war extended back from the battlefield into the factory and the office, the methods used in the office and the factory came back with a vengeance and began to govern the conduct of war. Like the operation of some huge industrial plant, trench warfare was a highly repetitive business—so many battalion hours a month, so and so many raids per division per week, and so many miles of barbed wire or tons of shell to protect or level so many miles of trench.[16] Like industrial production, this kind of war easily led itself to quantitative analysis and centralized, scientific control, often with disastrous results to all concerned, as happened, for example, on the Somme in 1916.[17] It should be remembered, moreover, that in warfare on this scale the traditional functions of the commander and his staff—intelligence, operations, supply—only constituted the proverbial tip of the iceberg; before they could even begin to fight, millions of men had to be fed, clothed, housed, provided with material and spiritual care, policed, and looked after in every way. As soldiers took over all these tasks, a situation was soon created in which their work and methods differed little, if at all, from those of civilian administrators in a city as large as Vienna or Berlin.[18] Of the 10,000 daily telegrams, 20,000 telephone calls, and 5,000 written messages that it took to manage a single British field army in 1918,[19] 95 percent or more were of the type described by Robert Graves in *Good-bye to All That*: "a warning about verdigris on vermorel-sprayers, or the keeping of pets in trenches, or being polite to our allies."[20] The most important single effect of economic mobilization on war, in other words, was to turn the latter into an exercise in scientific management, or perhaps one would rather say that it caused generals such as Douglas Haig to believe that scientific management was all that was needed in order to gain victory in war. As Ludendorff was to demonstrate in his offensives of 1918, and paradoxically in view of the above, the way out of trench warfare eventually consisted precisely in *not* surrendering to the belief in scientific management—but that is a topic on which no more can be said in the present context.

The second effect of economic mobilization of the conduct of war that deserves a brief mention here is the transformation of all warfare into a process of attrition. Where generals before the war had thought in Clausewitzian terms of strategic marches and decisive battles leading to the annihilation of the enemy,[21] there exists a sense in which all modern industrial warfare is attrition warfare, since it is opposed not merely by the enemy's armed forces in the field but by his entire politico-economic-social structure. Attrition warfare was brought about by barbed wire and the machine gun, it is true, but its continuation over a period measured in years would have been inconceivable without the factories in the rear. From the point of view of international relations, this shift probably signaled an increase in the time needed to plan and launch a war, and also in the war-making capacities of large states relative to those of smaller ones; but this is to anticipate the course of our argument.

That the extension of government controls over entire economies and states did not take place without conflict between, for example, officials and owners, and between employers and workers, may well be imagined and has indeed been extensively documented. Even more important than these struggles, however, were the disputes that took place between the brass on one hand and the top hats on the other. As economic mobilization gained in importance the former extended their interest from the employment of weapons to their production, whereas the latter tended to move in an opposite direction. The outcome of the clash reflected the relative balance of power in each country and society: whereas Germany was turned into a virtual military dictatorship from 1916 on, the allied governments gradually extended their control over military matters to the point where every major offensive on the Western Front had to be sold to Lloyd George, who alone could provide the resources required. Whatever the victorious party, the outcome was the appearance of modern mobilization warfare, accompanied by a vast upheaval in political, economic, social, and even sexual *mores* that helped create the world in which we live.[22]

The phenomenon of mobilization warfare, it cannot be too strongly emphasized, was the product of accident. Its coming had not been foreseen by any of the belligerents who, had they but possessed a dim understanding of the consequences, would probably have refrained from ever going to war in the first place. The reorganization of which it was both a cause and a consequence only took place in fits and starts and was not nearly complete in any country before two years had passed from the outbreak of hostilities. Its full implications were only understood, if at all, during the postwar years. It is to these implications, both as perceived in theory and as carried out in practice, that we must next turn our attention.

THE *BLITZKRIEG* STRATEGY AND MOBILIZATION WARFARE

Fundamentally and in principle, the end of World War I presented three different ways of coping with the problem of mobilization warfare. The first of these was to ignore it in the hope that it would go away; the second, to come to terms with the phenomenon and work out its full implications in preparation for the next round; and the third, to try to discover a way of going around it. During the 20 years' armistice that followed all three ways were tried out by various people, in various countries, and with various results.

The first, and most superficial, way of putting the genie back into the bottle was to regard mobilization warfare as a temporary aberration, a phenomenon that was the product of the peculiar conditions of trench warfare—in turn created by the momentary balance of tactical weapons and military technology—and therefore as irrelevant to the future except insofar as the discovery of new tactics and a new technology were necessary in order to prevent a repetition. As it happened, the closing years of World War I had already indicated a path towards both: there presented themselves the German infiltration tactics successfully employed by Ludendorff to smash a hole in the British lines in 1918 on the one hand, and the armored fighting vehicle used by the British to produce the same effect on the German side, on the other. It only remained to work out the implications of both in greater detail, a job that was largely complete by the early 1930s. There rose, in Germany, the elite 100,000-man army with its emphasis on thorough training, high mobility, and revolutionary tactics; whereas Britain saw in Liddell Hart and, to a lesser extent, Fuller (whose understanding of the socio-economic aspects of war was incomparably better) the prophets of a new form of armored warfare, the purpose of which was similar, namely to cut through opposing forces "like a knife through butter." Significantly, General von Seeckt—because he was forced to—as well as Fuller and Liddell Hart (not to forget de Gaulle and his *Armée de Métier*)—by their own choice—saw the future in terms of small, professional armies, it being assumed that the restoration of mobility in the field was all that was needed in order to prevent the recurrence of mobilization warfare and return to the good old days when war was little but a slightly more dangerous form of football. Not accidentally, there went with this solution a far-reaching emancipation of the armed forces from the subjection to, and concern with, civilian affairs that had been imposed on them by World War I; as Seeckt once put it when a meddlesome German chancellor asked whom the army supported, "the Army stands behind me!"

Whether they rode horses or tanks, the retreat from mobilization warfare would enable armies to return to "real soldiering" and "take the field" (if only that of polo) instead of sitting behind desks at home and participating in the administration of factories and the appeasement of unions. Novel as the tactics proposed by them were, therefore, the military reformers of the 1920s were conservative in aim: using the means put into their hands by modern industry, their aspiration was to effect a return to preindustrial warfare.[23]

The second, and in some ways more realistic, approach to mobilization warfare was to regard it as a product, not simply of weapons and tactics but of the industrial revolution itself and consequently as a phenomenon which, while possibly regrettable, would not go away and had to be dealt with on its own terms. There arose out of this approach Ludendorff's celebrated work, *Der totale Krieg*, published in 1936 and summing up the General's World War I experiences. As the man who, more than any other, had come close to running a large country's war effort single-handed—not merely commanded a company of infantry like Liddell Hart, or served as the chief of staff to a field army, like Seeckt—Ludendorff in spite of a certain senility that led him to dabble in antisemitism and occultism was perhaps in a better position than anyone to understand what modern mobilization warfare was all about. His starting point was that the need to engage in comprehensive economic as well as military mobilization had rendered Clausewitz's theories concerning the primacy of politics over strategy out of date; rather than being the handmaid of policy, war had become so total and all-embracing that it could not henceforward be successfully waged unless policy itself were made subject to its demands. Not merely field forces numbering millions, but the entire spiritual and material resources of the nation had to be mobilized and put to work in a concerted effort under the central direction of a supreme warlord. Thus mobilization warfare required, among other things, the most intimate collaboration between—or better still, a personal union of—the civilian ruler and the supreme warlord; the muzzling of political parties and of the press; the suspension of trade unions except as transmission belts for the implementation of the directives of the high command; and the organization of the entire country along strict military lines. All this, furthermore, was to take place not at the outbreak of hostilities, which was too late by far, but long before, in peacetime, peace itself being regarded essentially as nothing but a breathing space between wars.[24] Far from the object of war being a better peace, peace was seen as a prelude to a better war; a development which Ludendorff, the militarist, considered both inevitable and desirable.

It is one of the ironies of World War II, seldom understood, that Germany and Britain each adopted the military principles of the other. Whereas the German Army (supposedly) learned from Liddell Hart how to use tanks and prevent another tactical stalemate,[25] Britain under Churchill's direction had by 1941 achieved a degree of economic mobilization that went far beyond anything attempted in Germany before 1943. In Germany the adoption of British-made methods finally led to total collapse; in Britain the employment of German ones ended in economic eclipse.[26] Each side thus shaped its policies in far reaching agreement with the theories of the other, and in both countries the originators of those theories remained prophets without honor. Liddell Hart, after all, only gained recognition for his development of armored warfare in the years after 1945, whereas Ludendorff died in 1937 an embittered man who had just refused to accept the rank of *Feldmarschall* that Hitler had tried to confer on him.

The third, and in some ways most revolutionary, way out of the impasse presented by mobilization warfare consisted of lightning war, or *Blitzkrieg*. Blitzkrieg made use of the tactical methods advocated by Fuller and Liddell Hart, it is true, and to this extent consisted of the use of new weapons—the tank, the motor vehicle, the tractor-towed or self-propelled gun, and the aircraft—in new and coordinated ways for the realization of new tactics. What many of the early proponents of mobile armored warfare overlooked, however, was that tanks have to be produced before they can be deployed, and that the needs of production can play as important a role in shaping mobilization warfare as can any weapon system at the front. To put it in a different way, the essence of Blitzkrieg consisted not just of the tactical use of air and armor but, equally important, of a strategy that would make it unnecessary to produce truly large numbers of aircraft and tanks. It is this wider, strategic aspect of the Blitzkrieg with which we are concerned here.[27]

To be really effective in achieving its purpose—that is, to enable a country possessing an inferior demographic and economic base to wage war successfully under modern conditions—a Blitzkrieg strategy must do two things which are really different sides of the same coin. First, it must make its wars of such brief duration that the opponent will be knocked out before it has time to bring its superior resources to bear. Second, the industrial base must be so constructed as to render it capable, not of fighting a protracted war by means of an immense and sustained output but of rapidly and smoothly switching from one type of product to the next in accordance with the nature of the enemy of the moment. To do the first, it was necessary to rely on the tactics of mobile, armored warfare; to do the second meant "armament in width" (many guns with few ammunition reserves for each) rather than "armament in depth" (fewer guns with a lot of ammunition per barrel). The strategy of Blitzkrieg, in other words, is best understood as a way round the problems presented by mobilization warfare, or perhaps one should say that it constitutes a counterweight to the restraints imposed on small states (among which the Germans, save for a period of *Weltpolitik* megalomania before 1914, always counted themselves) by the evolution of that kind of warfare.

A curious fact worth pointing out at this point is that the strategic, as opposed to the tactical, doctrines of Blitzkrieg have nowhere been laid down in writing. In vain one looks for them on the pages of *Mein Kampf*; nor are they to be found in the writings of any German general of the period.[28] The closest approach to them is contained in that remarkable little book, Hermann Rausching's *Gespräche mit Hitler* (1934) which may however have been partly fabricated by its author and which does not in any case contain a single reference to tanks. Except as it appears with the benefit of hindsight, there is no positive proof that any of Hitler's generals, or indeed Hitler himself, really understood the theoretical foundations behind the kind of war that they waged, most successfully, for over two years. The generals had in fact distrusted the entire war from the outset, insisting that the Blitzkrieg idea would not work before being compelled to embark on two spectacularly successful campaigns—in Poland and in France—and beginning to believe that it was infallible just on the eve of the first campaign that was to overstretch the new form of war beyond its breaking point, the one against Russia. So much for military infallibility.

As things turned out, World War II as actually waged did not conform exactly to any of the three models that had been proposed for dealing with mobilization warfare. To take Blitzkrieg first, it was successful up to a point but ultimately failed to bring the decision when the spaces and forces confronting it were too large, as in Russia. Armored warfare, originally designed to reinforce the hand of the tactical offense, proved at least as successful in strengthening the defense—indeed more so, if the prolonged German resistance against overwhelming odds in 1943-1945 (and the 1973 Israeli defense against even greater odds on the Golan Heights) are any guide. Perhaps the closest to the mark was, after all, Ludendorff whose interest in tactics was limited but whose concepts concerning the need for total mobilization were adopted by all the belligerents, more or less, in 1939-1945. Ludendorff, however, turned out wrong in that he believed that the military were in the best position to direct this mobilization; whereas practice shows that it was most successfully carried out in countries such as Britain or the USSR, where policy was in the hands of a civilian warlord (even if he carried the title of Marshal, as Stalin did) dominating a small inner cabinet of which the minister of war was but a single member. In the end, civilian supremacy asserted itself even in Germany itself; it was only when economic power was taken away from the services (the *Wehrmacht* high command, the air force and the navy, all of which had originally done their own economic planning or produced their own weapons) and concentrated in the civilian ministry of Albert Speer that mobilizaton could start in earnest.[29]

This belated switch to total war did not benefit the Germans much, for it compelled them to engage in the very kind of struggle that Hitler had wished most to avoid. It lay in the nature of a war based on the total mobilization of the resources of entire nations, even continents, that it could only be decided by attrition, and World War II was in fact decided in this way in spite of many allegedly "decisive" battles.[30] However revolutionary in tactics and technology,

Blitzkrieg is therefore best understood as a reactionary attempt by the military (on whom, nevertheless, it had to be forced) to use the products of the industrial revolution in order to save something of their old dominance of war against the effects of that very revolution. The attempt ended in failure, and as World War II was coming to a close, it certainly looked as if the capacity to make war had now definitely shifted away from the warlords of old to the United States, a country with little military tradition to speak of but possessed of overwhelming industrial power.

MOBILIZATION WARFARE IN THE NUCLEAR ERA

As opposed to the period between the wars, when the questions of how economic mobilization for war should be carried out, by whom, and to what purpose governed the thought even of those who had the strongest interest in escaping from the attrition inherent in mobilization warfare, after 1945 the entire issue has been relegated to the sidelines. It is a paradox of mobilization warfare that at the very moment when it celebrated its greatest triumph it also produced the device that heralded its own demise; and that the very industrial base whose existence and functioning had made the manufacturing of the bomb possible by that very act decisively reduced, if not eliminated, its own relevance as an instrument for waging war.

Abrupt and dramatic as the shift from industrial to postindustrial warfare appears in retrospect, the first thing to be noted about it is that it was less so in practice. It is an often overlooked fact that the two nuclear devices dropped on Japan together caused only 3 percent of the damage inflicted on that country from the air during four years of war, and that for several years after 1945 first the United States and then the USSR only possessed a very limited stockpile of bombs. Since it had taken over 2 million tons of TNT before Germany was brought to its knees (if indeed it was strategic bombing that did bring her to her knees) it was clear to far-sighted strategists, if not to the public which was being fed such tales of global disaster as Aldous Huxley's *Ape and Essence* (1948), that a new war breaking out in the late 1940s would not be fundamentally different from the last one. Nuclear weapons would be freely used and would cause immense havoc, it was true, but calculations based on published sources showed that their power was not yet great enough to stop the armies of a superpower, much less to destroy entire societies with the continents on which they lived.[31] Though the difficulties would be greater, and the casualties larger, the men who set out to establish NATO implicitly and explicitly recognized the continued relevance of economic mobilization and, as important, the command of the sea which would make it possible. They also embarked on stockpiling strategic raw materials, machine tools, et cetera, a policy that speaks for itself.

As both sides started accumulating considerable stocks of atomic bombs in the early 1950s, however, and increasingly so after the appearance on the scene of the first hydrogen bombs in 1953-1954, the picture began to change. In a way, the advent of these weapons could be seen as a return to the situation as it had existed before 1914: just as people then had thought it inconceivable that war should be prolonged, so the Western strategists of the mid-1950s (and some even earlier) thought in terms of "massive retaliation" that would terminate any war almost before it began. Considered from this point of view economic mobilization had become an anachronism, and one that had been rendered both unnecessary and impossible by the potency of is own product.[32] People in the West preferring to regard nuclear war as inconceivable, the emphasis shifted to its prevention; the most important question now being, in the words of a famous pioneer of systems analysis, "How much is enough?"[33]—enough, to wit, to deter war with the traditional minimum of military expenditure in peacetime, not to wage it. Though its purpose was just the opposite, the doctrine of deterrence resembled that of Blitzkrieg in that it meant getting in the heaviest possible initial blow (even though that blow was to consist of a "second strike") rather than the capacity to deliver a succession of even heavier blows at some subsequent time. Like Blitzkrieg, too, it relied on armament in width—brought to an extreme in the form of silos which self-destruct by firing the single missile they contain—rather than in depth.

Though analogies should never be carried too far, the problems of economic mobilization under conditions of nuclear stalemate also resemble those faced by the originators of Blitzkrieg in another way. As Liddell Hart foresaw as early as 1946, the advent of this stalemate would not eliminate war as such but merely place a premium "on indirect methods of aggression, infiltration taking civil forms as well as military, to which nuclear retaliation would be irrelevant."[34] His prophecy was amply fulfilled to the extent that, in one way or another, every power possessing nuclear weapons has been involved in war since 1945. The problem confronting these powers has not been to carry though the type of total mobilization that was advocated by Ludendorff, but rather to construct an industrial basis that would be capable of meeting the—often, by no means insignificant—needs of limited war (or succession of limited wars) while leaving the rest of the economy comparatively untouched. Like the earlier Blitzkrieg economy, the basis thus created had to be flexible and therefore, to some extent at any rate, independent of the rest. As happened to the firms of Vickers-Armstrong and Krupp in an earlier age, this independence from the economy could only be brought at the price of an even greater dependence on the military who in turn found themselves compelled to nourish their suppliers in peace as well as war in order to maintain a certain level of expertise and always have some kind of industrial base and "surge capability" available. The result has been the rise of the modern military industrial complex, a system whose weapon-producing policies often seem geared to ensure its own survival and prosperity without regard to, and sometimes at the expense of, the country's ability to wage war.[35]

Finally, just as Blitzkrieg was designed to minimize the importance of a country's mobilization base and enable it to wage war against a potentially stronger opponent, so the advent of nuclear arms would appear to have diminished the importance of economic differences (provided only that enough of a base exists to produce or purchase the bomb and the means to deliver it) as a factor that governs war-making capacity. To use an extreme but interesting illustration of this truth, there seems to be no conceivable way in which a Libya (with her "mobilization base" consisting of 2 million illiterate Arabs), armed solely with conventional weapons of whatever type, could inflict any serious military damage on the United States. A nuclear Libya, on the other hand, would definitely pose some hazards, if only at the cost of her own suicide. To this extent, then, the advent of nuclear arms, by eliminating the need for a very strong economic base and for a prolonged process of mobilization, must be regarded as a destabilizing factor.

Another point to be noted in this context is that, of approximately 200 wars fought all over the world since 1945, a large proportion have been waged by states that did not have access to nuclear arms. To those countries, as the example of Israel facing the Arab states illustrates, the entire complex of questions surrounding mobilization warfare remains as vital today as it was to all powers 40 years ago. Like Germany before 1945, modern Israel can only hope to defeat its opponents in a rapid war before their full resources (and those of the entire vast Arab world) can be brought to bear.[36] As was the case in Germany, this constraint has implied reliance on Blitzkrieg tactics and "armament in width," resulting in very high firepower deliverable over a short period of time measured in days or weeks.[37] To the extent that they have remained free of nuclear weapons or close alliances with the superpowers, therefore, many states around the world have been able to engage in the time-honored games complete with all their economic implications. It would appear, however, that the number of nations still able to indulge in this luxury is gradually decreasing.[38]

However, the almost universally held Western view that any nuclear conflict would be a suicidal affair for both sides—"a war without a tomorrow," as Schlieffen put it in his inimitable style—is not the only one possible.[39] At first because they did not possess nuclear weapons, and later for reasons connected with their world-outlook which prevents them from staking as much on technology as the West does, the Soviets have never accepted that doctrine and instead have proceeded to construct a theory of war that puts far greater emphasis on the importance of the mobilization of a country's entire socioeconomic industrial system as a basis for waging all out (including nuclear) war. Whereas it is possible to read the works of the outstanding Western strategists —Bernard Brodie, Henry Kissinger, Oskar Morgenstern, and Thomas Schelling among others—and encounter hardly a reference to the question of economic mobilization for war, every Soviet work on military strategy opens with a discussion of the fundamental factors that govern war-making capacity: the stability and productivity of the economy, the cohesiveness of society, and the degree of ideologically inspired determination.[40] Nor, as even a cursory review of the Soviet defense system shows, is this view confined to words only. The spending, in peacetime, of some 15 percent of the gross national product (GNP) for military purposes; the system of universal conscription which provides a huge pool of at least partly trained manpower; the maintenance at various levels of readiness of some 160 divisions complete with their equipment; the existence of paramilitary and civil defense organizations with memberships numbering in the millions; and the gearing of industry to military needs, as exemplified by the fact that much civilian equipment is designed to be capable of operating in war also—these are but a few instances of the Soviet attempt to establish a proper basis for mobilization in peacetime and to make sure that the transition to a wartime economy will be carried out as rapidly and smoothly as possible.[41]

Thus, to the Soviets, the shadow of nuclear holocaust, far from being a convenient excuse for avoiding economic mobilization in war, merely renders it all the more necessary in peace. Seen from the NATO point of view, this doctrine is made even more dangerous by the fact that it is combined, not with any view of conventional warfare as a slow-moving process of attrition but, on the contrary, with the most highly developed machine for waging Blitzkrieg that the world has ever seen. Reaping the fruits of 15 years of economic mobilization, the Soviets now (1984) appear in a position to have their cake and eat it too. With their extensive programs of civil defense and mobilization they are in a position to wage total war on the one hand (at any rate more so than the hopelessly exposed and unprepared United States[42]) and at the same time have good hope of bringing about a rapid decision by annihilation rather than a slow one by attrition. To them Blitzkrieg is not a way round the full implications of modern industrial warfare but, on the contrary, its continuation and a means of rendering it even more effective.

Though Soviet doctrine has always placed far less emphasis on deterrence than does its Western counterpart, that objective too seems to have been admirably achieved by way, so to speak, of a side effect. Whereas dozens of American installations and ships have been subject to attack over the last 20 years, sometimes by the puniest of opponents and often with no fear of retaliation, the number of those who would play similar games with the USSR appears to be smaller by far. Soviet military doctrine seems to have made a most successful application of Chancellor Helmut Schmidt's dictum that one must be able to fight in order to avoid being compelled to.[43] To fully comprehend Clausewitz's doctrine that war, even missile age war, is merely the continuation of policy in the widest sense, not a simple outgrowth of the technology of the moment; that is the true secret of Soviet power and the ultimate cause behind whatever military superiority they may currently enjoy over the West.

CONCLUSIONS

Tracing the origins and developments of twentieth century mobilization warfare, this paper has suggested that it was a baby, accidentally conceived without parental foresight, which quickly demonstrated its demonic nature by growing to gigantic dimensions and threatening to devour those who had brought it into the world. Confronted by what was a most unwelcome phenomenon to many —unwelcome not merely because it transformed the entire nature of war but also because it enhanced the importance of economic differences and thus made it more difficult for small states to confront large ones—some countries and strategists responded by developing technologies and tactics which, they hoped would enable them to ignore it altogether. Others resigned themselves and expressed their determination to become giants themselves, whereas others still concentrated on finding ways to run between the giant's legs.

In the years after 1945, following the advent of nuclear weapons which were themselves the outgrowth and crowning glory of mobilization warfare, most American strategists assumed that such mobilization was obsolete and, by concentrating on deterrence, tried to avoid the cost of maintaining a gigantic military establishment in peacetime. By contrast the Soviets, though also in possession of nuclear arms, have opted to remain gigantic and learn to run at the same time. As a comparison of the two countries' military expenditures will show, it is more than doubtful whether the American solution has even been cheaper in absolute terms, though it certainly was in relative ones. Moreover, this solution undoubtedly points to a less profound understanding of war as something governed by "systems analysis" and "games theory" rather than as a social phenomenon involving the entire politico-economic-social-psychological makeup of nations. If this chapter has brought out the crying need for a Western doctrine concerning the relationship between economics and war that will be at least as profound and all-embracing as the Soviet one, it will have achieved something.

NOTES

1. As commonly employed, the term "total war" may carry any one, or several, of the following meanings: a. a war of annihilation aimed at totally overthrowing the enemy (*guerre à outrance*) as opposed to limited war; b. a war directed against the totality of the enemy's territory and resources rather than against its military forces alone; c. a war in which the normal constraints against atrocities are cast off; and d. mobilization warfare in the sense here employed.

2. All figures from C.M. Cipola, ed., *The Fontana Economic History of Europe* vol. 4 part 2, (London: Fontana/Collins, 1973), statistical appendix.

3. See M. van Creveld, *Supplying War; Logistics from Wallenstein to Patton* (London: Cambridge, 1977), ch. 3.

4. Quoted in G. Ritter, *Staatskunst und Kriegshandwerk* vol. i (Munich: Oldenburg, 1954), p. 141.

5. See I.F. Clarke, *Voices Prophesizing War 1793-1984* (London: Panther, 1970), ch. 2.

6. See M. Ferro, *The Great War 1914-1918* (London: Routledge and Kegan Paul, 1973), pp. 3-8.

7. See G. Ritter., *The Schlieffen Plan* (London: O. Wolf, 1957), pp. 90ff on what successive German chancellors were told, and were not told, of the Plan.

8. On this episode see H. Delbrück, *Friederich, Napoleon, Moltke, aeltere und neuere Strategie* (Berlin: Walther, 1892), introduction.

9. Ferro, op. cit., p. 27.

10. N. Stone, *The Eastern Front 1914-1917* (London: Hodder & Stoughton, 1975), p. 45.

11. For this and the following paragraph I must refer the reader to my own book (see note 3 above, chapter 4).

12. On Russia, see Stone, op. cit.; on Germany, G.D. Feldman, *Army, Industry and Labor in Germany, 1914-1918* (Princeton, NJ: Princeton 1966); on Britain, S.J. Hurwitz, *State Intervention in Great Britain, a Study of Economic and Social Responses 1914-1919* (New York: Columbia, 1949); and on France, J.C. King, *Generals and Politicians* (Berkeley: University of California Press, 1951).

13. On Rathenau, see his own *Deutschlands Rohstoffversorgung* (Berlin: Fischer, 1919); on Lloyd George, R.J. Adams, *Arms and the Wizard* (London: Cassell, 1978); on Clemenceau, Ph. Erlanger, *Clemenceau* (Paris: Grasset, 1968); and on Baruch, M.L. Coit, *Mr. Baruch* (London: Gollancz, 1957).

14. See A. Milward, *War, Economy and Society 1939-1945* (London: Allen Lane, 1975), especially pp. 54-55.

15. The best short summary is J.F.C. Fuller, *The Conduct of War 1789-1961* (London: Eyre Methuen, 1961), ch. 9.

16. On these aspects of war in the trenches, see T. Ashworth, *Trench Warfare 1914-1918* (New York, 1980), pp. 84-85.

17. I am currently writing a history of C^3 (Command, Control, Communications) in war which will include a chapter on World War I.

18. The way military headquarters now operated and the effect this had on outsiders are well described in J. Charteris, *At GHQ* (London: Cassell, 1931), pp. 208-210.

19. P.W. Evans, "Strategic Signal Communications in 1914," *Signal Corps Bulletin*, 1935, No. 82, p. 29.

20. R. Graves, *Goodbye to All That* (London: Penguin, 1975), p. 217.

21. See particularly, J. Wallach, *Das Dogma der Vernichtungsschlacht* (Frankfurt am Main: Bernard & Graefe, 1965).

22. This unheaval, it seems, has been most completely documented in Britain. See the review of the literature in A.S. Milward, *The Economic Effects of the World Wars on Britain* (London: Macmillan, 1970).

23. This presentation of Seeckt, Fuller, and Liddell Hart as military conservatives at heart will no doubt surprise many. Yet Seeckt was basically uninterested in modern technology, whereas Liddell Hart was constitutionally incapable of looking behind the employment of tanks to the conditions necessary for their production. Fuller was the only one of the three who fully understood that modern warfare was the product, not merely of tactics and weapons but of the industrial revolution as such, and his views in many ways paralleled Ludendorff's.

24. *Der totale Krieg* (Munich: Ludendorffs Verlag, 1936), p. 10.

25. See B. Bond, *Liddell Hart, a Study of His Military Thought* (London: Cassell, 1976), ch. 8.

26. Some, however, would argue that it was the discontinuation of wartime economic policy after 1945 that led to Britain's subsequent decline.

27. This and the following paragraph are based on the brilliant analysis in A. Milward, *The German Economy at War* (London: Athlone Press, 1965), ch. 1.

28. Guderian, the real father of the German Blitzkrieg, was basically nothing but a *Panzer* general whose knowledge of any subject except his own was close to zero. Hence, when told by Hitler in August 1941 that "my generals know nothing about the economic aspects of war," he could not but express agreement, click his heels, and drive his tanks into the Ukraine instead of to Moscow as he himself had previously suggested. See K. Macksey, *Guderian, Panzer General* (London: MacDonald, 1976), pp. 147-148.

29. On this shift see B. Carroll, *Design for Total War* (The Hague: Mouton, 1968).

30. The very number of battles dignified with the title "decisive"—Dunkirk 1940, Moscow 1941, Alamein and Stalingrad 1942, Kursk 1943, and Normandy 1944, among others—is itself proof that none of them were so in fact.

31. See P.M.S. Blackett, *The Military and Political Consequences of Atomic Energy* (London: Turnstile, 1948), p. 56; and V. Bush, *Modern Arms and Free Men* (New York: Simon & Schuster, 1949), pp. 115-116.

32. B. Brodie, *The Absolute Weapon* (New York: Harcourt, 1946), p. 89.

33. A.C. Enthoven and K. Wayne Smith, *How Much Is Enough?* (New York: Harper & Row, 1971).

34. B.H. Liddell Hart, *The Revolution in Warfare* (London: Faber & Faber, 1946), p. 87.

35. For a most interesting analysis of the modern military industrial complex in this sense see M. Kaldor, *The Baroque Arsenal* (London: Hill and Wang 1981), especially chapter 6; also M. Handel, "Numbers Do Count; the Question of Quality versus Quantity," *The Journal of Strategic Studies*, Sept. 1981, pp. 228ff.

36. The best short discussion of Israel's strategic problems remains M. Handel, *Israel's Political-Strategic Doctrine* (Cambridge, Mass.: Harvard University Press, 1973) which, however, stands in urgent need of updating.

37. Unlike Germany, however, Israel has shown that one can spend one-third of one's GNP on defense and yet remain a viable democracy, an interesting lesson to those who fear the effects of a large military establishment on liberal-democratic values.

38. See M. van Creveld, "Turning Points in Twentieth Century War", *The Washington Quarterly* 4, Summer 1981, pp. 3-8; also the interesting but unfortunately timed paper by L.J. Halle, "Does War Have a Future?" in *Foreign Affairs*, October 1973, pp. 20-34.

39. For a list of Soviet quotes to this effect see R. Kolkowicz, "US and Soviet Approaches to Military Strategy; Theory versus Experience", *Orbis*, Summer 1981, p. 212.

40. See, for example, V.D. Sokolovsky, ed., *Soviet Military Strategy* (Englewood Cliffs, NJ: Prentice-Hall, 1963), especially pp. 109-130, 269-276; N.A. Lomov, ed., *The Revolution in Military Affairs* (Washington, D.C., USAF trans. n.d.), pp. 187-218; and M.I. Cherednichenko, "Modern War and Economics," in *Selected Soviet Military Writings* 1970-1975, (Washington, D.C., USAF trans. n.d.), pp. 44-55.

41. Some recent publications discussing the Soviet defense system include J. Erickson and E.J. Feuchtwanger, eds., *Soviet Military Power and Performance* (London: Macmillan, 1979); and M. Augursky, "The Soviet Military Industrial Complex," *Jerusalem Papers on Peace Problems*, no. 31, 1980.

42. Just how exposed has been brought out recently in a conference held by the Institute for Foreign Policy Analysis, Inc. See for a preliminary report R.L. Pfaltzgraff Jr. and U. Ra'anan, eds., *The US Defense Mobilization Infrastructure: Problems and Priorities* (Cambridge, Mass: Archon, 1982).

43. "*Kämpfen zu können, um nicht zu müssen.*"

3

Restriction of Supply As a Strategic Choice

Alan S. Milward

The deliberate restriction of supply to a potential or actual enemy is one of the oldest of all strategies, the counterpart of seeking out his armed forces in battle. Throughout the history of warfare an extensive panoply of tactics has been devoted to serving this strategic purpose. As an aspect of combatant strategy the restriction of supply has been especially prominent in the United States and Britain. The geographical situation of both countries in relation to potential opponents, the lack until recent times of any large standing armed forces in either country, and the great influence and control which both have been able to influence over world trade and resources, have all tended to skew strategic choice in that direction. Close-cordon naval blockade, the control at source of raw materials and manufactured goods, pre-emptive purchasing, strategic embargoes, international economic blacklisting, and strategic bombing have all been important tactical choices in both countries, loosely collected under the unsatisfactory label *economic warfare*.

At the same time the relative geographical immunity from direct attack of both until virtually the end of the Second World War promoted the use against them by enemies and potential enemies of a similar range of tactics. Reverse blockade (the continental system), the extension of territorial occupation to deny both imports and exports, and large-scale submarine and aerial warfare against their ocean supply routes have all been used as substitutes for combat against their armed forces when that was either unattainable or undesirable.

In the history of all major modern wars, including the First and Second World Wars, such tactics were every bit as important as military combat. Nor does this judgement apply only to periods of declared warfare. Once we eliminate, as the whole world in any case now appears to have agreed to do, the arbitrary, legalistic distinction between declared war and peace we would have to conclude that for the United States and Britain such tactics have over the span of modern history been more important and more integral to strategy than military combat. A complicated array of such tactics dominated the "peaceful" relationship between the United States and Japan between 1937 and 1941. Their expressed purpose on the American side was to achieve much the same result as a military campaign, to force Japan to retreat from her more ambitious ventures in the Pacific sphere. If they ultimately provoked the opposite result of an attack by the Japanese armed forces on the United States and a declaration of war that only demonstrates that armed combat and denial of supply were potentially substitutable strategies whether in "war" or "peace." Similarly, much seventeeth and eighteenth century siege "warfare" was a deliberate attempt to avoid armed combat by a tactical choice closer to the optimal.

The judgement of the optimal was to a large extent in nineteenth and twentieth century British and American strategic thinking an economic one. Tactics, and within the necessary political and psychological constraints, strategy, were investment decisions, even though they were not so clearly seen in that light as they often should have been. Reduction of supply was seen in many cases as a more cost-effective tactic than combat. In the larger strategic context it was much more easily fitted into the political and psychological constraints which operated on the choice of strategy in Britain and the United States. It was less costly of human life, appeared to mean less destruction of fixed capital (although this may well not always have been true) and appeared also to mean less distortion of "normal" domestic economic activity. The desire to find a strategy more acceptable to liberal democratic society could, of course, lead to the choice of such a strategy when it was not necessarily optimal in the narrower sense of being more cost effective. There are certainly several instances where military combat would have produced a quicker result. It could also, of course, lead to a great deal of wishful thinking and hypocrisy as it did in the case of the extension of the naval blockade against Germany after the 1918 armistice, which was more costly of German civilian lives than further combat would have been, or in the case of the strategic bombing campaigns against Germany, which ended up by being an extension of an extremely costly form of armed combat for an economic purpose which was never sufficiently specified and which sometimes degenerated into killing civilians in the vague hope that that must also be of economic value.

It has also been the case that the strategic responses to restriction of supply have been numerous and successful. One is inherent in the mechanism of any economy, factor substitution. As soon as the statistical evidence from the Second World War (and the conclusion seems borne out by such evidence from the First World War) is reviewed in detail, it becomes clear that any undisputed list of raw materials of strategic importance would have to be a very short one. It would certainly, on the evidence which historians have now provided, have to be much shorter than the lists compiled for guidance in naval blockade or strategic bombing by the United Kingdom Ministry of Economic Warfare or the United States Board of Economic Warfare. The skeptical attitude toward such lists by air force commanders during the Second World War has been largely, although not entirely, justified. Given the long history of naval blockade as a reason for naval construction, similar skepticism was hardly to be expected from the navy. The paradox presents itself that whereas virtually every raw material is, given full freedom of strategic and tactical choice, important for large-scale combatant warfare, practically no raw material, if denied, is indispensable, providing the possibility of substitution is allowed for when strategic and tactical choices are made.

The most obvious instance appears to be nonferrous metals. A great part of the effort of the blockade against both Germany and Japan in the Second World War went to cutting off the supply of those metals which were thought to be indispensable to the manufacture of special steels, armor plate and high-speed cutting tools—chrome, nickel, tungsten, and molybdenum. But of these only tungsten proved nonsubstitutable given a satisfactory knowledge of experimental metallurgy, of which Germany was a prime source, and a willingness to produce military and other goods of less than 100 percent of specification, a policy which was in any case forced on all combatant powers. An equally telling instance is the substitution of artificial and reconstituted rubber for natural rubber in both Germany and the United States and the substitution of synthetic oil for natural oil in Germany through an expensive program of import-substitution whose capital cost was justified by the economic equations of war. Similarly, high-grade bearings, listed everywhere as a strategic commodity of the highest importance, could be and were substituted everywhere by lower-grade bearings given a careful consideration of the problem of which armaments could be produced to lower specifications.

Secondly, extension of the territorial area of control was highly effective. In the German and Japanese cases this was usually done by the extension of military occupation and the seizure of stockpiles and other forms of booty. As the tables that follow below suggest, the seizure of strategic stockpiles in France and other Western European countries in 1940 added to Germany's own supply of such materials to so great a degree as to nullify much British planning and strategy in this area. For Japan seizures were even more crucial. Both Germany and Japan also took control of areas producing raw materials of high strategic importance which were in short supply in their own economies. The Japanese seizure of the oil reserves of The Netherlands East Indies is a case in point and both this campaign and the German campaign in the Caucasus were directly influenced by such economic objectives. The most striking case is provided by the Germans, who sought to control sufficient bauxite resources for aluminum output never to become a bottleneck in aircraft production, even though Germany had no domestic sources of the raw material herself.

On the Allied side the obvious example was food. The combined boards extended their control in the Second World War over food supply and almost all the international trade in food and animal feeds which was not controlled by the Axis, including that of neutral countries. The shipping allocation decisions of the Allies determined levels of food supply and rationing in countries which were not otherwise involved in the war or, indeed, in some cases showed more than a little sympathy to the Axis side. Even before this level of official international organization was reached, multinational oil companies found themselves in 1938 and 1939 under extreme governmental pressures to direct Romanian oil exports away from Germany and Pacific oil exports away from Japan. By 1944 the movement of virtually every raw material in world trade was closely scrutinized and controlled by the major combatant powers, mainly of course by the United States and Britain. Much the same state of affairs had been reached in 1917.

A third answer was the traditional one of stockpiling. The list of indisputably strategic raw materials, the restricted supply of which would have caused major disruption and weakness, during the First and Second World Wars, would be even shorter were we to exclude from it raw materials which on the evidence of these wars could be stockpiled in sufficient quantities to negate the tactic of supply restriction. It is self-evident that there are great differences in raw materials in this respect. Some are necessarily consumed in extremely large quantities, others only in relatively small ones. In the Second World War, iron ore and gas and oil products fell in the first category. Even German planners working within a deliberate framework of import substitution estimated their annual import needs of iron ore from Sweden alone at 10 million metric tons. This proved pessimistic, but imports from Sweden averaged about 5 million metric tons annually over the period 1940-44 and the main reason why they were not higher was the seizure and control of the extremely large iron ore resources of France, the movement of which was not dependent on shipping. These quantities may be compared to the average annual German consumption of wolfram (tungsten ore) over the same period, 2,740 metric tons. The physical problem of stockpiling iron ore or gas and oil products was insuperable because the quantities were too large and to a certain extent because gas and oil stores were highly susceptible to enemy attack. But elsewhere, if supply could be obtained, stockpiling was an effective answer, as indeed the tables below show. It played a significant role in the bilateral trade negotiations which dominated intra-European and particularly German foreign trade in the 1930s.

Lastly, but of the greatest importance, the choice of strategy not only can but must take into account the likelihood of an attempt to restrict supply. This was central to the choice of strategy in Germany in the Second World War. Debate still rages over how clearly and expressly the Blitzkrieg strategy was formulated there. It remains undisputed, however, that strategy in Germany, whether it was chosen or whether it evolved, was designed to cope with a series of short wars in which Germany's raw material deficiencies and her vulnerability to supply restriction would not become a brake on production or military success. There is, indeed, a further debate in progress as to whether this strategy and even the timing of the invasion of Poland were not actually produced by perceived bottlenecks in the supply of raw materials in 1938. The potential which the economy may reasonably be required to reach to win any particular war must be one variable in the synthesis from which a chosen strategy emerges. This was true of the Blitzkrieg, and in most wars of the past, this in itself has constituted the best initial defense against the strategy of restriction of supply.

From all this it follows that the motives for waging war (or peace) by restriction of supply are very strong ones, but that the defenses against such a strategy are also very effective. Because in the Second World War Allied strategy was designed to expose the weakness of Germany's raw material base and German strategy designed to hide it, and because German strategy against the United Kingdom was likewise designed to restrict supply to the British economy, the best historical test of the effectiveness of such strategies seems to lie in the period 1939-45. There is a further advantage in examining this period inasmuch as information relating to the trade and stockpiling of strategic materials, which is normally kept out of the public realm, is much more fully available for Germany as a result of the unconditional surrender. The deficiencies of the data for Britain remain very great but the figures are used here as far as they go. They are supplemented by a consideration of the data relevant to certain Japanese imports against which American strategy was especially directed.

In the case of Germany the materials selected are those which were given priority by American and British "targeting" bodies, except where the "targets" themselves were admitted during the course of the war itself to have been wrongly selected. They consist of three major inputs into the German war economy in which the German economy itself was very deficient, gas and oil products, iron ore, and rubber, as well as the three nonferrous metal ores which proved the most essential (in the sense of being the least substitutable) inputs into armaments, steel and machine-tool manufacture, and on which Germany was completely import-dependent. For the United Kingdom the commodities chosen are the three principal food imports, against which the submarine campaign was particularly launched, and the biggest single animal feeds import.

The German figures have been recalculated from the official figures in order to eliminate the effect of territorial and stockpile seizures. The point of this is to show that the strategy of restriction of supply would in these cases have been ineffective *even if Germany had not made such great territorial and stockpile gains during the early part of the war.*

IMPORTS, STOCKPILES, CONSUMPTION AND AVAILABILITY OF STRATEGIC COMMODITIES TARGETED AS TRADE-DEPENDENT

Germany

(All statistics for the Third Reich have been recalculated on the basis of a constant territorial area of September 1939 to exclude booty and forced imports from occupied territories. Thus "imports" means only those commodities imported from neutral or allied countries and "stockpile" figures are given without the inclusion of commodities transferred from occupied territory whether as booty or through clearing agreements.)

Oil and Oil Products

These figures are to be treated with caution, insofar as they are sums of quantities which are not strictly comparable. Total availability for example is calculated as domestic crude oil output and imports of crude, semi-finished and finished oil products and finished output from synthetic oil works. One metric ton of crude oil, however, produces rather less than 1 metric ton of finished products and the gap varies according to the chemical composition of the crude or synthetic oil input.

TABLE 3-1: Oil and Oil Products (10^3 metric tons)

	Stockpile	*"Imports"*	*Output*	*Estimated Consumption*	*Hypothetical Availability*
1940	1508	2075	4813	6856	8396
1941	797	2807	5678*	8305	9282
1942	775	2359	6606*	7483	9740
1943	1120	2766	7631	7971	11517
1944	—	972	5584	—	—

*Imports from Hungary and Romania only. Possible error = ± 7.5%.

Sources: Reichsministerium für Bewaffnung und Munition, *Statistische Schnellberichte zur Kriegsproduktion und Mineralölbestände im Grossdeutschen Reich*; W. Birkenfeld, *Der synthetische Treibstoff 1933-45* (Göttingen, 1964).

---

*All stockpile figures are for the end of December unless otherwise indicated.

TABLE 3.2: Iron Ore (10^3 metric tons, ferric content)*

	Stockpile	*"Imports"*	*Output*	*Consumption*	*Availability*
1940	2014	6005	5884	10372	13903
1941	2618	5325	5539	14764	14451
1942	2437	5011	5136	15366	14237
1943	2910	5832	4603	16633	15017
1944	—	2711	4343	—	—

*It has been assumed throughout that the ferric content of stockpiles was in the same ratio to dryweight as the ferric content of imports.

Sources: *Statistische Schnellberichte*. M. Fritz, *German Steel and Swedish Iron Ore 1939–1945* (Göteborg, 1974); A. S. Milward, "Could Sweden Have Stopped the Second World War?" in *Scandinavian Economic History Review*, vol. XV, 1 & 2, 1967. J. - J. Jäger, "Sweden's Iron Ore Exports to Germany 1933–1944" in *ibid*; A. S. Milward, *The New Order and the French Economy* (Oxford, 1970).

TABLE 3.3: Rubber (10^3 metric tons)

	Stockpile	*"Imports"*	*Output*	*Reclamation*	*Consumption*	*Availability*
1940	1.9	17	40	43	67	101.9
1941	7.6	27	69	44	74	147.6
1942	3.6	25	98	41	92	167.6
1943	4.5	7	117	45	91	173.5
1944	—	0	104	42	96	—

Sources: *Statistische Schnellberichte*. United States, *Strategic Bombing Survey*, Oil Division, *Final Report*. *Statistisches Reichsamt*, *Monatszahlen*.

TABLE 3.4: Nickel (10^3 metric tons, metal content)

	Stockpile	*"Imports"*	*Output*	*Consumption*	*Availability*
1940	11.3*	5.4	0.8	11.6	17.5
1941	7.8	3.6	0.8	9.2	12.2
1942	10.4	2.4	0.6	8.0	13.4
1943	7.3	6.1	1.5	9.4	14.9
1944	6.7†	8.1	1.6	9.5	16.4

*November.

†Includes booty.

Sources: *Statistische Schnellberichte*. *Monatszahlen*. J. - J. Jäger, *Die wirtschaftliche Abhängigkeit des Dritten Reichs von Ausland* (Berlin, 1969).

TABLE 3.5: Wolfram (10^3 metric tons, metal content)

	Stockpile	*"Imports"*	*Output*	*Consumption*	*Availability*
1940	3.0	1.0	0.1	3.7	4.1
1941	1.9	1.5	0.2	3.4	3.6
1942	1.6	1.7	0.2	3.0	3.5
1943	1.5	1.4	0.5	2.2	3.4
1944*	1.3	1.3	0.5	1.4	3.1

*November.
Sources: Statistische Schnellberichte. Monatszahlen. J. – J. Jäger, op. cit.

TABLE 3.6: Chrome (10^3 metric tons, metal content)

	Stockpile	*"Imports"*	*Output*	*Consumption*	*Availability*
1940	29.9	3.5	0	35.3	33.4
1941	18.3	8.5	0	43.3	26.8
1942	20.9	30.1	0.1	38.4	51.1
1943	13.9	28.0	0.2	38.7	42.1
1944*	29.6	48.6	0	42.4	78.2

*November.
Sources: Statistische Schnellberichte. Monatszahlen. J. – J. Jäger, op. cit.

UNITED KINGDOM

TABLE 3.7: Wheat (10^3 metric tons)

	Hypothetical Surplus Transferred & Held in Stock	*Imports*	*Output*	*Consumption*	*Hypothetical Availability*
1940	1774	5754	1641	5621	7395
1941	2828	5393	2018	6357	7411
1942	2812	3487	2567	6070	6054
1943	3288	2824	3138	6369	5962

Sources: Central Statistical Office, *Annual Abstract of Statistics*, no. 86, 1938–1948. History of the Second World War, Civil Series, *Statistical Digest of the War.*

TABLE 3.8: Oilcake and Meal (10^3 metric tons)

	Hypothetical Surplus Transferred & Held in Stock	*Imports*	*Output*	*Consumption*	*Hypothetical Availability*
1940	57	417	969	1329	1386
1941	128	204	766	899	970
1942	91	55	810	902	865
1943	72	0	671	690	671
1944	69	68	715	786	783

Sources: Annual Abstract. Statistical Digest.

TABLE 3.9: Summary

	1940			1941			1942			1943			1944		
	(a)	*(b)*	*(c)*	*(a)*	*(b)*	*(c)*	*(a)*	*(b)*	*(c)*	*(a)*	*(b)*	*(c)*	*(a)*	*(b)*	*(c)*
GERMANY															
Oil & oil products	24.7	18.0	72.7	30.2	9.6	28.4	24.2	10.4	32.8	24.0	14.0	40.5	—	—	—
Iron ore	43.2	19.4	33.5	36.8	17.7	49.2	35.2	15.9	48.6	30.5	17.5	49.9	—	—	—
Rubber	16.7	2.8	11.2	18.3	10.3	28.1	14.9	3.9	14.4	4.0	4.9	64.3	—	—	—
Nickel	30.9	97.4	209.3	29.5	84.8	216.7	17.9	130.0	433.3	40.9	77.6	119.7	49.4	70.5	68.4
Wolfram	24.3	81.1	300.0	41.7	55.9	126.7	48.6	53.3	94.1	41.2	68.2	107.1	41.9	92.9	100.0
Chrome	10.4	84.7	854.3	31.7	42.3	215.3	58.9	54.4	69.4	33.0	35.9	49.6	62.1	69.8	60.9
UNITED KINGDOM															
Wheat	77.8	31.6*	30.8*	72.8	44.5*	52.4*	57.6	46.3*	80.6*	48.6	52.8*	101.0*	47.4	45.2*	102.0*
Oilcake and Meal	30.1	4.3*	13.7*	21.0	14.2*	62.7*	6.4	10.1*	165.4*	—	10.4*	—	8.7	8.8*	101.5*
Meat	51.3	2.3*	4.3*	54.3	17.1*	27.6*	57.6	25.8*	41.4*	58.2	33.9*	53.9*	60.1	38.6*	59.6*
Sugar	75.3	13.4*	15.7*	79.8	37.5*	39.8*	61.9	20.3*	41.8*	71.9	51.6*	55.0*	74.7	42.0*	59.6*

*Hypothetical stockpiles.
(a) Ratio of imports to availability in percent.
(b) Ratio of stockpiles to consumption in percent.
(c) Ratio of stockpiles to imports in percent.

The statistical evidence is overwhelmingly in one direction. Both on the Allied and German side most attempts at restriction of supply were failures. In the German case only rubber stockpiles were so low as to present a constant threat of exhaustion should additions to supply be curtailed. On the British side stockpiles of food were low in 1940 in relation to consumption, and in 1942 they appear to have fallen at the most intensive period of the submarine campaign. Otherwise for all the main 'targeted' commodities both Britain and Germany maintained a level of reserves sufficient to alleviate all real anxieties.

To this, however, there is one crucial exception which it is impossible to include in the summary table because of the lack of comprehensive data. This is the case of German supply of aviation fuel in 1944. The net withdrawal from the stockpile between April 1944 and the end of March 1945 must have been approximately 182,000 metric tons monthly, the level of consumption in the second quarter of 1944 when the German air force was operating at its full extent. This would have been more than 40 percent more than the total stockpile of all gas and oil products when it was at its maximum size at the end of December 1940. We know that German flight operations were severely affected from May 1944 onwards by what became an acute shortage of an essential input. What is more, it is clear that had the strategic air attacks on oil production and stockpiles not been diverted to other targets in August and September 1944 the supply of aviation fuel might have been stopped entirely.

This particular evidence relating to one product, which is so specialized a subdivision of the general category "oil and oil products" as to make the collection of accurate statistical data about its distribution extremely difficult, must give us cause for a different and more cautious conclusion. And this caution would be well warranted by any consideration of the evidence relating to

TABLE 3.10: Average Monthly Output and Consumption of Aviation Fuel (10^3 metric tons)

	Output	*Consumption*
1944		
1st quarter	168.0	137.7
2nd quarter	127.7	180.3
3rd quarter	20.7	103.7
4th quarter	31.7	46.0
1945		
1st quarter	11.0*	43.3*

*Estimates from factory figures.
Sources: *Statistische Schnellberichte*.

Japan. Success in restricting supply is properly measured only by measuring the restriction of supply of the exact product wanted at the exact place at the exact point in time. If we consider the global evidence on the restriction of supply to Japan of those commodities on which the Japanese economy had been thought to be particularly dependent, we could come, as in the case of Germany and Britain, to the conclusion that the strategy of restriction of supply was entirely ineffective. In this case there would be an additional reason which is of great relevance to present-day discussions about restriction of supply: Japanese consumption of the commodities examined here was much smaller than that of Britain and Germany. In the Second World War we are measuring the effect of attempts to restrict supply to large economies at exceptionally high levels of production and whose consumption of the commodities we are considering was very high. This was less so in Japan and it is much less so in the case of all the possible embargoes and blockades currently under discussion. Yet against this must be weighed the fact that Japan is a series of islands.

American strategy was deliberately aimed at destroying inter-island transportation links, and these links were in fact seriously and increasingly weakened. The effect of this on the restriction of supply could only be measured accurately at the individual enterprise level and the United States Strategic Bombing Survey was not allowed to pursue its studies at this level after its early reports on separate aircraft-manufacturing companies. We do not know the inter-island distribution of stockpiles nor is there any comprehensive data for inter-island movement of commodities. There is substantial evidence, but no consistent proof, that supply was restricted to important enterprises to the point where they were not producing at all. But the impact of that on the economy or on the fighting front can also not be measured accurately because of the missing information about important variables.

These variables, however, are central to the argument. Why should it be supposed that the possibilities of success in a strategy of restriction of supply, *once that strategy has been put into effect*, are any more measurable or sure than the possibilities of success in armed combat? Accident, unforeseen change, uncontrollable variables, human error, defects of administrative and military machinery used to implement the strategy—all are equally present and all must be taken into account. This very point can be exemplified by attempting to weigh the multitudinous different possible economic causes of Japan's gradual collapse in 1945 or of the downturn in German war production after July 1944. If these are then set in their full complexity against the no-less-complex consequences of armed attack on both countries, the vanity of trying to assess accurately the economic outcome of an uncontrolled strategic experiment is obvious. All that is possible is to draw a reasonable inference from the evidence. But the inference itself is so disputable that the best grounds for choosing restriction of supply as a strategy may well not be its predicted consequences at all, but the fact that it is more conformable to the overall political, economic, social, and ideological framework in which strategy has to be formulated at any given time. Precisely the same remark applies except in the most desperate circumstances to armed combat.

It follows from this that the restrictions on production in any of the industries consuming the raw materials examined here were also compounded of numerous variables of which the shortage of raw material inputs was only one. Tables 3.11 and 3.12 (referring to Japan) exemplify this point, unless, of course, the discrepancies between actual production and potential production, as measured by total availability of raw material, are explained by the growing difficulty of inter-island transportation.

TABLE 3.11: Supply of Coal in the Japanese Economy (10^3 metric tons)

	Stockpile at Start of January	*Production*	*Net Imports*	*Consumption*
1940	1473	57309	8632	—
1941	1762	55602	7846	60140
1942	3326	54178	7152	58797
1943	3159	55538	4929	56709
1944	3816	49335	2421	47471

Source: United States Strategic Bombing Survey, *Coal and Steel in Japan's War Economy*, pp. 21, 23.

TABLE 3.12: Supply of Iron Ore in the Japanese Economy (10^3 metric tons)

	Theoretical Requirement of Steel Industry at Full Capacity	*Stockpile in January*	*"Imports"*	*Total Available*	*Actual Consumption*
1940	n.a.*	3952	6846	10798	6986
1941	10567	3812	6625	10437	7832
1942	10567	2605	7669	10274	8875
1943	10567	1399	7524	8923	8131
1944	11313	792	6077	6869	6197

*n.a. = not available.

Source: United States Strategic Bombing Survey, *Coal and Steel in Japan's War Economy*, p. 70.

With all these reservations, the reasonable inference from the evidence of the Second World War might not therefore be very different from that to be drawn from the whole span of modern history. Restriction of supply can be a highly effective strategy but in the great majority of cases it cannot be shown that it has been so. This seems to apply in peace as well as war. As a strategy its outcome is as unforeseeable as armed combat. Economic "sanctions" in peacetime against a potential enemy must be assessed in the same way. Their outcome when applied against Japan before 1940, as in the case of their use against Italy in the mid-1930s, produced such changes of policy in both countries as to entirely alter the parameters of strategic action.

For restriction of supply to be effective, however, a genuinely accurate and detailed knowledge of an enemy's economy needs to be available. Both on the German and Allied sides in the two World Wars the problem was that neither side really knew enough about the detailed workings of the other's economy. Whether that has been sufficiently changed by the much more accurate intelligence-gathering methods now available is a moot point. The mechanics of substitution in a war economy are finally determined by cost calculations which are difficult for a combatant power to assess accurately even within its own economy. The same can be said about the policy of reduction of specifications. Had the restriction of supply of nonferrous metals to the German economy been concentrated more intensively on wolfram, together with the supply of industrial diamonds, this would have been much more effective than the dispersal of effort over the whole range of so-called strategic goods. It would have produced an immediate reduction in the input of machine-tools for shaping and cutting armor-plate. It is surely the case that a similar wasteful dispersal of effort goes into the control and embargo of strategic goods in international trade with the Eastern bloc now. The success of Allied restriction of aviation fuel supply in Germany in 1944 was achieved, quite literally, by hit and miss methods, although, had the purely economic and statistical advice of the "targeting" committees been followed, this would have been a higher priority target than it actually was. This, however, would also have been true of the attempt to restrict German ballbearing supply, which was by every measure, including cost effectiveness, a disastrous failure.

It may well be doubted whether in any future warfare the strategy of restriction of supply would come into consideration. But it has become an integral part of international strategy since the 1930s and shows no sign of diminishing in importance. If the historical lessons are of any value they would be of two kinds. The first is that however appropriate restriction of supply may seem to a power which is not only immensely important in world trade but must also synthesize a strategy within a complex mesh of democratic and liberal constraints, it is likely in many cases to be relatively unsuccessful no matter how strong the reasons for choosing it as a strategy. It is no less a risk than armed combat if success, rather than cost, is the criterion of choice. On several important occasions in modern history attempts to control supply at source have only succeeded in adding to the number of combatant powers which a country has had to face. The second is that restriction of supply depends for its effectiveness on an extremely accurate assessment of the likely direction of a very large number of interlinked microeconomic decisions in an enemy economy. It requires therefore not only an exhaustive and continuous input of accurate economic intelligence but also that such intelligence be regarded with a constantly skeptical eye. If the intelligence input about "enemy" economies is now sufficiently accurate, history might suggest a third lesson—it is that restriction of supply might well be a more effective policy if the risk of concentrating the effort on a significantly smaller number of commodities could be justified.

4

Economics, Strategy, and War in Historical Perspective

John H. Maurer

No examination of the history of war can ignore the pervasive influence of economic considerations on the strategies of Great Powers. Throughout history assumptions about the nature of economies have served as axioms guiding the strategic thinking of the statesman and the soldier alike. Economic considerations have also served to define the strategic options available to policymakers by acting as constraints on the duration, the geographical extent, and the intensity of combat operations. It must be emphasized that this is not an economically deterministic view of strategy, but a recognition of the importance of economic factors in shaping the strategic dogmas and operational approaches of decision makers in wartime.

The purpose of this chapter is to examine these underlying connections between strategy and economics. First, I explore the manifold ways in which economic considerations influence strategic thought and war planning. In the second part of the chapter I examine the development of strategic theories and operational doctrines that were predicated on the vulnerability of economies to attack.

ECONOMIC BACKGROUND TO STRATEGY

The relationship between strategy and economics has been the source of major strategic miscalculations. History records numerous examples of strategies that failed because they were based on flawed economic assumptions. This was certainly the case in 1914 when the European Great Powers went to war with the belief that the conflict would be short—lasting no longer than a few months.

Liberal dogmas about economics that were then fashionable—such as the interdependence of Great Power economies, the seemingly prohibitive cost of waging a modern war, and the supposed limited ability of the state to intervene in national economies—seemed to dictate the necessity of short wars in the modern era. Like the campaigns of Napoleon a century earlier and the wars conducted by the elder Moltke at the middle of the nineteenth century, a military decision regarding the war would be reached by the initial battles and by the subsequent pursuit the victorious army conducted deep into the interior of the enemy's country. Kaiser Wilhelm well captured this widespread notion when he told his soldiers leaving for the front during the first week of August: "You will be home before the leaves have fallen from the trees."[1]

Guided by this belief that a war between modern European states would be short, military planners in the general staffs of the Great Powers concentrated on elaborating what they saw as the ingredients for decisive success: railway schedules to expedite deployment and operational plans aiming for the destruction of the enemy's armies in battle. A.J.P. Taylor is certainly correct in saying that the Great Powers of this era "were, as their name implies, organizations for power, that is in the last resort for war . . . the basic test for them as Great Powers was their ability to wage war."[2] The ability to wage war, however, was narrowly measured in terms of the time needed for deployment, the number of artillery pieces in a division, and the sum of the divisions that could be placed in the field. Industrial capacity, agricultural production, and the concomitant institutions capable of organizing people and resources for a protracted conflict played no part in the calculations of military planners. This restricted focus of war planning precluded military planners from looking beyond the first battles and imagining how the war would be fought if the initial engagements produced no decision. After all, a protracted conflict, lasting beyond the initial battles, could not be reduced to the precision of a railway schedule or the daily march rate of a body of troops in an operations plan. Military planners could not provide an operational solution to the problems of a long war of attrition that would test the industrial, social, and political stamina of the Great Powers. Rather than dwell on contingencies that seemed problematical, the purpose of war planning was to ensure a knock-out blow to the enemy's armies in the first round—the *Entscheidungsschlacht* (decisive battle) or *Vernichtungsschlacht* (battle of annihilation).[3] This "decisive battle of annihilation" would overwhelmingly determine the outcome of the wars fought between continental European states. Bereft of its army, a continental state would have no alternative but to seek an armistice and negotiate for the best terms it could obtain to end the war.

Since the initial battles would decide the outcome of a modern war, economic preparations for a conflict were primarily limited to keeping stockpiles of bullion on hand in central banks, harvesting crops and purchasing grain in order to provide essential supplies of food. The relatively limited importance attached to economic considerations was due in part to the experience of the last major war between European Great Powers—the Franco-Prussian War of 1870–71. In 1870 the economic position of France and Germany was roughly equal: French heavy industry produced as much iron and steel as did the whole of Germany, and, although Germany possessed a slightly larger population, Paris' financial position was undoubtedly superior to that of Berlin, as can readily be seen by the rapidity with which France, burdened by defeat and torn by a bloody civil war, paid off the huge indemnity that had been saddled on her by Germany after the war. Had France's relative military position with regard to Germany more closely resembled its relative economic position, a rapid German victory would have been unlikely. As the organized and large-scale French resistance after the opening defeats around Metz and at Sedan demonstrated, France possessed the economic resources to carry out a much larger mobilization of military forces than what it deployed in Alsace and Lorraine at the war's beginning. The opening German victories, however, robbed France of the time it needed to accomplish this transformation by exploiting the military potential of its economy to expand the army. In the Franco-Prussian War the ability to deploy superior forces during the initial battles had proved to be decisive.[4]

The essential component of the short war dogma, then, was the climactic battle of annihilation. At the beginning of this century military planners and commentators had a distinct type of battle in mind when they spoke of a "battle of annihilation." This type of battle was characterized by the winning side capturing large numbers of prisoners, standards, and cannon. These outward signs of a battle marked the broken morale and ruptured organization of the defeated army. Captured trophies, rather than grisly "body counts," were the distinguishing feature of a successful *Feldherr* (field commander). A distinction was therefore drawn between battles that resulted in a limited victory—or what Napoleon called an "ordinary victory" and what Clausewitz termed an *einfachen Sieges* (simple victory)—and a battle of annihilation. An ordinary victory, while it could result in the defeated army retreating and suffering heavy losses, did not destroy an adversary's organized power for resistance and would not produce a short war. The Battle of Borodino during Napoleon's Russian campaign of 1812 is perhaps the best known battle of this type. Operations planners on the general staffs thus sought to avoid fighting these types of battles and instead aimed at annihilating their opponent's army. The battle of annihilation was the solution to avoiding an operational stalemate and a protracted conflict.[5]

To postwar historians and military commentators seeking answers to how the cruel deadlock of the trenches came about, the focus of military planners before 1914 on deployment plans aiming at decisive battles seemed to be unduly narrow and far removed from the reality of the type of war that followed. For one, Gerhard Ritter decried the "purely military" nature of staff planning that was not bound by any meaningful political guidelines or constraints.[6] Others, like Winston Churchill, were appalled by the horrible slaughter caused by modern weaponry and shocked that military planners had failed to take account of this development in their planning.[7] Rather than being solutions, the deployment plans of the general staffs were said to be blueprints for disaster. In France, parliamentarians conducted investigations into the reasons for the French General Staff's inadequate preparations in the prewar era to defend the industrial regions of Lorraine and Flanders. In writing about the disastrous failure of France's Plan XVII in 1914, Bernard Brodie remarked that this "was neither the first nor the last time that bad anthropology contributed to bad strategy."[8] It was also an instance of bad economics. The "short-war paradigm" of the French High Command had permitted the Germans to occupy these important industrial and mining areas, thereby crippling France's efforts during the First World War to sustain a war of material attrition. Yet the French were not alone in 1914: military planners in all of the European Great Powers failed to appreciate the importance of industrial production and technological innovation in modern warfare.[9]

These criticisms are perhaps only clear with the advantage of hindsight, however. T.S. Kuhn has noted in his analysis of the process lying behind scientific inquiry and discovery that a paradigm "is declared invalid only if an alternate candidate is available to take its place. . . . The decision to reject one paradigm is always simultaneously the decision to accept another."[10] A similar pattern of reasoning provided the underpinnings of military theory and planning in the years immediately before the First World War. There seemed to be no alternative paradigm to the dogma of the battle of annihilation. To be sure, there were some notable dissenters to the notion that the next war would be short. There was the famous warning of the elder Moltke, who prophesied in his farewell speech to the German Reichstag that if "war should break out . . . it might be a Seven or even a Thirty Years' War."[11] Hans Delbrück also became involved in a celebrated and lengthy debate on strategy when he articulated the concept of *Ermattungsstrategie* (strategy of attrition) that was at odds with the operational tenets of the Great General Staff in Berlin.[12]

The most extensive critique of the short war dogma appearing before 1914 was written, however, by the Polish financier Ivan Bloch. His massive study, entitled *The Future of War in Its Technical, Economic and Political Significance*,[13] argued that wars between industrial societies, fought with modern weaponry, would not be decided by a single campaign. Bloch ridiculed the historical approach to war of the general staffs that sought to bring about a modern Cannae, Austerlitz, and Sedan. "What is the use," he wrote,

> of talking about the past when you are dealing with an altogether new set of considerations? Consider for a moment what nations were a hundred years ago and what they are today. In those days before railways, telegraphs, steam ships, etc., were invented each nation was more or less a homogeneous,

> self-contained, self-sufficing unit. . . . All this is changed. . . . Every year the interdependence of nations upon each other for the necessaries of life is greater than it ever was before . . . . Hence the first thing that war would do would be to deprive the Powers that made it of all opportunity of benefiting by the products of the nations against whom they were fighting . . . . The soldier is going down and the economist is going up.

The growing economic interdependence of the Great Powers thus was making war a form of economic suicide.

In addition, Bloch argued that the development of modern weaponry had reached the stage where the "soldier . . . has so perfected the mechanism of slaughter that he has practically secured his own extinction." If war did occur, he predicted:

> At first there will be increased slaughter on so terrible a scale as to render it impossible to get troops to push the battle to a decisive issue. They will try to, thinking that they are fighting under the old conditions, and they will learn such a lesson that they will abandon the attempt forever . . . . The war . . . will become a kind of stalemate, in which neither army being able to get at the other, both armies will be maintained in opposition to each other, threatening each other, but never able to deliver a final and decisive attack.

The stalement and heavy losses on the battlefield, coupled with the economic dislocation caused by the conflict, would only end with the economic collapse and social revolution of the belligerents. Bloch hoped that his study would demonstrate the practical impossibility of war: "Even in the leading circles of Europe hardly anyone will dare deny that it will be possible to bring our means of annihilation to such a degree of perfection that war must become completely impossible. But the question is: have we not already reached such a stage of development in military apparatus, does the sum total of conditions not already exist under which we must eliminate war, since it has not only become a shattering experience, but also politically fruitless?"[14]

Yet Bloch's avowedly pacifist stance was criticized at the time as being naive. Delbrück argued that despite the growing economic interdependence of states, international political rivalries would continue, and that peace could only be maintained by the ability of military power to deter conflict. The ancient Roman adage, *si vis pacem, para bellum,* best expressed what was considered to be the only realistic approach to ensure peace.[15] Moreover, Bloch's stark portrait of the course and consequences of some future prolonged war of attrition could be used to buttress the argument that there was no alternative to planning for a short war decided by a battle of annihilation. Count Alfred Schlieffen, the high priest of the dogma of the battle of annihilation, emphasized this point. He believed wars of attrition "are impossible in an age when a nation's existence is founded on the uninterrupted continuance of its trade and industry; indeed a rapid decision is essential if the machinery that has been brought to a standstill is to be set in motion again. A strategy of exhaustion is unworkable when the maintenance of millions demands the expenditures of billions." The "degeneration" of the military operations during the Russo-Japanese War in Manchuria into trench warfare further convinced Schlieffen of the importance of seeking an early decision: "Out there in Manchuria they may face each other for months on end in impregnable positions. In Western Europe we cannot allow ourselves the luxury of waging a war in this manner. The machine with its thousand wheels, upon which millions depend for their livelihood, cannot stand still for long. . . . We must try to overthrow the enemy quickly and destroy him."[16] Outside of pacifism or a protracted war of attrition, there seemed to be no alternative to the short-war paradigm propagated by the general staffs in the continental Great Powers. The battle of annihilation would thus be used to forestall the horrors of military stalemate, economic collapse, and political revolution.

In order to avoid this catastrophe, all the continental Great Powers assumed the offensive in the attempt to overthrow their adversaries quickly at the outbreak of war. The Russians carried out an amended version of Plan 19, which called for simultaneous offensives against both Germany and Austria-Hungary.[17] In Austria-Hungary Conrad von Hötzendorf committed his forces to offensives against Russia and Serbia.[18] Joffre's Plan XVII sent the French army onto the offensive into the Rhineland.[19] Finally, Germany attempted to carry out the famous *manoeuvre sur les derrières* through Belgium that Schlieffen and the younger Moltke had developed during the preceding ten years.[20] When all of these plans failed to bring the expected rapid defeat of the enemy, the inadequacy of prewar economic preparations for a longer conflict became readily apparent. By late October 1914 the prewar stockpiles of arms and ammunition were exhausted and the belligerents were forced to rely upon current production, which did not match the rates of wartime consumption. This resulted in the curtailment of military operations amid talk of a "shell shortage" and "munitions crisis." With the onset of positional warfare during the first war winter and the great battles of *matériel* beginning in 1916, strategy could no longer be equated solely with operations plans. A new conception of strategy had emerged for the industrial age that saw war not only as a clash of armies on the battlefield, but as the competition of economic systems to produce the tools of war. Modern warfare between Great Powers required more than the call-up and deployment of armies, it demanded the mobilization of entire economies to produce large quantities of war materiel. As Bloch had predicted, in a war of attrition the plant manager would play as important a part in the war effort as the military officer. One of the marks, then, of a Great Power is the ability to sustain a long war of attrition if the opening military operations do not produce a decision on the battlefield.

In a war of attrition, when a knock-out blow cannot be delivered in the first round of fighting, economic considerations begin to play a much larger role in determining a Great Power's strategy. Instead of viewing warfare predominantly in operational terms, decision makers pay much more attention to the relative economic strengths and weaknesses of the belligerents in their assessments of the likely outcome of a conflict. The objective of policymakers in a war of attrition is quite simply to muster the resources to outlast an adversary while at the same time preventing him from delivering a decisive military blow. This is the strategy Britain and France pursued when they went to war in 1939. At that time the British and French did not feel that it was possible to obtain a decisive military victory over Germany in a short war. As a consequence, their operational plans were essentially defensive and their view of the likely duration of the war was that it would last over several years. In a war of this duration, Britain and France pinned their hopes for victory on the belief that they possessed the superior economic resources required for a long conflict. The war would not be decided by the opening military operations. British and French leaders believed that the war would ultimately be won by the side with the stronger economy.[21] What is more, Germany's political and military leadership agreed with this assessment about the relative economic and strategic position of the European powers. As Alan Milward has argued, Germany adopted what he has termed a "Blitzkrieg strategy" in order to avoid having to fight the war of attrition its adversaries planned to wage.[22] Policymakers, then, who advocate a strategy of protracted conflict have generally done so because they see their own country's economic position to be stronger than that of their adversaries.

Another fascinating example of the dynamics of a war of attrition can be found in the great war between Athens and Sparta for mastery of the Greek world that is the subject of Thucydides' monumental history. This conflict, which began in the spring of 431 B.C., would ultimately drag on for 27 years and result in the destruction of the Athenian Empire. Actually it is composed of two major wars, each of ten years' duration, with a period of seven years of uneasy peace sandwiched in between. The first of these ten years' wars has come to be known as the Archidamian War, after the Spartan king who commanded the Peloponnesian forces in its initial campaigns. Perhaps the war might have been more aptly called the Periclean War, however, in recognition of the central role played by the great Athenian war leader Pericles in shaping the war's dynamics and outcome. Athenian strategy under Pericles rested on two assumptions: first, that Athens could withstand a protracted war of attrition better than the Spartan-led coalition of Peloponnesian Greek states, and, second, that the Athenian army had no chance of victory in a short war decided by a battle between the armies of the two sides.[23]

In order to understand the strategy of Pericles, it is necessary to take a brief look at the structure and nature of the Athenian Empire. The Athenian Empire had its beginnings during the winter of 478/477 B.C. when a group of Greek states located on the islands and coastlines of the Aegean Sea banded together into a confederation known as the Delian League. The primary purpose of this confederation was to maintain a standing fleet to fight the war then taking place against Persia. The construction, manning, and support of this fleet was an expensive undertaking, however, that required a system of regular payments by the league's members into a central treasury located on the island of Delos. Being the largest, most powerful, and most prestigious state in the league, Athens determined the contributions to be made by the league's members for the upkeep of the fleet. Some states furnished ships and men, while others provided only money to the central treasury for the upkeep of the fleet. Thucycides tells us that over time "most of the allies allowed their assessments to be changed from ships to money because of their reluctance to embark on military campaigns and so that they might not be away from home." With the allies shrinking from the arduous duties of combat, "the Athenian navy grew strong at their expense," and Athens shouldered most of the league's fighting. When some states refused to continue making contributions and sought to leave the league, "they always found themselves inadequately armed and inexperienced in war," and thus unable to prevent Athens from using her powerful fleet to force them to resume their payments into the central treasury.[24] By the outbreak of the Peloponnesian War, the naval alliance formed to fight Persia had been transformed into a naval empire ruled by Athens. This transformation of the Delian League into the Athenian Empire is perhaps best symbolized by the movement of the central treasury in 454/453 B.C. from Delos to Athens. Another important step in this transformation of Athens into an empire was the construction of three long walls connecting the city of Athens to the sea and the port of Piraeus. In ancient Greece the capture of a walled city was a difficult task. The three-year siege of Platea during the Archidamian War shows how only a relatively small group of defenders could hold off a besieging force many times their own number. When a city did fall, it was generally not on the account of an assault, but do to deception, treachery, or starvation.[25] The long walls thus made Athens virtually impregnable to a land assault. In effect, Athens had been changed into an "island" empire when the long walls were finished in the spring of 457 B.C.: so long as the Athenian fleet remained strong enough to protect the seaborne movement of grain from the Black Sea, Athens could not be starved into submission by an enemy attacking only from the landward side. This conjunction of tribute from the empire, the security of the long walls, and naval supremacy in Greek waters provided the foundation for Athenian power.

The sources of Athenian power were much different from that of her principal antagonist Sparta. Unlike Athens, the main repository of Spartan power rested in its large, well-trained, and experienced hoplite army. While Thucydides does not provide detailed figures for the size of the Peloponnesian army led by Sparta, modern historians have calculated its strength to be two or three times the size of the Athenian army. With their superb army, which Pericles believed "could stand up to all the rest of Hellas in a single battle,"

Sparta could confidently expect to defeat the Athenian army if it came out from behind the protection provided by the long walls. Even if the Athenians did not oblige and refused to fight a major engagement, the Spartans believed that "they would destroy the power of Athenians in a few years if they wasted their land." Moreover, most Greeks shared Sparta's assessment of the time needed to defeat Athens. Thucydides says that at the beginning of the war "some thought that, if the Peloponnesians invaded Attica, Athens might survive for a year, and while others put the figure at two or three years, no one imagined she could last more than that." Stated briefly, Sparta's strategy was based on the assumption that the Athenian Empire could be defeated in a short war by invading Attica with a powerful army, destroying the Athenian army in battle, and ravaging the countryside surrounding the city of Athens.[26]

The Spartan King Archidamus was less sanguine, however, about Sparta's chances for quickly defeating Athens. Instead of being forced to surrender after the destruction of its territory in Attica, Archidamus believed that Athens possessed the resources in its empire to carry on the war. If that occurred, he asked his fellow citizens how they expected the war could be brought to a successful conclusion. Since Sparta and her allies lacked a fleet capable of seriously challenging the Athenian navy, as was clearly shown by Corinth's defeat at the naval battle of Sybota, there was little hope of striking at Athens in the Aegean by encouraging and supporting revolts in its empire against Athenian rule. Archidamus warned that "we must not bolster ourselves up with the false hope that if we devastate their land, the war will soon be over. I fear that it is more likely that we shall be leaving it to our children after us."[27] As we know, Archidamus' counsel was rejected by the Spartans, but his prediction was nonetheless borne out by the events of the war. As J.K. Anderson has observed: "Spartan offensive strategy . . . was based on the assumption that . . . an opponent's submission could be obtained by mastery of the open field. . . . a destructive march through the enemy's farm lands might be both profitable and enjoyable. For this method of warfare, the hoplite army was the perfect instrument. The Spartan mistake lay in supposing that this strategy was as applicable to Periclean Athens . . . as to the country towns of the Peloponnese."[28]

While Sparta began the war with a major offensive into their enemy's territory, Pericles argued that Athens must remain on the defensive and demonstrate to the Spartans that they did not possess the strength to overturn the Athenian Empire. With the tribute from the empire, Athens possessed the economic resources to maintain its fleet and feed its population even if the farmlands of Attica were ravaged by the Spartan army. Athens could thus make the war last much longer than what the Spartans and most Greeks anticipated. Moreover, the economic weakness of the Peloponnesian states would prevent the Spartans from challenging Athenian naval mastery by sending expeditions into the Aegean. In a speech recorded by Thucydides, Pericles pointed out to the Athenians that the military operations of the Spartans would be circumscribed by their limited economic resources: "The Peloponnesians cultivate their own land themselves; they have no financial resources either as individuals or as states; then they have no experience of fighting overseas, nor of fighting that lasts a long time, since the wars they fight against each other are, because of their poverty, short affairs. Such people are incapable of often manning a fleet or often sending out an army, when that means absence from their own lands, expense from their own funds . . . . this is the main point: they will be handicapped by lack of money and delayed by the time they will have to take in procuring it." As long as the Athenian army remained behind the Long Walls and refused to be drawn into a major land engagement, and the fleets of the Peloponnesian states remained insignificant, there was no means for the military power of the two sides to be brought together in a manner that would produce a decision to the war. The war would be decided by the side better able to stand the economic and psychological strain of a long conflict. Because of its economic strength, Pericles believed Athens could maintain this strain better than Sparta. Thucydides says that Pericles' argument was: "the strength of Athens came from the money paid in tribute by her allies, and victory in war depended on a combination of intelligent resolution and financial resources."[29]

The influential German historian Hans Delbrück used the term *Ermattungsstrategie*, or strategy of exhaustion, to describe the strategy of Pericles. According to Delbrück: "The greatest strength of a strategy of exhaustion is time, and hence one of the fundamental laws, the economy of resources."[30] Without a doubt, economy of resources lay at the center of Pericles' strategy. Pericles warned that Athens must remain on the defensive and not try to expand her empire during the war with Sparta. On the eve of war he told his countrymen that Athens had the resources to defeat Sparta so long as "you are willing not to try to extend your empire at the same time as you are fighting the war and not to add self-imposed dangers, for I am more afraid of our own mistakes than the strategy of our opponents." Offensive schemes to expand the empire would be expensive and would probably only result in a disaster, weakening the ability of Athens to outlast the Spartans. Thucydides recalled Pericles saying that "if the Athenians would remain quiet, take care of their fleet, refrain from trying to extend their empire in wartime and thus put their city in danger, they would prevail."[31]

Pericles' strategy also depended on the Athenians husbanding the gold and silver collected in tribute from the empire and stockpiled on the Acropolis. This supply of precious metals would pay for the Athenian war effort. Unlike the Spartans, Pericles believed that "accumulated wealth, not forced contributions, sustain a war." Because of its importance, Thucydides provides a detailed picture of Athenian gold and silver revenues and reserves on the outbreak of war in 431 B.C. The annual income of Athens was approximately 1,000 talents. Of this amount, 400 talents came from internal sources of revenue, such as rents, custom duties, market taxes, and court fees; however, this sum provided the treasury with no surplus since it went to pay for current expenses of the state. In addition to these revenues generated from internal sources, Athens received a further 600 talents from imperial sources that would be available to help pay for the war's expenses. This sum, though considerable, could not pay the annual costs of waging war, however. The annual expense incurred by Athens to wage a major war has been estimated by Donald Kagan to be approximately 2,000 talents. The difference between the annual cost of making war and the revenue from the empire had to be met by borrowing from the stockpiles of gold and silver on the Acropolis. There the Athenians had 6,000 talents of coined silver. In addition, uncoined gold and silver worth at least 500 talents was deposited there. Finally, the gold plate on the statue of Athena on the Acropolis, worth at least 40 talents, could be used in the case of dire need, but, as Pericles pointed out, "if they did use this gold for their own preservation they must restore it again afterwards in the same or in a greater quantity." Of these sums in reserve, a special fund of 1,000 talents was set aside to be used only in the extreme emergency "of their enemies coming to attack them with a fleet by sea." In order to preserve this special reserve fund, the Athenian people passed an extraordinary law providing the death penalty "for anyone who should suggest or should put to the vote any proposal for using this money" for any purpose other than for a final naval effort to avert surrender. Pericles believed that Athens possessed the resources to defend its empire and, over time, to weaken the resolve of Sparta to carry on the war.[32] F.E. Adcock has described the strategy of Pericles well: "Pericles must prove that the existence of Athens and of the Athenian Empire could not be destroyed . . . . It was a reasonable calculation that the nerve and will-power of her opponents might well be exhausted before the treasures on the Acropolis, and they might admit that the power and determination of Athens were invincible."[33] And, according to Delbrück: "Everything depended on who first reached the point of no longer being able to bear the pain, who first became exhausted."[34]

In the event, Athenian reserves of silver and gold proved to be inadequate as the war dragged on much longer than anyone had predicted. By 428 B.C., that is after the three years of war which some considered to be the longest Athens could hold out, one authority has calculated that the reserve on the Acropolis had been reduced to 945 talents, not including the special fund of 1,000 talents set aside for an emergency. This meant that, unless the scope or intensity of Athenian operations were curtailed, Athens would have to increase its annual state revenues. Perhaps the only way to accomplish this, however, was by increasing the assessments of tribute paid by the states comprising the empire. Yet such a move would be unpopular and carried with it the danger of bringing about a revolt in the empire against Athenian rule. Already in 440 B.C., before the outbreak of the war with Sparta, Athens faced a major rebellion within her empire when the states of Samos and Byzantium rose up in revolt. This rebellion, which tied down a large army and fleet for an entire year before it was crushed, showed the extreme peril Athens would be in if confronted by large-scale revolts in the empire. Of course, this peril would only be greater if it occurred while Athens was engaged in a war for survival with the dogged Spartans. Athenian policymakers therefore were caught in a dangerous dilemma: they hestitated to demand increases in tribute from the empire while at war with Sparta for fear of inciting a revolt, but the successful conduct of this war required more resources which could only be found from tributary states. Fortunately for Athens, the Spartans suffered a heavy defeat at Pylos in the fall of 425 B.C. In the wake of this victory, Athens felt strong enough to increase the tribute from the empire. By this measure the annual revenues from the empire rose almost threefold from the amount of 431 B.C. to 1460 talents. This increase thereby permitted the Athenians to maintain their war effort at a high level until they were finally defeated at sea in 404 B.C. in the decisive naval battle of Aegospotami.[35]

The examples of the First World War and the Archidamian War clearly illustrate how deeply rooted strategic thinking is in the economic dogmas of the day. In both instances, on account of their misunderstanding of the ability of economies to adapt to the requirements of wartime, policymakers made serious strategic miscalculations about the likely duration and outcome of the conflict. Since the initial operations did not result in a rapid end to hostilities, both these wars dragged on much longer than what had generally been thought possible before the outbreak of hostilities. When military forces failed to bring a rapid decision to these conflicts, then the economic strength and social stability of the belligerents became crucial in determining their outcome. As the following section on the interplay of economics and operations will show, many other examples could be used to illustrate the increased importance of economic considerations in shaping the competing strategies of belligerents during a protracted conflict. Napoleon's mercantilist assumptions about the nature of economies, for instance, certainly shaped his strategic decisions during the war against Britain. Despite his impressive military victories over the continental Great Powers of Europe, Napoleon could not decisively challenge Britain on the high seas on account of France's naval weakness after Trafalgar. Napoleon therefore sought to bring the war to a conclusion by striking directly at Britain's economy. His Continental System, whereby he attempted to restrict British trade with Europe and drain Britain's supplies of bullion, failed to produce Britain's defeat.[36] It is critical therefore that decision makers understand the important role economic assumptions play in shaping their approaches to strategy.

THE INTERPLAY OF ECONOMICS AND OPERATIONS

Great Powers have often undertaken military campaigns to capture or protect economic centers or movements of resources that are perceived to be of vital importance for its security. Strategy—in the sense of the planning and carrying out of military operations designed to bring about the defeat of an adversary—is frequently concerned with the attack and defense of the economic basis for military power. The vital commodity of oil, for instance, played a crucial role in determining the geographical scope and the intensity of military operations during the Second World War. The safety of Romanian oil fields was a constant preoccupation of Hitler and German military planners. On account of its importance, Hitler could not afford to be indifferent to Balkan political developments and could only look on the Soviet military advance in Bessarabia as a threat to Germany's security.[37] Later, when Germany attacked the Soviet Union, one of the principal objectives of German military operations was the conquest of oil-producing regions of the Caucasus. This drive to capture oil led to the dangerous overextension of German forces and to the crucial Soviet victory at Stalingrad during the winter of 1942–43.[38] Throughout the war German naval, air, and ground operations were hindered by shortages of oil supplies. Germany's adversaries sought to heighten these shortages by various means. Britain and France tried to prevent Romanian oil from reaching Germany by making large preemptive purchases there; the Soviet Union undertook massive demolitions in the oil fields located in the foothills of the Caucasus that fell into German hands during the summer of 1942; and Allied air forces made major efforts to destroy oil-producing facilities throughout German-occupied Europe.

In the case of Japan, access to the oil fields of the Dutch East Indies exercised an important hold on Japanese strategic thinking and planning during the Second World War. By bringing this oil-producing region and the raw material supplies of Southeast Asia under Japan's control, Japanese leaders were trying to end their country's dependence on rival Great Powers for supplies of vital commodities. In 1940, for instance, Japan had to rely on its most dangerous potential adversary, the United States, for approximately 80 percent of its oil supplies. When negotiations to obtain reliable access to the oil of the Dutch East Indies failed, Japanese decision makers became increasingly convinced that the conquest of this region was the only way to solve Japan's long-term security problem. Indeed, the Japanese decision for war against the United States and Britain owed much to Japan's critical shortage of domestic oil production. When the United States government moved to stop shipments of oil to Japan at the end of July 1941, it became of critical importance that Japan obtain access to oil before its carefully husbanded stockpiles were exhausted. After all, as Admiral Shimada, the navy minister at the time, pointed out: "If there were no supply of oil, battleships and any other warships would be nothing more than scarecrows."[39] Like Germany's attack on the Soviet Union, Japanese military operations aimed at seizing control of oil-producing regions.

The close interplay of economic considerations and military operations historically can perhaps be seen most clearly in naval warfare. The attack and defense of ocean-going commerce has long been a prominent feature of naval strategy. There have been many instances throughout history of Great Powers that have depended on the seaborne transportation of vital commodities for their economic livelihood, social stability, and political cohesion. The rise and decline of these states has been intimately bound up with their ability to use naval power to protect the movements of these vital commodities along trade routes. To be sure, what constitutes a vital commodity has changed from age to age. Periclean Athens depended for its food supply on the grain-producing regions bordering the Black Sea. The safe transportation of grain through the Straits and the Aegean Sea thus was the lifeline of the Athenian Empire. As has been noted earlier, when the Spartans severed this line after their great naval victory at Aegospotami, a small city located on the narrow Dardanelles, Athens was forced to surrender less than six months later when it exhausted its stores of grain. On account of Athens' inability to keep open this vital line of supply, the long, drawn-out Peloponnesian Wars came to a sudden end with the collapse of the Athenian Empire. In a similar fashion, the seaborne movement of grain supplies was a crucial consideration in the military and naval campaigns of the Roman and Byzantine Empires. Another notable example is the important role the treasure *flota* of gold and silver from the New World played in providing the economic underpinnings for imperial Spain's far-flung military campaigns. On several occasions Philip II found his military enterprises disrupted when shipments of bullion from New Spain failed to arrive on account of Dutch and English attacks, and, as a consequence, the Spanish government had to declare its bankruptcy after failing to meet payments on loans it had contracted. While the impact that these attacks had on her ability to wage war has often been exaggerated, Spain's rivals—England, France, and Holland—nonetheless repeatedly sought to cripple Spanish power in Europe by attempting to capture, destroy, or delay this important source of income.

The strategic importance given to these supplies of bullion in the wars that occurred during the 200 year period between the late sixteenth and late eighteenth centuries can be likened to the emphasis that has been put on the security of Persian Gulf oil over the last ten years.[40] In addition to the gold and silver from the New World, all the major Atlantic naval powers during the era of sailing warships—Britain, France, the Netherlands, and Spain—depended on access to "naval stores," such as timber, masts, spars, pitch, tar, flax, and hemp, from the region of the Baltic Sea. When the Baltic states of Russia, Sweden, and Denmark joined together into agreements with one another during the eighteenth century to restrict the movements of these supplies—in effect, an OPEC for naval stores—the navies of the Atlantic powers faced the bleak prospect of being denied access to these critical commodities in wartime. Given the importance of these naval stores, it is not surprising that the Atlantic powers attempted to build stockpiles of these supplies or look elsewhere for alternative sources of supply, as Britain did in North America.[41]

One of the most fascinating examples, however, of naval operations being guided by the seaborne movements of commerce is the First Anglo-Dutch War, which came about as a consequence of trade and commercial rivalries between England and the Netherlands. Favored by its geographical position astride some of Europe's most important sea lanes and inland waterways, the Netherlands had become by the middle of the seventeenth century the world's leading commercial power. It has been estimated by Professor Charles Wilson that the Dutch carried approximately three quarters of the trade in grain and between a half and three quarters of the trade in timber from the Baltic region to the rest of Europe. In addition, the Dutch controlled the important trade of Swedish metals. The return trade to the Baltic was also dominated by the Dutch: three quarters of the salt from France and Portugal was carried by Dutch ships, while more than half the cloth reaching the Baltic was made or finished in the Netherlands. European consumption of colonial wares was also to a large extent in Dutch hands. In order to carry this trade, the Dutch merchant marine had grown to enormous proportions. The shipping industry of the principal Dutch state of Holland, for instance, was reputed to have by itself employed 168,000 seaman. On account of this dominance of Northern Europe's trade, the Dutch earned the accolade of "carriers of the world." This Dutch maritime predominance was further reinforced by the thousands of boats employed in its massive and thriving fishing industry.[42]

These Dutch commercial successes rankled in England, however. English commercial circles wanted to break what they perceived as the Dutch stranglehold on Europe's trade, and, according to the mercantilist theories propagated in that age, England's share of this commerce could only be increased by a drop in that of the Netherlands. In the words of the English Admiral Monck, "The Dutch have too much trade, and the English are resolved to take it from them."[43] War against the Netherlands was one way in which England could hurt Dutch trade and, presumably, increase its own. This commercial rivalry erupted into fighting in the spring of 1652 when Dutch warships escorting a homebound convoy of merchant ships through the English Channel became involved in combat with English warships. What began as a skirmish rapidly escalated into a major naval engagement as the main battle fleets of both sides clashed with one another after they had moved into the Channel to provide support for the ships around the convoy. This initial battle did not prove in any way decisive, but acted as a spur to both governments to hasten their preparations for war and to issue instructions to guide the naval operations of their war fleets.

In the orders to the commander of the English fleet, Admiral Blake, the Commonwealth government of Oliver Cromwell made clear that the destruction of Dutch seaborne commerce and their fishing industry was the primary English objective. As soon as the English fleet could be made ready, Blake was "directed to take and seize upon" a homeward bound convoy of Dutch merchant ships from the East Indies and "take and surprise, or otherwise to burn, sink or destroy" Dutch shipping in the North Sea engaged in the Baltic trade and in the fishing industry. The Dutch fleet, on the other hand, had orders to prevent the English from ravaging their trade. In order to accomplish this task, the principal Dutch commander, Admiral Tromp received orders to "miss no serious opportunity which you can seize . . . to attack the English fleet . . . and do all imaginable damage to it." The major battles of this First Anglo-Dutch War can thus be described as "convoy battles" since each of them came about in response to Dutch attempts to shield important convoys from attacks by the English fleet. After 15 months of bitter fighting, which included five large and hotly contested fleet actions, the English fleet achieved a measure of naval superiority that enabled them to restrict severely the movement of Dutch trade and to inflict heavy losses on Dutch shipping: well over 1,000 Dutch vessels were captured at a time when the English merchant marine amounted to perhaps only half that number. One Dutch correspondent complained: "Our trade is nearly gone, our Banks begin to be blank and lose their credit every day and cannot hold out long." Another observer recorded: "The sources of revenue that had always maintained the riches of the state, such as fisheries and commerce, were almost dry. Workshops were closed, work suspended. The Zuyder Zee became a forest of masts; the country was full of beggars; grass grew in the streets, and in Amsterdam 1,500 houses were untenanted." While this description might be overdrawn, the Dutch did indeed suffer from high unemployment, the closing down of the fisheries, soaring food prices, riots in the cities, and mutinies in their armed forces. Clearly, the Dutch decision to conclude a rapid end to hostilities was the best means of preventing the complete ruination of their economy. The English onslaught against Dutch seaborne trade and industries thus had succeeded in a relatively short period of time to defeat the premier maritime power of the age.

The First Anglo-Dutch War, however, had been fought between two navies of roughly equal combat power: neither fleet possessed a decisive superiority over the other at the outbreak of fighting, and the English had only gained the upper hand at sea by dint of hard fighting and a large shipbuilding program. Yet history also offers numerous examples of conflicts where the naval power of one side was markedly inferior to that of the other. In these situations, the question to be faced by the weaker side is to what purpose should its navy be put since it stands little chance of success in battle against the fleet of a superior adversary. One role that has often been adopted by the weaker navy is commerce raiding, designed to strike directly at an adversary's ocean-going trade without first having to fight its fleet. The objective, then, is to cripple an adversary by attacks on his economic sources of power, rather than his naval forces. Maritime powers, like Britain and Holland, which have been heavily dependent on overseas trade for their economic well-being, seemed to be particularly vulnerable to this type of onslaught. As has already been noted about the First Anglo-Dutch War, the English fleet, even though it was not inferior to the Dutch, was nevertheless given as its main objective the destruction of the seaborne trade of the Netherlands. While the English fleet happened to be strong enough to engage the Dutch on even terms, Cromwell's government nonetheless saw commerce destruction as the best means to defeat the Dutch. An inferior navy, however, could not hope to follow this example and attempt to defeat its adversary in battle; instead, inferior navies have sought to duplicate the English successes in the First Anglo-Dutch War of disrupting an enemy's commerce without first overcoming the superior fleet of a maritime opponent.

In the long series of wars fought between England and France that began in 1688 and lasted until 1815, the French navy sought to undermine England's ability to make war by repeated attacks against her commerce. One of the leading advocates of commerce warfare was none other than Sebastien le Prestre de Vauban, the great military engineer of the reign of Louis XIV. In 1706, during the War of Spanish Succession, he argued:

> If we were to be quit of the vanity of great fleets which can never suit our needs and to employ the ships of the navy partly on commerce warfare and partly in squadrons to support it, we should bring about the downfall of the English and the Dutch within about two or three years, in consequence of their great trade to all parts of the world.[44]

Although French attacks could at times be remarkably successful—as in the case of the Nine Years' War when English shipping losses reached 4,000 merchant vessels[45]—France never succeeded in crippling England's economy to the extent that the Dutch economy had been hurt during the First Anglo-Dutch War. Despite heavy shipping losses, England was never forced to make peace on account of French attacks on its commerce. In fact, England's overseas trade, and the state revenues derived from it, continued to grow throughout this period in the face of French depredations. This experience of the French navy in these wars thus appeared to demonstrate that an inferior fleet could not expect to defeat a maritime power by commerce raiding alone. This lesson, espoused by Mahan and other naval thinkers in the English-speaking world, seemed clear: commerce warfare, or *guerre de course*, could not by itself be decisive.

This dogma of naval strategy was challenged, however, by a school of naval thought known as the Jeune École, or "Young School," that originated in France around the middle of the nineteenth century.[46] Like Vauban, the Jeune École advocated commerce warfare as the primary means for an inferior navy to defeat a stronger maritime adversary. In what was the first major work of the Jeune École, entitled *De la Guerre Maritime* by Baron Richard Grivel and published in 1869, the dominance of commerce warfare is clearly stated. According to Grivel: "Commerce warfare, the most economical for the poorest fleet, is at the same time the one most proper to restore peace, since it strikes directly . . . at the very source of the prosperity of the enemy." While commerce warfare by itself had not been successful in earlier wars, the Jeune École argued that the economic conditions underlying naval warfare and strategy had been fundamentally changed by the industrial revolution, and, as a consequence, the vulnerability of maritime powers to attacks on their trade had dramatically increased. This argument seemed to be supported by the example of the highly-successful Confederate commerce raider C.S.S. *Alabama*, which had created a panic among Northern shipping owners. Here, then, was striking proof of the damage that could be done by commerce raiders to the shipping industry of a major maritime power. French naval writers further contended that attacks on merchant vessels would have an even greater impact in the case of Britain than did Confederate raids on Northern shipping. The industrialization of Britain had made that country heavily dependent on overseas trade for raw materials and foodstuffs in a way that she had not been during the eighteenth century. In 1894 it was estimated that the value of Britain's trade annually amounted to the enormous sum of over 1 billion pounds. British naval planners and commentators clearly recognized that the interruption of this trade would be a grievous blow to Britain's economy and they feared the consequences of a major attack on their country's seaborne trade. Lord George Hamilton, First Lord of the Admiralty at the time of the Naval Defense Act of 1889, described the "freedom of sea communication between Great Britain and the outer world . . . as essential to her existence as the passage of air through the windpipe of any human being is to the preservation of his life." And one British journalist, writing on naval affairs during the agitation to increase the Royal Navy in the 1880s, posed the question: "If one Alabama . . . could cause a loss of trade of over £50,000,000, what loss would be inflicted on our trade if half a dozen or a dozen, or two dozen French . . .cruisers were let loose on the immense ocean-going trade of England?"[47]

It was thus widely believed that Britain's economy could be wrecked if these commerce-destroying cruisers delivered a massive blow against British seaborne trade at the outset of a war. In a famous passage the central figure of the Jeune École, Admiral Theophile Aube, described how these attacks against shipping would take place: "Tomorrow war breaks out, a torpedo boat has sighted one of those ocean steamers freighted with a cargo of greater value than the richest galleons of Spain, the torpedo boat will follow at a distance, keeping out of sight, and when night comes on will unobserved close with the steamer and send to the bottom cargo, crew, and passengers, not only without remorse but proud of the achievement. In every part of the ocean similar atrocities will be seen." These attacks would produce a panic in Britain's financial, shipping, and insurance communities similar to the one that had occurred in the North during the American Civil War. Once this panic had taken place, Britain's economic life would be paralyzed by shortages in essential raw materials and of food. "As soon as her [Britain's] factories stop," one *Jeune École* writer predicted, "thousands of workers will be plunged into misery, and a terrible economic crisis will break out. Little by little, even famine will come on with all its horrors." Economic collapse and social upheaval would signal the end of Britain's ability to continue the conflict, even though her fleet was still intact and undefeated in battle.[48]

On account of this new vulnerability, the Jeune École argued that it was possible to defeat a major maritime power at sea without first undertaking an expensive program to build a fleet of battleships. Instead of battleships, the Jeune École pressed for the construction of torpedo boats and cruisers to be used as commerce raiders. The teachings of the Jeune École had enormous influence on the shipbuilding programs of the Great Powers. The French navy, for instance, ordered its first torpedo boat in 1875 and over the next ten years had acquired 70. These torpedo boats, based on French ports in the Channel and Mediterranean, would prey on British commerce in European waters. Two prominent Jeune École writers, Louis Vignot and Paul Fontin, asserted in an influential study entitled *Essai de stratégie navale* that with a force of 200 torpedo boats and 60 cruisers France could bring about Britain's defeat in a war. Great Power navies other than the French also adopted the theories of the Jeune École and built fleets designed for commerce warfare. Russia, Germany, Austria-Hungary, and Italy followed France's lead and acquired large numbers of torpedo boats. In addition to torpedo boats, France and Russia embarked on expensive programs in the early 1890s to build large cruisers, capable of steaming great distances to attack Britain's trade outside of European waters. When the Russian armored cruisers *Rurik* and *Rossia* first appeared they created a sensation in Britain since they were thought to be superior in speed, armament, and coal supply to all existing first-class cruisers in the Royal Navy. One English writer imagined the Russian cruiser *Rurik* as "a roaring sea-lion, going up and down the world devouring any British cruiser that might have the temerity to withstand her." In response to this Russian threat, the British Admiralty decided to build two cruisers—the *Powerful* and *Terrible*—that were designed to be superior to Russia's commerce raiders. Britain also sought to overcome the threat posed by France's cruisers and torpedo boats by providing the Royal Navy with a superior force of cruisers and torpedo-boat destroyers. The teachings of the Jeune École thus played a crucial role in shaping the international naval competition between the Great Powers during the last two decades of the nineteenth century.[49]

In the two world wars of this century, however, attacks on the ocean-going trade of major maritime powers, like Britain, Japan, and the United States, did not bring about their rapid defeat as had been anticipated by some of the more strident advocates of commerce warfare. Despite the appearance and development of what can be considered the ideal commerce raider in the submarine, commerce warfare failed to deliver a knock-out blow. Instead, commerce warfare resulted in a war of attrition with commerce raiders trying to sink merchant ships at a faster rate than the shipbuilding industries in the maritime powers could replace shipping losses.

Germany tried in both wars to sever the vital North Atlantic sea lanes on which enemy men and supplies moved to the various war fronts. In the First World War, German military and naval leaders saw an unrestricted submarine campaign against British shipping as the best means of dislocating the economies of Germany's adversaries and bringing an end to the war in 1917. The Commander-in-Chief of the High Seas Fleet, Vice-Admiral Reinhard Scheer, recorded in his diary on February 1, 1917, the day Germany's submarine campaign began: "We now enter a new stage of the war in which the submarine arm is to bring the decision by strangling British economic life and sea communications." Just as they had pinned their hopes for a rapid victory in 1914 on the Schlieffen plan, Germany's military leaders in 1917 anticipated the defeat of their country's enemies within six months from unrestricted submarine warfare. Germany's unrestricted submarine campaign did indeed come close to bringing victory in the spring of 1917 when it inflicted catastrophic losses on merchant shipping. Before it could prove decisive, however, the British Admiralty took the long-overdue step of instituting the convoy system to protect seaborne commerce. This step dramatically reduced shipping losses during the second half of 1917 and, coupled with increased construction of merchantmen in British and American shipbuilding yards, defeated Germany's bid for victory by a submarine offensive. Like the Schlieffen plan, unrestricted submarine warfare turned out actually to have been a desperate gambler's throw.[50] During the Second World War Germany again tried to defeat her adversaries by means of a massive submarine offensive. As in the First World War, German submarines inflicted heavy losses on Allied shipping—some 8 million tons of merchant shipping in 1942 alone—but failed in the objective of cutting the North Atlantic sea lanes. In its attempt to defeat the Allies at sea, the German submarine force paid a suicidally high price: of the 863 submarines that Germany made operational during the Second World War, it lost 641, or almost 75 percent. These losses make clear that commerce warfare was not a "cheap" way to victory.[51]

In the Pacific during the Second World War the unrestricted submarine campaign conducted by the United States against Japan's merchant fleet enjoyed considerably more success in dislocating the Japanese economy and military operations. Japan, however, was extremely vulnerable to this form of attack in a way that the other maritime powers were not. The Japanese economy was heavily dependent on overseas sources of supply for a number of vitally important raw materials, such as petroleum, iron ore, bauxite, rubber, and coking coal. In addition, the Japanese merchant fleet, which had been barely adequate for Japan's peacetime needs, never possessed sufficient ships to meet the requirements of fighting a major war in the vast expanses of the Pacific Ocean. This problem was compounded by the inability of the Japanese high command—riven by bureaucratic rivalries between army, navy, and civilian authorities—to distribute the available shipping in the most efficient manner. Finally, the Japanese Navy was doctrinally, technologically, and materially unprepared to defend against an unrestricted submarine campaign on Japan's shipping. On account of the Japanese Navy's inability to offer effective protection against the submarine threat, Japan's merchant fleet suffered practical annihilation during the war. At the war's outbreak in 1941 the Japanese merchant fleet contained more than 1,700 ships of over 500 tons gross registered displacement, totaling approximately 6 million tons of shipping. This shipping was supplemented during the war by 3 million tons of new construction and the capture of a further 800,000 tons. By 1945, however, over 8 million tons, or approximately 80 percent of its shipping, had been destroyed. Of these losses, almost 5 million tons had been sunk by U.S. submarines. Even more remarkable is that these devastating shipping losses had been inflicted at the low cost of only 47 submarines lost by the United States.[52]

The heavy losses suffered by the Japanese merchant marine wreaked havoc with Japan's war effort, as can readily be seen in the role oil shortages played in shaping Japanese naval movements. While Japanese forces overran the oil fields of the Dutch East Indies with relative ease, the transportation of this oil to refineries and to the fleet proved to be a much more difficult task. By the summer of 1944 the losses inflicted on Japan's merchant marine had reached the point where shortages of oil seriously circumscribed Japanese naval operations. In order to ease the burden of these shortages, the main Japanese battle fleet used as bases various anchorages in the East Indies, like Tawi Tawi and Brunei Bay, that were in close geographical proximity to the oil fields. Even this expedient to save shipping, however, could not solve the problem of insufficient quantities of refined oil. As a result, the Japanese battle fleet was forced to burn in its boilers unprocessed Borneo oil, which was a greater fire hazard and a less efficient naval fuel than refined oil. The Japanese battle fleet thus steamed into the crucial battles of 1944 in the Philippine Sea and Leyte Gulf hobbled in its movements by severe fuel shortages.[53]

Of course, other historical examples, such as the massive Allied bombing campaign against Germany during the Second World War, can be used to illustrate operational doctrines that sought to defeat an adversary by directing attacks against his economy rather than his armed forces. As has been mentioned, the Jeune École argued that this approach could produce a rapid decision in a war with a maritime power. Similarly, advocates of aerial bombardment in the era between the two world wars maintained that bombing campaigns against population centers and industrial targets would decide any future war between Great Powers during its initial stages. Air power, so it was widely thought at the time, would prevent a repetition of the military deadlock and attrition warfare of the First World War by striking directly at an adversary's economic base and civilian population. The experience of the two world wars did not confirm, however, the predictions made by the extreme advocates of operational doctrines calling for selective attacks against economic targets. Commerce warfare, bombing, and blockade demonstrably failed to bring short wars. Even the extremely successful submarine campaign by the United States against Japanese merchant shipping did not, by itself, bring about Japan's economic collapse or force her surrender. Economies of major powers have shown themselves to be remarkably capable of regeneration during wartime. These operational approaches became therefore but another means of striking at an adversary during a war of attrition. Despite their failure to confirm the extravagant claims made by doctrinal theorists, doctrines seeking to change the balance of military power between states by changing their relative economic position have nonetheless been an important component in the development of modern strategic thought.

CONCLUSION

As has been the case with Great Powers throughout history, the strategic outlook of both the United States and the Soviet Union has been shaped by economic assumptions. One recent study chronicling United States efforts to contain Soviet expansion since 1945, for example, has drawn attention to the correlation that exists between the domestic economic policies of American administrations and their strategic approach to the Soviet Union. Its author, John Lewis Gaddis, contends that "the economic orientations of particular administrations, defined in light of domestic priorities, do have profound influences on national security policy, nor is it surprising that this should be so . . . What is surprising is the *primacy* that has been accorded economic considerations in shaping strategies of containment, *to the exclusion of other considerations.*"[54] Meanwhile, the Soviet economy all too clearly reflects the strategic imperatives that has guided its development since the First Five Year Plan. From the time of Stalin's famous speech to plant managers in 1931 to the present day, the Soviet Union's leadership has doggedly persevered at great economic cost in its attempts to keep Soviet armed forces abreast of those possessed by rival powers. Moreover, in their analysis of the dynamics of change in international politics, Soviet theorists stress the importance of economic and social factors in determining the "correlation of forces." Since 1945, then, each of the superpowers could be described as having pursued an *Ermattungsstrategie* against the other. Both the United States and the Soviet Union have sought to deny the other any opportunity for launching a decisive and overwhelming attack, while at the same time attempting to restrict and undermine the influence of the other on world politics. Traditional approaches to strategy that emphasize economic considerations thus have been employed by both superpowers: the restriction of supply in vital commodities, the posing of military threats to critical resource areas and lines of supply, and, ultimately, the targeting of economic and population centers with nuclear weapons. Since a comprehensive political settlement between the United States and the Soviet Union is not a realistic possibility, the outcome of their global rivalry will depend, to paraphrase Delbrück, on who first reaches the point of no longer being able to bear the pain, who first becomes exhausted.

NOTES

1. The best general accounts on war planning before 1914 are L.L. Farrar, *The Short-War Illusion* (Oxford: Oxford University Press, 1973), and Paul Kennedy, ed., *The War Plans of the Great Powers, 1880–1914* (London: George Allen and Unwin, 1979).

2. A.J.P. Taylor, *The Struggle for Mastery in Europe, 1848–1918* (Oxford: Oxford University Press paperback edition, 1971), p. xxiv.

3. On the importance of the "battle of annihilation" in German military doctrine, see the superb account by Jehuda L. Wallach, *Das Dogma der Vernichtungsschlacht: Die Lehren von Clausewitz und Schlieffen und ihre Wirkungen in zwei Weltkriegen* (Frankfurt am Main: Bernard und Graefe Verlag für Wehrwesen, 1967), pp. 52–103, 125–188.

4. On the Franco-Prussian War, see Michael Howard, *The Franco-Prussian War* (London: Methuen, 1961); and, on the financial position of France and Germany, Fritz Stern, *Gold and Iron: Bismarck, Bleichröder, and the Building of the German Empire* (New York: Knopf, 1977).

5. Carl von Clausewitz, *On War*, edited and translated by Michael Howard and Peter Paret (Princeton: Princeton University, 1976).

6. Gerhard Ritter, *The Sword and the Scepter*, vol. 2: *The European Powers and the Wilhelmine Empire* (Miami: University of Miami Press, 1970); and idem. *The Schlieffen Plan: Critique of a Myth* (Westport, Connecticut: The Greenwood Press, 1979).

7. Winston S. Churchill, *The World Crisis*, five volumes (London: Butterworth, 1923–1931).

8. Bernard Brodie, *Strategy in the Missile Age* (Princeton: Princeton University Press, paperback edition, 1971), p. 52.

9. On French military planning before 1914, see Douglas Porch, *The March to the Marne: The French Army, 1871–1914* (Cambridge: Cambridge University Press, 1981); and Joel A. Setzen, "The Doctrine of the Offensive in the French Army on the Eve of World War I" (Ph.D. dissertation, University of Chicago, 1972).

10. Thomas S. Kuhn, *The Structure of Scientific Revolutions* (Chicago: University of Chicago Press, 2d, 1970), p.8.

11. Hajo Holborn, "Moltke and Schlieffen: The Prussian-German School," in *Makers of Modern Strategy*, edited by Edward Mead Earle (Princeton: Princeton University Press, paperback edition, 1971), pp. 172–186.

12. Gordon A. Craig, "Delbrück: The Military Historian," in *Makers of Modern Strategy*, pp. 260–283.

13. I.S. Bloch, *The Future of War in Its Technical, Economic and Political Relations: Is War Now Impossible?* (New York: Doubleday and McClure, 1899).

14. Ibid., pp. vii–lxi.

15. Roger Chickering, *Imperial Germany and a World Without War: The Peace Movement and German Society, 1892–1914* (Princeton: Princeton University Press, 1975), pp. 403–405.

16. Holborn, "Moltke and Schlieffen," pp. 186–205.

17. Norman Stone, *The Eastern Front 1914–1917* (New York: Scribner's 1975), pp. 37–91.

18. Ibid., pp. 70–91; Norman Stone, "Die Mobilmachung der österreichisch-ungarischen Armee 1914," *Militärgeschichtliche Mitteilungen*, 2 (1974), pp. 67–95.

19. Porch, *March to the Marne*; and Setzen, "Doctrine of the Offensive."

20. Ritter, *The Schlieffen Plan*.

21. N.H. Gibbs, *Grand Strategy*, vol. 1: *Rearmament Policy* (London: Her Majesty's Stationary Office, 1976), pp. 441–529, 605–688.

22. Alan S. Milward, *War, Economy and Society* (Berkeley: University of California Press, 1977), pp. 25–30; Wallach, *Das Dogma der Vernichtungsschlacht*, pp. 305–413.

23. This reconstruction of Athenian strategy during the Archidamian War is based primarily on Donald Kagan, *The Outbreak of the Peloponnesian War* (Ithaca: Cornell University Press, 1969), pp. 317–342; idem. *The Archidamian War* (Ithaca: Cornell University Press, 1974), pp. 17–42; Hans Delbrück, *History of the Art of War Within the Framework of Political History*, vol. 1: *Antiquity* (Westport, Connecticut: Greenwood Press, 1975), pp. 135–143; idem., *Die Strategie des Perikles erlaütert durch die Strategie Friedrichs des Grossen* (Berlin: Mittler, 1890), passim; Thomas Kelly, "Thucydides and Spartan Strategy in the Archidamian War," *American Historical Review*, 87, 2 (February 1982), pp. 25–54; and, of course, Thucydides, *History of the Peloponnesian War*, trans. Rex Warner (Penguin Books, 1976), passim.

24. Thucydides, *Peloponnesian War*, pp. 92–94.

25. Kagan, *Archidamian War*, pp. 102–105, 171–172.

26. Thucydides, *Peloponnesian War*, pp. 132–139.

27. Ibid., pp. 82–86.

28. J.K. Anderson, *Military Theory and Practice in the Age of Xenophon* (Berkeley: University of California Press, 1970), pp. 8–9.

29. Thucydides, *Peloponnesian War*, pp. 118–123.

30. Delbrück, *Die Strategie des Perikles*, p. 113.

31. Thucydides, *Peloponnesian War*, pp. 118–123.

32. Ibid., pp. 132–133.

33. F.E. Adcock, "The Archidamian War, 431–421 B.C.," *Cambridge Ancient History* (Cambridge: Cambridge University Press, 1940), pp. 195–196.

34. Delbrück, *History of the Art of War*, p. 136.

35. Kagan, *Archidamian War*, pp. 205–251.

36. E.F. Heckscher, *The Continental System. An Economic Interpretation* (Oxford: Oxford University Press, 1922).

37. Martin van Creveld, *Hitler's Strategy: The Balkan Clue* (Cambridge: Cambridge University Press, 1973).

38. Barry Leach, *German Strategy Against Russia, 1939–1941* (Oxford: Oxford University Press, 1973).

39. Arthur J. Marder, *Old Friends, New Enemies: The Royal Navy and the Imperial Japanese Navy; Strategic Illusions, 1936–1941* (Oxford: Clarendon Press, 1981), pp. 166–167.

40. On these naval campaigns, see Peter Padfield, *Tide of Empires: Decisive Naval Campaigns in the Rise of the West*, two volumes (Boston: Routledge and Kegan Paul, 1979–1982).

41. See Robert G. Albion, *Forests and Sea Power: The Timber Problem of the Royal Navy, 1652–1862* (Hamden, Connecticut: Archon edition, 1965); and P.W. Bamford, *Forests and French Sea Power, 1660–1789*. (Toronto: University of Toronto Press, 1956).

42. This account of the First Anglo-Dutch War relies primarily on the studies by Padfield, *Tide of Empires*, vol. 1, pp. 152–234; Paul Kennedy, *The Rise and Fall of British Naval Mastery* (New York: Charles Scribner's Sons, 1976), pp. 43–59; and C. Wilson, *Profit and Power: A Study of England and the Dutch Wars* (London: Longmans, 1957).

43. Kennedy, *Rise and Fall of British Naval Mastery*, p. 48.

44. Herbert William Richmond, *The Navy as an Instrument of Policy*, edited by E.A. Hughes (Cambridge: Cambridge University Press, 1953), p. 43.

45. Kennedy, *Rise and Fall*, p. 79.

46. On the Jeune École, see Theodore Ropp, "Continental Doctrines of Sea Power," in *Makers of Modern Strategy*, edited by Edward Mead Earle (Princeton: Princeton University Press, paperback

edition, 1971), pp. 446–456; and idem., "Development of a Modern Navy: French Naval Policy, 1871–1904" (Ph.D. diss., Harvard University, 1937). At present, there does not exist in English any comprehensive and comparative study of the naval doctrines of the European continental powers.

47. Arthur J. Marder, *The Anatomy of British Sea Power: A History of British Naval Policy in the Pre-Dreadnought Era, 1880–1905* (New York: Knopf, 1940), pp. 84–104; and Bryan Ranft, "The Protection of British Seaborne Trade and the Development of Systematic Planning for War, 1860–1906," in *Technical Change and British Naval Policy, 1860–1939*, edited by Bryan Ranft (London: Hodder and Stoughton, 1977), pp. 1–22.

48. Ropp, "Development of a Modern Navy," pp. 269–341.

49. Marder, *Anatomy of British Sea Power*, pp. 163–164.

50. Arthur J. Marder, *From the Dreadnought to Scapa Flow: The Royal Navy in the Fisher Era, 1904–1919*, vol. 4: *1917: Year of Crisis* (London: Oxford University Press, 1969), passim.

51. Bodo Herzog, *60 Jahre Deutsche U-boote, 1906–1966* (Munich: J.F. Lehmans, 1968), pp. 112–113.

52. Clay Blair, *Silent Victory* (Philadelphia: Lippincott, 1975), p. 900; Atsushi Oi, "Why Japan's Anti-Submarine Warfare Failed," *United States Institute Proceedings*, 78, 6 (June 1952), pp. 587–601.

53. Paul S. Dull, *A Battle History of the Imperial Japanese Navy, 1941–1945* (Annapolis: Naval Institute Press, 1978), pp. 281–337; Clark G. Reynolds, *The Fast Carriers: The Forging of an Air Navy* (Huntington, New York: Robert E. Krieger edition, 1978), pp. 190–210, 218–220.

54. John Lewis Gaddis, *Strategies of Containment: A Critical Appraisal of Postwar American National Security Policy* (New York: Oxford University Press, 1982), p. 356.

II

Economic Structure and Political Control

5

The Importance of the Economic Base to National Security

Richard E. Bissell

The idea that a strong economy is an important factor in a nation's ability to defend itself and to pursue its national interests is hardly new. The history of foreign policy is replete with examples of broken or expanding economies that accompanied the failure or success of their related political systems. However, the national actors in the Westphalian system since 1648 have only gradually adjusted their domestic economic planning to meet the ever-expanding demands of warfare. Because the development of mobilization warfare was largely a haphazard process, as Martin van Creveld made clear in Chapter 2, expansion of economic supporting structures was also largely unforeseen. The momentum of larger armies and longer ranges of operation, as well as the demands of peacetime eras, have simply made necessary the provision of men, material, and money to support the efforts. The consistent resistance to such an economic base on the part of Western nations like the United States in the nineteenth and twentieth centuries is in large part a result of the prevailing "liberal" view of economics and its relationship to politico-military needs of the state. Some states even refused entirely to provide for an adequate economic base, and a gradual erosion of their national political strength ensued.

In any discussion of the concept of the economic base, a range of questions arise. First, one must ask how the economic base is defined and how that definition changes over time, given its relationship to the maintenance of national security. Second, one must examine an implicit assumption of the term, that the economic base underlies and is thus an independent variable in relation to the politico-military strength of the state. To what extent must the economic base conform to the demands of defense strategies, even to the point of war strategies taking into account the expansion of the economy? A third question must deal with conditions in the late twentieth century and the extent to which present characteristics of warfare and economic systems may affect our conception of an appropriate economic base. Is the twentieth century structurally different (particularly in the 1980s) from earlier eras in the demands that issues of war and peace make on economic systems? And fourth, it is helpful to examine the limitations of democratic societies in accepting the role of the economy as a "base" for national security. To what degree are national security needs competing in the marketplace along with "business as usual" for available resources?

We must begin with a working definition of the *economic base*. That term will be used here to denote the structure and extent of economic behavior available to support the political and military goals of the state. It is not the entire economy, but that part of the economy actually supporting or available to support in emergencies political/military goals. In that sense, it applies to all states, not just the more powerful. Indeed, all states should undertake planning for an economic base, even if most are unsuccessful or successful for only a short time. All states must set aside manpower, physical resources, and financial resources for national security. This concept of an economic base is very general, and the debate over an appropriate economic base arises in the context of national needs at a particular time. It is in the latter sense that changes in the relationship between the economic base and national security need to be examined.

THE ECONOMIC BASE AND NATIONAL SECURITY

The extent of the economic base, in national security terms, is defined in large part by the definition of threats facing any nation. Changing conditions of warfare and peaceful conflict alter political leaders' views of what kind of economic base is appropriate. At the same time, important theoretical considerations have frequently intruded on political leaders' decisions as to how to structure the economic base and which sectors of society should bear the cost of accumulating surpluses of defense needs.

For instance, the traditional view of the mercantilists emphasized accumulation of domestically controlled assets to sustain a state's military capability. With only limited surpluses and very limited credit available to kingdoms, the pursuit of war in the seventeenth and eighteenth centuries was based on a fragile economic base. Indeed, manpower, horses, and fodder counted much more than money in the treasury. Strategic direction of forces in the field could easily be determined by the available fodder for the horses and grain for the men.[1] The need to generate wealth to support war led to the expansion of empires, particularly into the New World, where available gold and silver specie could easily be translated into the ability to wage more European wars. But the move to incorporate overseas empires into the economic bases of European kingdoms had a curious effect on the viability of those bases. By extending the base to include the Americas, the economic base was also made vulnerable. The British were quick to take advantage of this opening as in the commissioning of privateers to interrupt Spanish trade with the American possessions. In the prevailing economic view of the time, the sinking of one major bullion fleet played havoc with the stability of the Spanish currency, and the resulting unavailability of gold directly undermined the ability of the Spanish Crown to field armies. Because the ability of the European nations to transfer resources to the mother countries was generally sustained, however, the colonial system was a major development, an important expansion of the economic base of those European nations engaged in hegemonic warfare.

The organization of warfare on a more systematic basis, requiring more extensive resources from the domestic populations, is frequently dated from the French supply planning of the Napoleonic era.[2] That development could have introduced a long era of onerous burdens on the economies of Europe, but the extended peace of the nineteenth century had the opposite effect. The colonial system remained largely intact, notwithstanding the putative independence of Latin America and the division of Africa, and the rapid industrialization of Western Europe and the United States expanded more rapidly than the international system consumed such production in war. The interdependence of economies reached a dramatic new plateau, whether between industrial societies such as Britain and the agricultural societies, or between expanding industrial powers. The underlying philosophy of the international economy has generally been called liberalism, referring in large part to the following characteristics of the economy: (1) On the whole, freedom of trade and of financial transactions from governmental restriction prevailed; (2) because governments did not, by and large, control international trade and payments, conditions of doing business throughout the trading world were reasonably calculable; and (3) national economies were mutually responsive and adaptable to one another.[3] Although such liberal principles were dependent in large part on British control of the international economy, unrestricted British political influence did not result. Indeed, on a number of occasions challenges to British expansion of influence ensued.

The "liberal" view of the economic base was not universally respected. Some, of course, viewed mankind as reaching a new plateau of enlightenment from which there could be no fall. Auguste Comte's thesis about the industrialization of societies and the resulting expansion of international trade rendering war impossible is interesting in this regard.[4] Such a sociological view of the relationship between the economic base and national security planning was a premonition of functionalist arguments of the mid-nineteenth century, but it was also shattered by the events of the early twentieth century. The direct challenge to liberal economies came in several forms, however. One was the influence of Friederich List's argument for nation industrialization—addressed to French, German, and American audiences in a British-dominated world—foreshadowing the creation of protective tariffs and a secure *national* economic base. List and his followers emphasized the division of the world into industrial and agricultural powers and pointed out that Britain's global hegemony derived from its position as the premier industrial power. On agricultural nations, List said:

> Trade with manufacturing nations is subject to interruption by war or commercial regulations, and then comes the double inconvenience of finding no buyers for an agricultural surplus, and deprivation of manufactured articles in common use. A purely agricultural nation . . . is like an individual who, wanting an arm, employs the arm of another, the use of which, however, he is not always sure of obtaining; a nation, both agricultural and manufacturing, is like an individual in full possession and use of his own two arms.[5]

These economic calculations were matched by the romanticism of political nationalism in the nineteenth century, in Italy, Germany, the United States, and elsewhere. The desire of these and other states to create their independent financial centers and industrial infrastructure and to establish "new" colonial presences meant that the relatively liberal order of the nineteenth century was increasingly identified as British and thus open to attack as hegemonic. In this way, the military and political purposes of the governments began to place a strain on national economies, as seen in the debate over the arms race of the pre-World War I period.[6]

The nineteenth-century revolution in the economic base (from agricultural to industrial) made possible the popularization, increased cost, and improved technology of warfare in the twentieth century. "Industrialized warfare" meant that steel battleships and submarines replaced wooden sailing ships; that accurate, heat-resistant machine guns replaced single-shot muskets; and that large armies could stay longer in the field with greater independence of movement. A vast economic surplus was at the disposal of the state as a result of industrial enterprise. And finally, revolutionary new ideological and political movements that arose from the industrial class structure created an extended, and continuing, international systemic struggle that embraces both the military sphere and the economic sphere.

In these ways, the relationship between the economic base and national security was drastically transformed in the twentieth century. An initial reaction to the disorder of this century was the embracing of fascist ideologies and related economic autarky: the creation of an extremely secure economic base, mobilized by an infusion of political ideology for the ultimate abnegation of the individual. With the defeat of the fascist powers in World War II, the greater part of the world attempted to create a relatively open system, almost a replication of the nineteenth-century British system, although one in which the United States is far more integrated into the global economy than Britain was. Perhaps equally important is the extent to which the systemic conflict focused on the superpowers at the present time does not have an analogy in the nineteenth century. The parallels are also not accurate in that the present armed peace requires an economic base for the United States that Britain could ignore. The indeterminacy of current defense planning, envisioning conflicts of both a nuclear and conventional character for most states, creates an atmosphere of uncertainty and a potential demand on the economic base that is quite unlimited. Given the simultaneous pressures on most states for extensive social expenditures, it is hardly surprising that the relationship between the economic base and national security is for most observers confusing.

The other major bequest of the industrial revolution was technological. Technological changes have always influenced warfare, as in the ability to bridle a horse or the invention of gunpowder, but the devotion of the industrial revolution to technological change is unprecedented in human history. The independent dynamic of the economic base produced new technologies for use by the military, and specialists in military technology have made demands on the industrial base that are frequently beyond its capability to deliver. At the same time, the ability of military bureaucracies to command government funds without cost-effectiveness criteria to develop new technologies has been a useful impetus for the eventual dissemination of technology to the civilian economic base, as with the American Manhattan Project in World War II. A clear area of steadily expanding military demands on the industrial base is transportation, dating back in the U.S. experience to government-built roads over the Appalachian Mountains for supplying the Indian Wars. This was followed by subsidies for construction of ships under national control, the knitting together of the nation by railroads, and eventually the use of air power, both in inner space and now in outer space. Such technologies can almost become symbolic, particularly in an era of armed peace; the Chinese, for instance, have undertaken a major heavy missile program in recent decades even at a time when miniaturization of nuclear weapons makes such bulky delivery systems less relevant to military balances. The missiles can still be used for weapons delivery, but smaller systems could readily be developed at lower cost to the overall economy.

A final point about the twentieth-century transformation should be made: With the dividing line between peace and war becoming increasingly blurred, traditional views of the economic base have been rendered obsolete, particularly for the United States. During peacetime, the U.S. economic base has paid little attention to military requirements, and to a slightly lesser degree, the same has been true of other economies. With other societies becoming willing to maintain a consistently higher degree of peacetime mobilization, however, the United States and its allies have been forced to reexamine their view in recent decades. For instance, as recently as 1972, Charles Schultze, then at the Brookings Institution and later a member of the Carter administration, could say,

> Does our national security depend upon maintaining a healthy rate of growth in our economy—is it dependent on our economic strength? Surprisingly, perhaps, my answer is that our capability to maintain an appropriate Military Establishment does not fundamentally depend on our economic strength . . . . Within the range of likely possibilities over the next 10 years, whether for example the GNP grows at 2 percent or 4 percent a year, our economic strength will not really make much difference in our capability to sustain whatever defense establishment we deem warranted."[7]

There is always pressure to return to old thinking habits, however. A former Treasury Department official has testified:

> I think that our military and diplomatic planners really have no alternative but to devise strategies which will minimize our foreign exchange costs. To put it bluntly, it will be increasingly difficult to earn the foreign exchange to keep large numbers of troops, planes, and ships stationed outside the United States.[8]

Such is a classic and not unusual example of the view that in peacetime the economic base should not have to strain merely to acommodate the national security interests of the nation. For a view of wartime conditions, however, a vast and rewarding literature exists with regard to the responsiveness of the economy and the ability of economies under siege to adapt and respond with increased productivity and physical delivery of goods to meet the war effort.[9] In large part, the principal issue in recent limited wars has not been the capacity of the economic base to respond but the willingness of particular sectors of the democratic publics to shoulder the costs of war in financial terms and to mobilize the economy outside the peacetime economic base.

THE ECONOMIC BASIS OF POLITICS

Some ask whether the strength of the economy determines national security, or the national security strategy determines the shape of the economy. Any particular country will have a bias in one direction or the other, determined by the historical pattern of setting priorities. Quite clearly, the perpetual quest for national security on the part of the Soviet Union has forced the development of an economy at the service of the military structure, first and foremost. Other factors clearly contribute to the shape and strength of the Soviet economy, but military factors are clearly paramount. On the other hand, many of the Western economies begin from the premise that the first obligation of the economy is to deliver market-determined quantities of goods, and that military goods should be produced and allocated as a part of the complex bargain imposed by the economic and political marketplace. Another way of describing this dispute over priorities has been the idea that "economic man" and "political man" compete for control of the state; the notion deserves greater examination.

In his *The Economic Basis of Politics,* historian Charles Beard argued that in the era after 1914 there also existed a "military man" competing for control of the state. "From Aristotle's time down through the centuries the theory of the economic basis of politics had been limited by the condition that economic forces operate freely only in the absence of military forces."[10] That last clause, Beard believed, had been conveniently forgotten during the prevailing peace of the nineteenth century but had seen its validity reconfirmed in the first five decades of the twentieth century. Even Karl Marx was seen as a child of nineteenth-century industrial liberalism in his argument for materialist determinism and the eventual withering of the state. Beard's description of the struggle for the state as involving three types of "men" is interesting, but it is evident from his writings that he assumed tacit alliances between "political man" and "economic man" in the determination of politics. In the Anglo-American democratic culture, Beard's assumptions have largely held up in the light of experience, and in the broader context of global ideological developments, "political man" is generally given sway over "military man" in constitutional documents and other normative statements of political systems.[11] What was not anticipated was alliances between "military man" and "political man" that have served to alter significantly the role of the economic base as an independent determinant. In the national socialist experiments of the 1930s, and then more thoroughly in the development of the Soviet system, the shape of the economy is determined to a large extent by military demands, with a wide range of consequences, including a greater capacity for mobilization of available resources and an overall inefficiency that effectively lowers national output owing to the absence of individualistic economic incentives.

In the framework of political debate in the Western democracies, however, the relationship between the economic base and national security has generally remained indeterminate, almost as though governmental allocation of resources is in every case cause for a reexamination of priorities and establishment of a new compromise. Only in subsystems of the economic base focused largely on defense production has a firm alliance appeared between "military man" and "economic man" (a phenomenon somewhat akin to the often-cited "military-industrial complex"), and even the "political man" has marshaled resources to prevent formation of firm national priorities. In most industrialized democracies, the trend has been toward identification of mass political groups with welfare priorities rather than with "military man." In that sense, the Beardian conditional clause ("in the absence of military force") is once again being ignored, with the economic base able to determine some of the parameters of defense spending and thus the definition of national security. It is evident that certain absolute limits are set by the available economic resources for national security, and history is replete with the effect of such limitations. What is interesting about the present period is the very limited proportion of the national budget and the gross national product that is allocated in public perceptions for national security.

For the most part, the economic elites tend to view the economic base as an independent variable. Some scholars have identified the independent development of the economic base with the rise of the middle class in nineteenth-century Europe: the liberal ideology then developed remains influential into the twentieth century as a statement of economic optimization of domestic and international transactions and a normative view of subordination of national security needs in calculation of state priorities. With economic elites, however, it is necessary to distinguish between global powers and secondary powers. The aspirations of global economic powers to expand their presence in international markets argues for a strategy of expanding trade networks rather than the use of military tools (unless a small dose of force is helpful to establish an economic presence). On the other hand, some economic elites with primarily domestic interests argue for what is essentially a mercantilist approach, using protective tariffs to develop an indigenous economic base not dependent on overseas suppliers. Middle ground can be found, as in Albert O. Hirschman's study of the interwar economies, when large nations sought to expand trade with small nations unlikely to pose a security threat.[12] Secondary powers are more likely to seek a protective approach, especially if they perceive a technological or industrial gap that can be bridged only by artificially stimulated domestic development. In either case, the economic elites will attempt to pursue what they consider economic logic: as Schultze argued, "Securing national economic prosperity and healthy growth are most important objectives in their own right. They ought to be pursued for their own sake, not because they are overwhelmingly important determinants of our ability to maintain the defense establishment."[13]

The extent to which construction of an economic base will entail parameters for national security is sometimes not foreseen. The reliance of industrialized nations on petroleum for transportation, power generation, and other basic industrial needs in the mid-twentieth century created a national security problem for those nations, especially when the political leadership was persuaded that a shortfall of only 7 percent in oil imports would cause disruptive hardship. With the consequent threat of political stability, maintaining foreign oil supplies as a part of the economic base was incorporated into national security planning. Political and economic stability was so threatened by a potential shortfall of oil supplies, especially in the minds of the leaders of relatively weak West European governments, that the energy system became wrapped up in modern notions of the "economic base." Where energy supplies had formerly been of domestic origin, the protection of that flow was not an international concern, even though it did prompt substantial reserve measures of a national character (such as the U.S. Naval Petroleum Reserves of the early twentieth century). Instead, with rising dependence on energy imports for functioning of the economy in general, combined with a political decision that stability would be shaken with a shortfall of 7 percent, it is clear that the expansion to a global resource base had caused major changes in strategic calculations. In effect, the growth of the liberal trading economy fostered an expansion of national security concerns.

There are numerous examples of economies that adapted well to stringent demands of national security, including the entire restructuring of international ties. The adaptability of economies is nearly always underestimated, despite evidence of significant adaptations in World War II (as in the Soviet Union, Britain, and elsewhere). Alan Milward cites the cost of manufacturing a long-range bomber in the United States: $15.18 per hour in 1940, and $4.82 in 1944.[14] Schultze argues that in present circumstances, the U.S. economy "would adapt amazingly well" and cites the results of the Strategic Bombing Survey of World War II: "After more than two years of heavy bombing and the reduction or elimination of many overseas materials, industrial production in Germany was higher in 1944 than at the beginning of the War."[15] But when political leaderships have to consider the possibility of economic dislocation and the attendant political costs, these bits of evidence are frequently cast aside in democracies. If the environment becomes highly unpredictable, the answer frequently is protectionism, in which case the domestic economy profits, at least in the short run.

When the protectionist option is taken, however, a government faces the likelihood of problems in procuring particular production unavailable through domestic resources. A traditional strategy was that of conquest, whether in quest of additional grain, manpower for the army, precious or base minerals, or access to transportation links, such as the sea.[16] The growing legal and moral sanctions against conquest as a national strategy in the twentieth century do not make it irrelevant to our discussion. Indeed, the movement of German thinking toward incorporation of European areas into the imperial system of the Third Reich provides us with detailed case studies of the relevance of conquest for industrial societies.[17] What is striking is the extent to which the German leadership apparently saw particular nations such as Norway as candidates not for plunder but for incorporation into the economic base. One can argue that it was not economic logic as much as an assessment of the racial purity of the Norwegian people that was involved, but it is evident that long-range strategic planning led the Germans to plan for an expansion of the economic base, with attendant outflows of German capital into Norway. Under the stress of war, such an expansion of the economic base did not really occur, but postwar planning was explicit and comprehensive. As Milward points out, Hitler's plans for European conquest were logical outgrowths of the need to avoid the domestic stress associated with economic growth: additional resources, then, would have to be generated through conquest.[18]

In the case of conquest, then, the definition of national security takes the initiative in making demands on the economic base, but the nation will also physically expand the economic base for strategic purpose. The process made sense for the Third Reich in that Hitler found ready allies in the German economic elite anxious to expand into the energy- and mineral-rich economy of Norway. Such an approach, however, is the aberration in a period of several centuries in which the influence of liberal economics ensured a degree of independence for the economy and the right to dispose of its surplus as it wished.

THE ECONOMIC BASIS OF WAR

The particular circumstances of twentieth-century warfare were mentioned earlier in this chapter as a major factor in the reconsideration of the economic base. For the United States in particular, the advent of nuclear weapons has eliminated the geographical and temporal cushion that allowed Americans to give only slight attention to the economic base until the actual declaration of war. As already indicated, however, planning for nuclear war has not eliminated the conventional alternative—the need to establish the economic base for a three-year rerun of World War II. Between those two demands on the economic base, the United States is forced to deal with indeterminate needs or, put another way, to deal with a range of strategic options each of which places major demands on an economic base with major existing commitments to nonmilitary expenditures. The issue, however, is not limited to the United States. Other countries have been affected as well by the existence of nuclear weapons, the spatial/global demands on major powers, the infusion of postindustrial technologies into war planning, and the hegemonic conflict caused by the universalist ambitions of the Soviet Union and the United States.

The strategies designed to conduct nuclear war and to prevent an outbreak of nuclear war raise major problems for the economic base. The nuclear powers have never agreed on "rules of encounter" that would establish the extent to which the economic base is to be a focus of attack or the extent to which a nuclear engagement would be a one-salvo affair or an extended war. The ambiguities, combined with the fact that the world has not yet experienced a nuclear exchange, means that strategies (and their related implications for the economic base) are quite speculative. Even gaming scenarios based on best guesses leave a wide range of variables. It is thus understandable that there is much dispute over what measures are required for the economy to deal with nuclear warfare. The question of dispersing industries or providing shelters for workforces and manpower pools is a point of great contention in nearly all nations. The demands that maintenance of a credible nuclear deterrent make on the economy are relatively insignificant; in most nations the portion of the defense budget given to strategic weapons is not a burden. The monumental challenge that the economic base faces is rather the implications of a nuclear war-fighting doctrine. For an economy to survive any particular war scenario requires costly (politically and financially) decisions well in advance with regard to siting and protecting industries, populations, and resources. The unwillingness of democratic countries to consider survival of and preparation for a nuclear war means that the economy has not yet come to terms with the full implications of nuclear weapons development. The issue, when posed, generally provokes responses based upon simple fear, rather than any financial or strategic calculations of the relationship between weapons and the economy.

Another major characteristic of the late twentieth century is the truly global nature of security planning. Even Britain during its hegemony of the nineteenth century chose not to intervene directly in certain parts of the world, knowing that it would mean overextension of its resources. With weaponry and control mechanisms capable of reaching all parts of the world simultaneously, a hegemonic power must be able to control political developments in all parts of the globe. This is not to argue that there presently exists a global hegemonic power (the Soviet Union does not possess the international economic power to do so, and the United States lacks the strategic direction and political will to do so) but to state that the resolution of the present superpower confrontation is likely to result in the emergence of a truly global power.[19] The economic base to support such an order may not yet exist, but present growth rates in the international economy and particularly in the industrialized nations suggest that it is not far away, or if present, simply needs ordering. Walt W. Rostow has put together the figures for global industrial production. (See Table 5.1.) These figures show the aggregate growth of the industrial sector, which is impressive even if the world is approaching the end of a Kondratieff cycle, considering what is likely to ensue in the next cycle. There is also the additional issue of the concentration of industrial production (see Table 5.2), if one is to consider the emergence of an economic base for hegemony. While the United States remains the greatest single economy, it is clear that a gradual dispersion of industry throughout the world is also distributing the economic base in a large number of nations, with the role of Europe greatly diminished.

What needs to be considered at the same time, however, is the extent to which national security planning may be going through a technological revolution. The measurement of heavy industrial strength may be as irrelevant to future military strength as the gross agricultural output became less relevant in

TABLE 5.1: World Industrial Production, 1700–1971 (1913 = 100)

1701-10	0.55
1781-90	1.81
1802-12	3.18
1820	4.16
1830	5.78
1840	7.40
1860	14.70
1870	19.50
1880	26.90
1890	41.10
1900	58.70
1913	100.00
1929	153.30
1938	182.70
1948	274.00
1971	950.00

Source: Walt W. Rostow, *The World Economy: History and Prospect* (Austin: University of Texas Press, 1978), p. 662.

the course of the nineteenth century. The proverbial postindustrial age is already having a dynamic effect on the projected conduct of war, as in the case of electronic warfare, new communications modes, the use of plastics in place of metals, miniaturization of weaponry, and space-based weapons. Warfare periodically reaches a new plateau as it goes through technological transformations that not only put the technologically advanced nations into a league entirely different from the remainder but also render useless past measures of the strength of the economic base. One small sample would be the present replacement of titanium alloys in airplanes with advanced plastics that cost less, have better performance characteristics, and do not depend on the importation of minerals into the United States. Indeed, the entire field of materials use in weapons is undergoing such a reformulation in the research and development stage that the material needs of U.S. defense industries as defined by past practice are greatly diminished.

The evolution of weapons design in the direction of using esoteric, "postindustrial" materials places a major strain on relations between the defense establishment and the economic base. For instance, at a time when a major rationale exists to protect a domestic ferroalloy industry in order to preserve a war-supplying capacity, the technology of many weapons systems on the drawing boards is moving away from ferroalloys. The nature of communications systems is changing so rapidly that old vulnerabilities of cable-based systems—as in sealed cables and critical domestic transmission nodes—may be

TABLE 5.2: Distribution of World Industrial Production, 1820–1971 (in percent)

Year	*U.K.*	*France*	*Germany*	*Russia*	*Belgium*	*U.S.*	*Canada*	*Japan*	*Other*
1820	24	20	15	n.a.	n.a.	4	n.a.	n.a.	37
1840	21	18	17	n.a.	n.a.	5	n.a.	n.a.	39
1860	21	16	15	n.a.	n.a.	14	n.a.	n.a.	34
1870	32	10	13	4	3	23	1	0	14
1881	27	9	14	3	3	29	1	0	14
1898	20	7	17	5	2	30	1	1	17
1908	15	6	16	5	2	35	2	1	18
1913	14	6	16	6	2	36	2	1	17
1926	9	7	12	4	2	42	2	3	19
1936	9	5	11	19	1	32	2	4	27
1963	5	4	6	19	1	32	2	4	27
1968	5	3	4	16	1	34	3	4	30
1971	4	3	5	16	1	33	3	5	30

Note: n.a. = not available.
Source: Adapted from Walt W. Rostow, *The World Economy: History and Prospect* (Austin: University of Texas Press, 1978), pp. 52–53.

eliminated without knowing the nature of future vulnerabilities in the new communications of the economic base. For example, scientists have only gradually come to realize the vulnerabilities of microwave communications. The priorities of the private sector are different from those of national security planners, and yet the introduction of new technologies by the private sector and the publication of new research is so rapid that hazards for national security are created quite frequently. At one level, national security is undermined by the rapid rendering of military technologies obsolescent. The private sector may incorporate new technical ideas into their publicly sold services and products before they are even available to the defense technologies industries for application. At another level, sectors of the economy that have traditionally been suppliers for the defense establishment may go out of business as a result of changes in the private economy, and be unavailable to supply products and services to the defense sector. The most recent example of this change in the United States is in the forging industry, essential for heavy weapons manufacture. Major structural changes are occurring in the advanced nations of the world, but unsynchronized introduction of those structural changes, whether appearing first in military systems or in the economic base, creates problems and severe political tensions.

The last factor that creates problems in the relationship between national security and the economic base is the continuing hegemonic conflict between the Soviet Union and the United States. Since many other nations are involved as allies of one or the other, the continuing status of "no peace–no war" causes disruptions in many social systems. A perpetual state of perceived mobilization, when combined with a constant turnover of military systems as new technologies are introduced, effectively undermines whatever intentions political leaders may have had to maintain liberal economic systems. Leaders of the United States and Soviet Union cannot allow their conflict to shift to open warfare, thus becoming a conflict of attrition, fought politically, economically, and in small conventional wars through proxies, and the economic base has to be designed to meet the needs of partial mobilization. Small states then align with the superpowers, not so much to join the battle, but to find an umbrella under which they can allow their economies to emphasize material gain. This has been a source of grievances on the part of the United States with its European allies, as well as on the part of the Soviet Union with its Eastern European allies.

The tendency of small states to seek protection from larger states is not always unwelcome. The principal Chinese criticism of the Soviet Union since their break in the early 1960s has been that the Soviet Union is using allies merely to establish the hegemony of that nation in the international system, the infamous crime of hegemonism. Couched in different terminology, the West Europeans complained about likely U.S. motives in the creation of the International Energy Agency in 1974, some arguing that the United States saw the petroleum shortage merely as an excuse to reaffirm U.S. control over Western Europe and thus consolidate the anti-Soviet forces.[20] With the apparent unwillingness of either the Soviet Union or the United States to press its state of partial mobilization to full warfare, one finds that the economies of both sides have contributed to the continuing stalemate. On the Soviet side, the economy does not have the strength to control effectively those nations it would like to bring under its hegemony. On the U.S. side, the economy is so strong and extroverted that it repeatedly ignores the conditions of political warfare in order to make profitable arrangements with the putative enemy of the United States. This mutual paralysis and the other factors described above are likely to make the late twentieth century a time of unresolvable problems between the economic base and the needs of national security. The relationship between the two, which in other times has been mutually supportive, now tends to provoke policy dilemmas and is far more frequently adversarial.

CONCLUSIONS

Major difficulties confront democratic states that attempt to increase the allocation of resources for national security purposes. Public opinion would rather see government budgets devoted to consumer-oriented, nondefense items. As a result defense needs are often treated on a par with hospital construction, day-care centers, education loans, and other discretionary functions of government. At a time when the economy is expanding, the surplus can be freely allocated to national security as well as other purposes, as happened in the mid 1960s, but finding funds for national security in times of economic retrenchment is a much more arduous process. Military managers do not make it easier for themselves: for example, abandonment of mandatory military service by many nations has thrown the armed services into the same competition for manpower as any private company in the economy. Such a move reinforces the perception that national security needs hold no special place in national priorities and that the armed services have to pay the same wage as any other employer.

Even the decision to determine what resources are available for national security evokes painful debate in most democracies. Since armies no longer exist on bread and horsefeed, advance planning for productive capacity is required to ensure harmonious relations between the military and the private sector. With the wide swings in political sentiment that are apt to occur in democracies, however, the mandate for defense spending can vary tremendously, generally causing more headaches for defense contractors in the private sector than the work is worth. The types of compensation then created for contractors, such as cost-plus contracts, become objects of scorn for the vast majority of the private sector, who are accustomed to working competitively. The sophistication of the weapons being procured in this era implies even greater problems: the defense establishment can obtain its necessary resources only from a narrow segment of the economy. As the number of aircraft manufacturers declines, as the materials required become more esoteric, and as the sophistication required to maintain and operate the weapons increases, the defense establishment is constantly operating from a narrower economic base—even as the measure of the overall economy, the gross national product, is growing substantially.

If national security expenditures are simply one more budget line in the eyes of the public and its representatives, national defense becomes part of the general political bargaining. Issues of military allocations become tied to various coalitions. The domestic lobby against the construction of nuclear power plants finds a useful ally in the lobby for unilateral disarmament of nuclear weapons. Those opposed to the construction of expensive new battle fleets find a coalition with bankers opposed to larger deficits. The issues of national security are then treated less on their own merits and more on the neutral currency of money, budgets, and economic transactions, thus avoiding a real understanding of defense issues. In liberal economic systems all transactions and resource transfers can be debated in terms of common pricing elements, but this can obscure the substantive implications of allocative decisions. In addition, using such transactional units to measure international behavior can enable economic actors to avoid the other implications of their decisions. For instance, money loaned abroad is evaluated according to "neutral" economic criteria designed to exclude the political implications of such loans. Trade is conducted on the basis of market values that measure only the goods and the currencies, not the ultimate use of those goods. Such is the problem that is characteristic of democratic societies. Having once drawn great strength from the liberal economies of the past, they are reluctant to face the possibility that such liberalism may spawn serious vulnerabilities.

It should now be clear that construction of a viable economic base is a fundamental component of national security in the twentieth century. The evolution of warfare and peacetime mobilization into more popular and more sophisticated phenomena has made the relationship between national security and the economy a central one. The important characteristics of that relationship highlighted in this survey include:

- The economic base (human resources, industrial production, and capital) is in part defined by the national security needs of a nation. At the same time, the independent momentum of the economy, whether growing or contracting, will influence the availability of the economic base for national defense.
- The choice of economic system—mercantilist/autocratic or liberal—affects the way a government can coax additional resources out of the

economic base. In some cases, states choose to add territory through conquest rather than tolerate the domestic dislocations associated with economic growth.

- Conditions in the late twentieth century are peculiar in that they contain political and military characteristics that undermine traditional assumptions of the economic base. These characteristics include the possibility of nuclear war, the hegemonic struggle between the United States and the Soviet Union, and the emergence of new technologies from the economic base that may push certain states towards different economic structures.
- The problem of synchronizing the economy and national security is particularly acute in democratic systems, where the capacity of the state to dispose of the economic surplus as it wishes is limited by the wisdom of the elected representatives of the people. In addition, it could be argued that the perspective of the private sector in many democracies is counterproductive from the perspective of national security where planning of political and military programs is necessarily long-term in scope. In such cases, a rarely acknowledged behavioral conflict emerges, not to be settled until one sector of the society changes its fundamental values.

NOTES

1. Martin van Creveld, *Supplying War: From Wallenstein to Patton* (New York: Cambridge University Press, 1968).
2. Ibid.
3. *The Political Economy of American Foreign Policy: Its Concepts, Strategy, and Limits*, report of a study group sponsored by the Woodrow Wilson Foundation and the National Planning Association (New York: Greenwood Press, 1968), pp. 24–25.
4. See Edward L. Morse, *Modernization and the Transformation of International Relations* (New York: Free Press, 1976), pp. 78–81.
5. Friederich List, *National System of Political Economy*, translated from the German by G.A. Mattle (Philadelphia: J.B. Lippincott Co., 1856), p. 268.
6. *The Political Economy*, p. 43. See also Robert Gilpin, "Economic Interdependence and National Security in Historical Perspective," in Klaus Knorr and Frank N. Trager, eds., *Economic Issues and National Security* (Lawrence, Kansas: Regents Press of Kansas, 1977), p. 67.
7. Statement of Charles L. Schultze, in Hearing-Symposium before the Subcommittee on National Security Policy and Scientific Developments of the Committee on Foreign Affairs, House of Representatives, 92d Cong., 2nd Sess., June 7, 1972, p. 148.
8. Ibid., p. 145.
9. On World War I, see the studies commissioned by the Division of Economics and History by the Carnegie Endowment; on both world wars, see Alan S. Milward, *The Economic Effects of the World Wars on Britain* (London: Macmillan & Co., 1970).
10. Charles A. Beard, *The Economic Basis of Politics* (New York: Alfred A. Knopf, 1947), p. 75.
11. Ibid., p. 104.
12. Albert O. Hirschman, *National Power and the Structure of Foreign Trade* (Berkeley: University of California Press, 1969), esp. pp. 87–116.

13. Schultze, p. 149.

14. Milward, *Economic Effects*, p. 35.

15. Schultze, p. 150.

16. See Milward's discussion of the changes in the concept of conquest in *The New Order and the French Economy* (Oxford: Clarendon Press, 1970).

17. See ibid. and Milward's *The Fascist Economy in Norway* (Oxford: Clarendon Press, 1972).

18. Milward, *The New Order*, p. 21.

19. As suggested by Robert Gilpin, *War and Change in International Politics* (New York: Free Press, 1981).

20. See Bissell, "The West in Concert: A Very Complex Score," in *Oil Diplomacy* (Philadelphia: Foreign Policy Research Institute, 1979).

6

Structural Constraints on Economic Leverage: Market-Type Systems

Robert Gilpin

The subject of this chapter is structural constraints on economic leverage, with particular reference to capitalist or market economies. It seeks to determine whether there are peculiar features of such economies which restrict their use of economic leverage against other states. Does this type of economy have institutional features or behavioral characteristics which distinguish it from command or state-controlled economies in terms of its capacity to exercise various forms of economic power?

In the light of recent experience this question has become highly pertinent. During the past decade there have been a number of efforts to employ economic leverage in the form of trade and other sanctions against states whose behavior has been offensive to a substantial number of states. The Iranian seizure of American hostages, Rhodesian racial policies, and Soviet aggression in Afghanistan are cases in point as is the violation of the Polish government (with Soviet complicity) of the human rights of its own citizens. In every one of these efforts to force policy changes through the use of economic leverage, the general consensus among scholars who have studied them is that they had relatively little effect in achieving their stated policy objectives and, as in the case of Iran, may have been actually counterproductive. As we shall undoubtedly see future attempts by capitalist states to employ economic leverage as an instrument of foreign policy, it is important to inquire into the prospects of their success.

In this chapter I shall use the term *capitalist* to characterize the economies of the United States and its major allies, Japan and Western Europe. The principal characteristic of this economy is the private ownership of the means of production. Although the government can and usually does play a major role in the economy, the driving force in these economies is the private sector in its search for profits in a competitive market situation. As this type of economy in theory, and to a considerable degree in practice, is independent of the government and its foreign policy, to what extent does this situation impose a structural constraint on the government's use of economic leverage over other societies?

Although economic leverage may be exercised in a positive or negative manner, the focus of this chapter will be on negative forms of economic leverage. It will concentrate on the use of economic sanctions and other forms of denial rather than on the use of positive inducements such as promises of foreign aid, favorable trading arrangements, and the granting of access to capital markets. These positive instruments of foreign policy are certainly important but they do not raise to any significant degree the issue of the competence of capitalist economies to employ them as do negative leverage such as trade embargoes and other forms of economic sanctions.

The questions raised by positive economic leverage are primarily that of the price one is willing to pay and whether that price is high enough to influence the policies of another country. Unless the government intends to give away the property rights of individual citizens or firms, as Secretary of State Henry Kissinger frequently proposed in the realm of technology transfer, the nature of the economy is hardly relevant. It is merely a matter of resource transfers and their effects on the behavior of other governments. In the case of negative economic leverage, however, the nature of a capitalist economy and, more importantly, its relationship with other capitalist economies become of considerable importance. Whereas positive leverage is usually a unilateral action, negative leverage in almost all cases must be multilateral. To be effective, other states must give it their support. For this reason the focus of this chapter is on the structural constructs of capitalist economies with respect to the issue of international cooperation in the use of negative economic sanctions.[1]

This coercive use of economic policies is but one aspect of the tendency of states to restrict international commercial relations for political purposes. Although it is frequently difficult to draw clear and unambiguous boundaries among them, two other types of politically motivated actions in the realm of international economic relations may be identified. In the first place, the purpose of economic actions and boycotts may be to reduce the military and economic base of an adversary; such economic warfare is a supplement to or substitute for military actions.[2] In the second place, a state may control certain types of trade in order to deny particular weapons and strategic technologies to a state or group of states in order to inhibit the growth of military power.[3] These other political uses of economic restrictions will not be treated directly in the present chapter. It should be noted, however, that the reasons for the limited utility of economic sanctions in changing the policies of other states are also applicable to cases of economic warfare and strategic embargoes.

The three types of state actions listed above have in common the manipulation of economic relations for political objectives. In addition, there is the broad category of state interventions in international commercial relations such as tariffs and nontariff barriers whose primary purpose is economic rather than political. The aim of such actions is primarily to protect domestic economic interests, to retaliate against foreign trade barriers, or to force economic concessions from other countries. Although we will not treat this subject directly, two points should be made.

The first is that the use of trade or other control for economic ends is an accepted, though frequently criticized, aspect of international life. It is a recognized part of the game of international economic relations and as such usually does not lead to the political consequences associated with the use of trade control for political purposes. Moreover, in contrast to the political use of trade control, tariffs and nontariff barriers are subject to generally accepted sets of rules and understandings. In contrast, there are no generally accepted "rules of the game" or understandings with respect to the use of trade control for coercive purposes.[4] For this reason, the issues and problems related to the use of tariffs and nontariff barriers for economic purposes are quite distinguishable from the political use of trade controls and therefore fall outside the scope of this chapter.

Secondly, we recognize that the line between the use of trade or other controls for economic or political purposes is not always an easy one to draw. In many situations, the erection of trade barriers may have a politically coercive purpose as well as an economic one. However, when this is recognized to be the case, tariffs and nontariff barriers entail all the problems associated with economic sanctions in general. As a consequence the overall conclusions of this paper regarding the effectiveness of economic sanctions for coercive purposes are equally applicable to these mixed-motive cases.

The primary focus of this chapter, then, is on the coercive use of economic sanctions and, more specifically, the imposition of trade controls to achieve political objectives. This emphasis on trade restrictions is due to the fact that trade embargoes have become a salient feature of contemporary international relations and in particular a frequently employed policy instrument of the United States. This reliance on trade controls to achieve political objectives was an important feature of the foreign policy of the Carter administration and now of the Reagan administration as well. It is for this reason they deserve a detailed examination with respect to their effectiveness and consequences. The generalizations regarding the utility and effectiveness of trade sanctions to achieve political purposes, are equally applicable, however, to other types of economic leverage.

While trade controls have long been regarded by political leaders as an appropriate means to advance foreign policy objectives, the objectives themselves have changed over time. In the 1930s, for example, economic sanctions were regarded as the most effective means to deter and punish aggression; this hope of preventing war was based on the belief that economic sanctions were the worst punishment that could be inflicted upon a potential aggressor. Today, the belief in the effectiveness of economic sanctions is still alive but they are now regarded as the best way to change undesirable political systems and the repugnant policies of states such as Rhodesia, South Africa, or the Soviet Union.[5]

More specifically, the imposition of economic sanctions on other states has long been regarded by American political leadership as an effective and inexpensive means by which to achieve foreign policy objectives. In the 1930s, as mentioned above, trade sanctions were used by the United States as the primary means to deter Japanese aggression in Asia. In the 1940s and 1950s they were used in an attempt to weaken the Soviet Union. More recently the United States has imposed economic sanctions on other states to combat terrorism and promote human rights. Unfortunately, as numerous scholars have demonstrated, such coercive uses of economic sanctions not only fail to achieve their stated purposes, however laudable they may be, but they entail high costs for the United States as well and very frequently are counterproductive in their consequences.

This conclusion with regard to the limited utility of economic sanctions to change the policies of other states does not mean that they should never be employed. They can serve a useful purpose as a symbolic gesture. They also do inflict costs on the sanctioned state but seldom of a magnitude by themselves to force it to change its behavior. The threat to use them may help deter another state from pursuing particular policies. In conjunction with other actions they can influence the decisions of an opponent. They do not constitute only meaningless or completely ineffectual gestures.

The basic problem with respect to the use of economic sanctions is rather that the United States has tended to overrely on them as a response to the repugnant policies of other states and has failed to take proper account of the fact that they entail costs for the United States as well. If sanctions fail, they become a symbol of impotence and thereby lose their future deterrent value. They are costly to particular American economic interests and to the American ideals of free trade and an open world economy. They produce severe strains with allies whose interests and historical experience make them reluctant to impose strong economic sanctions on other states. The task for the policy makers, therefore, is to appreciate that economic sanctions as an instrument of foreign policy have inherent limitations and should be employed only following a detailed consideration of both their benefits and associated costs.

The specific issue to be explored in this chapter is whether the reason for the limited effectiveness of economic sanctions is due to the inherent features of a capitalist economy or whether the answer lies with the nature of economic sanctions themselves: Do economic sanctions ever work regardless of the type of economic system that imposes them? For these reasons, I begin with a general analysis of economic sanctions as an instrument of foreign policy. I, then, discuss the specific case of the use of economic sanctions by capitalist states in the present era. Finally, I draw the relevant conclusions from this analysis.

THE THEORY OF ECONOMIC SANCTIONS

The definition of economic sanctions used in this chapter is one provided by Johan Galtung: "actions initiated by one or more international actors (the "senders") against one or more others (the "receivers") with either or both of two purposes—to punish the receivers by depriving them of some value and/or to make the receivers comply with certain norms the senders deem important."[6] From this perspective, economic sanctions have a deterrent and/or compellence function. In either case, the essence of economic sanctions is the coercive use of trade and other economic policies in order to deter, compel, and/or punish other states in order to achieve one's foreign policy objectives.

In simplest terms, economic sanctions threaten or execute economic punishment in order to coerce a society to change its policies or its government.[7] Indirectly, they may also be employed against a state in order to deter third parties from undertaking undesired behavior. Not least in importance, they also serve to satisfy the emotional or political needs of the punishing state itself. Whatever the objective, the purpose is to understand in general terms how sanctions work and what factors determine their success.

Although economic sanctions may involve any type of normal commercial relationship, the most frequently employed and important form of economic sanctions is the trade boycott. The sanctioning state limits or stops exports to or imports from the target state. Thus, through economic deprivation and punishment a trade boycott seeks to achieve its purpose of changing policy in one of two different ways. First, sanctions seek to create and accentuate divisions within and among the ruling elite(s) of a society. Or, second, the imposition of sanctions attempts to split the ruling elite of a society from the general populace, thereby weakening internal support for the regime and its policies. In either case, the success or effectiveness of economic sanctions are dependent upon the degree of punishment inflicted and the internal situation of the target society.

More specifically, the success and effectiveness of a trade boycott are dependent upon three broad sets of factors. While these factors are not independent of one another, for analytical purposes it is best to treat them separately. The first of these factors influencing the ultimate success of a trade boycott is the cost of compliance. The second is the vulnerability of the target state to a cutoff of imports or exports. And the third is the internal social, political, and psychological situation of the target state. Each of these sets of factors will be treated in turn.

Costs to Sanctioned and Sanctioning States

In evaluating the factors which affect the effectiveness and utility of economic sanctions two sets of costs must be taken into consideration. In the first place, there are the costs of compliance for the target or sanctioned state. In the second place, there are costs to the sanctioning state itself in imposing the trade cutoff. Each of these sets of costs will be discussed in turn.

It is a fairly straightforward proposition that the greater the cost to the target state of compliance with the purpose of a boycott, the less probable that the boycott will be successful; it is certainly much more difficult, for example, to unseat a government than to force a change in one of its policies. Yet, the matter of costs is not as simple as it may seem on first glance.

For the target state the costs of compliance are determined primarily by the availability and costs of other options to compliance with the boycott. Are other markets or sources of supply available, and at what cost? What are the transition costs of diversifying exports or sources of supply? Such matters relate to the more general question of vulnerability and will be treated in more detail in the next section. Here several other aspects of compliance costs will be discussed.

The first point is that the costs of compliance or noncompliance are not always clear for a number of reasons. The imposition of economic sanctions by one state or group of states against a target state is a hostile act and it is never unambiguous how far the sanctioning states are willing to go. For example, if the target state complies with the expressed demands of the sanctioning state with respect to even a minor issue will this only whet the desires of the sanctioning state to increase its demands? Or, vice versa, if the target state fails to comply will this stimulate a more aggressive, and even military, response from the sanctioning state? The imposition of sanctions has a dynamic all its own and can trigger an action-reaction process which leads to dire consequences which neither sanctioned nor sanctioning state desired. Unfortunately, such considerations as these are not mere theoretical speculations but are well illustrated by historical experience such as the American embargo of oil to Japan in 1941 which played a major role in the Japanese decision to attack Pearl Harbor.

A trade boycott always has powerful political consequences because it is such a highly publicized action and thereby engages the prestige of both sanctioning and sanctioned state. Once involved in a boycott situation, even regarding a minor question, if either state capitulates its prestige and international standing suffer. Thus, even though the object of the boycott may be a seemingly minor one, a much higher matter—the prestige and credibility of the participants—is always involved. For these reasons, states are very resistant to changing their behavior or policies in response to economic sanctions.

This is a political consideration that the ancients knew. In Thucydides' *History of the Peloponnesian War*, there is a telling passage in which the Athenian leader Pericles rebuts his political opponents who desire that Athens lift its trade boycott of Megara, an ally of Sparta, in response to a Spartan ultimatum:

> I hope that you will none of you think that we shall be going to war for a trifle if we refuse to revoke the Megara decree, [instituting the trade boycott] . . . and the revocation of which is to save us from war . . . . Why, this trifle contains the whole seal and trail of your resolution. If you give way, you will instantly have to meet some greater demand, as having been frightened into obedience in the first instance.[8]

It was the imposition of the Athenian trade boycott of Megara and Athens' refusal to lift it in response to the Spartan ultimatum that precipitated the Great Peloponnesian War.

The point of relating this dramatic event is that the imposition, the compliance with, or even the lifting of a trade boycott of whatever magnitude can involve unanticipated and potentially very high costs. A trade boycott is an act bordering on economic warfare. As in the case of any act of war, it should not be undertaken lightly.

Prior to leaving this discussion of costs, it must be appreciated that there are costs for the sanctioning state as well. The probable success of economic sanctions may very well turn on whether the ultimate costs involved are higher for the sanctioned or the sanctioning state. For this reason, what are the costs involved for the sanctioning state(s)?

In the first place, there are the dangers and potential costs of a political nature. As in the case cited above, sanctions may precipitate untoward political developments, leading in some cases to war. More likely, sanctions will fail causing a loss of prestige for the sanctioning state. The history of economic sanctions demonstrates that these political costs can be real and in particular cases have been far greater than were initially anticipated.

In the second place, there are in almost every instance economic costs to the sanctioning states. As Klaus Knorr points out, when normal trading arrangements are disrupted trade is forced into less economic channels for all concerned.[9] As a consequence, there are transitional difficulties and expenses in switching to other markets or sources of supply. Additionally, a state which is prone to use economic sanctions for political purposes is obviously not regarded as a reliable trading partner by other states and they will avoid becoming dependent upon it. Finally, in a democratic and capitalist economy, the costs of imposing sanctions fall heaviest on particular sectors and usually cause deep resentments as in the case of the American grain embargo of the Soviet Union. Thus, while the imposition of economic sanctions tends to unify the sanctioned country (see below) it is more likely to cause internal dissension in the sanctioning country. For this reason, those economic interests in the sanctioning state(s) which will be harmed by the imposition of economic sanctions should be compensated by the rest of society; otherwise the imposition of economic sanctions become divisive in the sanctioning state. It is, unfortunately, not enough to ask those particular sectors on whom the costs fall to accept them as their patriotic duty.

Thirdly, the use of economic sanctions for political purposes by a capitalist country committed to an open world economy and free trade is destructive of these ideals. While this is a more intangible cost than the ones above, it is no less real. As will be argued in greater detail below, the use of economic sanctions to promote goals however worthy undermines the type of world order the United States has sought to promote since the end of the Second World War.

In brief, when one speaks of the costs of economic sanctions the costs to both the sanctioned and sanctioning states must be kept in mind. These costs may be economic or political. They range from relatively minor transition costs to precipitating a conflict from which neither sanctioning nor sanctioned state benefits.

Vulnerability of the Target State

The most crucial determinant of the effectiveness of a trade boycott is the vulnerability of the target state to a cutoff of trade. The degree of vulnerability in turn is influenced by several international factors. In the first place, as one of authority has put it, "the key to the understanding of vulnerability seems to be *concentration*: the more a country's economy depends on one product, and the more its exports and imports are concentrated on one trade partner, the more vulnerable is the country."[10] For this reason, developing and commodity-exporting countries tend to be much more vulnerable to trade boycotts than do advanced economies exporting many products to many markets.[11]

A second and related aspect of vulnerability is the relative importance of foreign trade for the economic welfare of a society; or to put it another way, the vulnerability of a society is influenced by the degree of openness of the economy where the degree of openness is determined by the ratio of imports to national income (gross national product or GNP).[12] All other things being equal, the greater the openness of an economy the greater the vulnerability of the society to a trade boycott, and also, it should be added, the more reluctant it is to engage in trade boycotts. The high degree of openness of America's European and Japanese allies makes them very vulnerable to trade sanctions and therefore reluctant to encourage the widespread use of this instrument of foreign policy. As they have been subject to punishing trade embargoes in the past and even more recently, they have a powerful negative attitude toward them. As communist societies are more closed than capitalist ones, they tend to be less vulnerable and less reluctant to use them. In fact, only the Soviet Union rivals the United States in the use of economic sanctions against other states, witness its imposition of economic sanctions against Albania, Yugoslavia, and Communist China. This low vulnerability of communist economies is of course declining as they develop and enter the world economy.

A third set of factors affecting vulnerability relate to the elasticity of supply and demand for a particular product. The effectiveness of a trade boycott is determined by the availability of other sources of supply (or substitutes) and/or the flexibility of demand for a particular product. These factors in turn are profoundly affected by the state of the world economy, technology, and the level of economic development of the target economy. While in theory new sources of supply (or substitutes) can be found and the strength of demand will adjust, this may take a considerable period of time. For this reason, the extent and duration of a trade boycott must be taken into account. One of the very few successful boycotts on record—the Arab oil embargo against Western Europe and Japan in the winter of 1973–74—was due to the confluence of a number of favorable factors which caused an effective thorough and relatively brief export restriction of a product for which there were no readily available substitutes. Fortunately or unfortunately, there are few, if any, similar sets of conditions favorable to the success of an export embargo.

Yet it must be emphasized that even under conditions of extreme vulnerability and severe punishment states will tenaciously resist economic sanctions, especially where their independence is involved. Two of the harshest recent examples of the use of economic sanctions to force the submission of other states were Soviet sanctions against Yugoslavia (1958–59) and against Albania (1960). In the Albanian case, 56 percent of Albania's imports and 45 percent of her exports were with the Soviet Union, most of the rest were with Soviet satellites in Eastern Europe. Yet at a great cost to her economic development, Albania resisted Soviet pressures to align with the Soviet Union against China.[13]

In summary, one state has coercive economic power over another state if the former has a high degree of control over the supply of an important commodity or constitutes the overwhelmingly critical market for a good. In reality, however, these conditions seldom exist. The supply of commodities is too dispersed and other markets are usually available. Although costs are involved, the sanctioned state can usually find alternative sources of supply and markets. On the basis of an extensive examination of many cases of economic boycotts, Klaus Knorr concludes that, "the historical record shows very few cases in which control over supply by a single state was sufficient to produce effective economic coercion when the conflictual issues at stake were important to both actors. The international markets, and even though some are much larger than others, even the largest for any one good seldom controls an overwhelming share.[14]

Internal Conditions of the Target State

The third set of factors influencing the effectiveness and consequences of economic sanctions is the internal set of conditions of a target society. Whereas the vulnerability of a target state affects the extent of punishment economic sanctions will exact, the internal conditions of the target society affect how the punishment will be distributed among various groups in society, the level of punishment that can be tolerated, and the psychological effect of sanctions on the elite and population. Thus, social, political, and psychological factors internal to the society strongly determine the response of the target state to the imposition of economic sanctions.

In contrast to the analysis above of the factors influencing vulnerability, there appear to be few generalizations which can be made regarding the internal situation of a society and its potential response to economic sanctions. On the contrary, the few generalizations that do exist are more apt to mislead rather than to be good indicators of probable success. It is frequently posited, for example, that the dependence of the ruling elite on trade-generated income make a society particularly vulnerable to an economic boycott. Such an argument has been made, for example, with respect to a boycott of Ugandan coffee, Rhodesian chrome, and South African exports. As Klaus Knorr has concluded, however, on the basis of his examination of past cases, this does not appear to be an important factor.[15] More likely, as critics of these African boycotts point out, the victims too frequently are the hapless black Africans whose interests the boycott are allegedly supposed to serve.

Despite the difficulty of assessing in general terms the internal factors conditioning a society's response to a trade boycott, such an assessment is imperative when imposing sanctions. If these domestic factors are not taken into account, economic sanctions may not only be ineffective but, more importantly, they may be highly counterproductive and bring about developments contrary to the interests of the sanctioning state.[16] In particular, trade sanctions tend to have counterproductive and deleterious effects because they are public and usually highly publicized, thereby accentuating their emotion-laden nature. As such, they may force the sanctioned society to rally round the flag and support the sanctioned government.

The three most important counterproductive consequences of trade boycotts are the following: first, the imposition of a trade boycott more frequently than not bolsters the government of the target state and promotes national unity in the face of the hostile boycotting state. In response to a boycott societies may make economic sacrifices and accept political decisions they would ordinarily not find acceptable; the American boycott of Poland in the winter of 1981 is an exception to this rule. Second, a trade boycott forces a society to build up domestic capabilities in a boycotted area or in those areas which are under the threat of boycott. For a society such as the United States which has a commitment to international trade, the encouragement of autarchic policies on the part of other states is clearly not desirable. And, thirdly, trade boycotts have frequently strengthened the most belligerent elements in the target state and have in fact forced target states to undertake aggressive policies.

A paradoxical feature of economic sanctions is that they may have greater potency as a threat than they do in actual practice. It can be argued that the actual imposition of sanctions increases the credibility of the threat in future cases. Yet, if the sanctions prove to be ineffective, they are weakened as a deterrent. For this reason, sanctions must be used with discretion in order to maintain their deterrent or compellent value.

In conclusion, there are a number of general points about economic sanctions and the conditions under which they are apt to be successful.[17] In the first place, the threat of economic sanctions tends to be successful when minor issues are at stake, when the threat is implicit, and when it is made privately. Such threats do not challenge the prestige of the target economy and create a powerful internal resistance. In the second place, the costs of compliance must be lower than the costs of noncompliance if sanctions are to be successful, And, thirdly, an economic threat is most often successful if it is in the same policy area as the desired compliance. States, for example, tend to accept as part of the game threats involved in tariff and economic bargaining generally whose purpose is to gain economic concessions. They deeply resent and resist, however, the use of economic threats for political objectives. This psychological aspect of economic sanctions makes trade boycotts, for example, a particularly poor means to achieve such political objectives as combatting terrorism and promoting human rights. Yet, it would be quite wrong to conclude that sanctions are never a justifiable instrument of national policy. They can impose serious costs on the sanctioned state and for this reason do have a deterrent value. They also serve an important symbolic value. These objectives, however, must always be weighted against the costs to the sanctioning state itself and the potential loss of prestige if the sanctions are ineffective.

WESTERN EXPERIENCE WITH ECONOMIC SANCTIONS

Despite the inherent limitations of economic sanctions as an instrument of foreign policy, the Western powers due to American pressure in recent years have turned to them as a means to pressure particular foreign governments to change repugnant domestic and foreign policies. Unfortunately, in no case has the Western use of economic sanctions had more than a marginal effect on these policies. For example, the invocation of economic sanctions against the Soviet Union for its direct aggression in Afghanistan and its indirect aggression in Poland has had a symbolic importance and has inflicted punishment, but there is little evidence to suggest that it has resulted in significant policy changes.*

The question to be asked is why this experience has been so unsuccessful from the point of view of the West. Is it due to the nature of the economies? Or, is it due to the restricted conditions discussed above under which economic sanctions are effective? Or is it a combination of these two factors? Only when one answers these questions can the West develop appropriate policies in this area.

The first cause for the failure of economic sanctions does reside in the inherent nature of capitalist economy. In contrast to state-controlled economies, capitalist economies have a strong propensity to expand exports. There are two primary reasons for this difference in the two types of economies. In the first place, exports play a demand stimulant or Keynesian role in capitalist economies which they do not in a planned economy.[18] Exports have a powerful multiplier effect stimulating both growth and employment as they work their way through the economy. This means capitalist economies have a strong motive to expand exports and resist restrictions on these exports. It should be noted, however, that the American economy with its relatively small foreign sector is less sensitive to this situation than its allies, explaining in part its greater willingness than other capitalist economies to embargo exports. Secondly, capitalist economies more than planned economies seek to maximize returns on capital and therefore have a powerful incentive to expand output. This is especially true in high technology goods where the export market must be added to the home to make them profitable.[19] For these two sets of reasons, capitalist economies are inherently more reluctant than planned economies to impose economic sanctions against trading partners.

The slowdown in world economic growth and international trade has greatly accentuated the importance of the demand or Keynesian stimulant aspect of foreign trade. With sluggish economies and rising unemployment, few governments indeed are willing to forego foreign market opportunities. This is particularly true if they suspect that a foreign competitor will step in and take advantage of the situation. Under these circumstances it becomes very difficult for a government to embargo exports which would create jobs. This restraint on the use of economic sanctions, however, may be due as much to the fact that the society is democratic as it is that the economy is capitalist. It is usually the case of course that these economic and political systems go together.

---

*It should be stressed that this analysis refers to the use of trade sanctions as a response to specific Soviet actions. We are not treating the Western embargo of strategic goods such as computers and other advanced technologies to the Soviet bloc. The effectiveness of the latter policy is a quite separate issue.

The reluctance to use economic sanctions has become particularly strong in the case of America's most powerful allies—Japan and, even more so, West Germany. Both are highly dependent upon export markets in high-technology goods. As the growth of Western trade has slowed, their reliance upon trade with Communist countries has increased because of the complementarity of their exports in manufactures and the East's exports of raw materials, including fossil fuels. For West Germany this economic interest is reinforced by its political desire to maintain contacts with East Germany and to lessen the confrontation in Central Europe. Trade with the East is also seen as a way to encourage moderation and evolution in a more liberal direction. For this reason the Germans in particular are extremely reluctant to take measures which might destroy what they regard as the benefits of East-West détente. Both economic and political factors therefore inhibit the use of economic sanctions by America's two most powerful economic allies.

The second factor explaining the failure of Western economic sanctions is a divergence between the United States and its allies regarding the utility of economic sanctions. In part these contrasting perspectives are due to the differences in dependence on foreign trade mentioned above. But it is much more than this. The American belief in the usefulness of economic sanctions to achieve foreign policy objectives has deep roots in American history. One of the first major foreign policy actions of the American Republic in fact was a series of trade embargoes during the period 1807 to 1812 to force changes in British policy toward the United States, in particular Britain's interference with American trade and impressment of American sailors. The American embargo was eventually successful—one of the few on record—though it was extremely costly to American economic interests, caused great internal dissension, and gave rise to vast smuggling operations. Ironically, the American government—believing the boycott to have failed and unaware of events in London—declared war against Great Britain, two days after the British had met the American demands.

The deep American belief in the effectiveness of economic sanctions may perhaps be best illustrated by quotations from two American statemen who are separated in time, party affiliation, and political ideology:
President Woodrow Wilson, Autumn 1919:

> If any member of the League breaks or ignores these promises with regard to arbitration and discussion, what happens, war? No, not war but something more tremendous than war. Apply this economic, peaceful, silent, deadly remedy and there will be no need for force. The boycott is what is substituted for war.

Future Secretary of State John Foster Dulles, 1932:

> The great advantage of economic sanctions is that on the one hand they can be very potent, while on the other hand they do not involve the resort to force, which is repugnant to our objective of peace.[20]

Thus, for both Wilson and Dulles, economic sanctions were not only an effective but a bloodless and relatively costless way to achieve American foreign policy objectives.

The tendency of the United States to believe in and rely upon economic sanctions is due to a number of factors. In the first place, even before the founding of the Republic, American political leaders believed in what Felix Gilbert in his classic study of the origins of American foreign policy, *To the Farewell Address*, called the "new diplomacy." This was the close connection between commerce and foreign policy, and the associated notion that the United States could use trade and commerce to influence the course of international politics. It was the firm conviction of Alexander Hamilton, America's first Secretary of the Treasury, to quote Gilbert, that "commerce was a weapon in the struggle of power politics."[21] Through his influence on President George Washington and his role in the drafting of the Farewell Address—Washington's Political Testament and advice to the American people—Hamilton's views on commerce became embodied in American foreign policy.[22]

A second reason for the tendency of the United States to employ economic sanctions as opposed to the disinclination of other capitalist states has been vastly different economic circumstances. Until very recently, the United States was a relatively self-sufficient economy. The United States raised most of its own food and the subsoil held the raw materials which were required for industrial development. The United States did not need to import. Nor was there an imperative to export though the United States began to export great quantities of food and other commodities, especially in the later decades of the nineteenth century. The United States possessed a vast and rapidly expanding internal market. Foreign trade in fact was a relatively small percentage for America's total economy. Moreover, Americans were (and still are) a highly innovative people and while industrial goods were imported in great quantities, from the latter part of the nineteenth century onward there was a growing world demand for American technology. From the strong world demand of American agricultural and industrial products and, until recently, the lack of a reciprocal American need for imports and exports, there developed the notion that the United States could use this asymmetrical economic situation as a source of political leverage.

A third, and more cynical, reason for the American reliance on economic sanctions has been its attractiveness to political leaders. The declaration of economic sanctions against an unpopular and unsavory government, amidst much publicity and fanfare, has always been a relatively popular and inexpensive expedient for American political leaders. Regardless of the actual effectiveness of such sanctions, it is a way of seeming to be doing something and of courting favor with public opinion in general or with particular interest groups. In the face of popular or congressional demand "to do something," sanctions are far preferable to risking war, or seemingly doing nothing.

The first concerted effort on the part of the United States to use its economic power to reform the behavior of other states came in the 1920s. The First World War had transformed the United States into a creditor nation and the United States came out of the war as the world's dominant financial and industrial power. Though withdrawing into political isolationism, the United States sought to use its new-found economic power to reform international relations and the internal workings of other societies. Then Secretary of Commerce, Herbert Hoover, expressed to the Third Pan-American Commercial Conference in 1927, this American faith in the capacity of economic power to reform the world and derelict societies: ". . . if nations would do away with the lending of money for the balancing of budgets, for purposes of military equipment or war, or even that type of public works which do not bring some direct or indirect public return, a great number of blessings would follow to the entire world.[23]

American belief in the efficacy of American economic power in the 1920s and 1930s is in fact remarkably reminiscent of the dubious effort of the Carter administration to foster human rights through the threat and imposition of economic sanctions on delinquent governments. As Herbert Feis recounts this earlier history in his *The Diplomacy of the Dollar, 1919–1932*, American political leadership hoped that it could use economic leverage to foster the adoption by foreign governments of "a form of political system resembling our own" and "of constitutional government, under which individual freedom and justice would be respected."[24] While the United States achieved some good, Feis concludes that the American people were ultimately disappointed that through economic means alone, they could "spread American ideals, foster good will and trust between ourselves and foreign countries, encourage disarmament, and bring reconciliation and peace."[25] Unfortunately, this lesson from the past has been insufficiently learned by many policy makers in Washington.

In contrast to the American proclivity to use economic sanctions for political purposes, Japan and Western European countries have a deep negative attitude toward them. The United States, for example, has had to pressure them to enforce boycotts of China and the Soviet bloc. When they could, America's allies evaded the boycott and as soon as they were sufficiently strong to resist American pressures, they fought to have the boycott lifted. Such an attitude reflects in part their longer and unhappy experience with boycotts (such as the League boycott of Italy or American trade sanctions against Japan in the 1930s) and, more importantly, their lesser degree of self-sufficiency and greater need to export to be able to purchase vital imports.

The best and most representative statement of the European attitude toward the boycotting of East-West trade was that of Sir Hartley Shawcross, then president of the Board of Trade, in a speech delivered in August 1951. Shawcross reminded the United States that unilateral dictation to Europe and lack of confidence in Europe's good judgment was no way to treat an ally.

Moreover, Western Europe required East European resources and to deprive Eastern Europe of trade would not eliminate communism. The heart of the difference with America, however, lay in the contrasting economic circumstances:

> Our position was wholly different in East-West trade as in many other matters from that of the United States, because of the importance of this trade to us. America had not, and did not, need to have any significant trade with the Soviets; it meant little or nothing to her to discontinue the imports of furs, caviar and crab. With us things were quite different. We obtained from the Soviet bloc essential foods and raw materials—and we believed that in these trade exchanges we got as good as we gave, economically and strategically.[26]

Thus, though Europeans have accepted the rationale of restricting the export of "strategic goods" to the Soviets, they have rejected as ineffective and contrary to their interests the more restrictive embargoes favored by the United States.

The third factor underlying the impotence of Western economic sanctions is the relative economic decline of the United States. The United States is decreasingly able to enforce a sanctions policy on reticent allies. Acting alone it cannot succeed nor can it force its allies to overcome their reluctance to join it in such a policy. This is the stark lesson to be learned from the effort of the Reagan administration to impose sanctions against the Soviet Union for its role in the suppression of Polish Solidarity.

Earlier, in the general discussion of the theory of economic sanctions, the point was made that sanctions can succeed only if the sanctioning state or states have market power; they must, in other words, enjoy a monopolist or monopsonist position in world markets. Furthermore, it was argued that this situation seldom, if ever, exists, and for this reason sanctions have almost never succeeded. In the modern world only two countries have come even close to possessing such market power—Great Britain at the height of her power in the nineteenth century and the United States at the end of the Second World War. With the rise of new industrial and economic powers, however, British market power and capacity to impose sanctions on others declined.* Though not nearly as great, a similar relative decline in market power characterizes the United States in the last quarter of the twentieth century.

At the end of the Second World War, and for some years thereafter, the United States was in a sufficiently powerful market position to be able to exercise considerable political influence. The United States for example, used this market position to force its Western European and Japanese allies to participate

*Great Britain it should be noted, almost never used economic sanctions against other states, though it did engage in gunboat diplomacy.

in its trade boycott of the Communist bloc. By the 1960s, however, this monopoly position had vanished and America's allies in combination with the general appreciation that the boycott was not working, succeeded in bringing the highly restrictive boycott to an end. In the light of current American efforts to seek once again to achieve political objectives through the exercise of American economic power, it is instructive to review how this monopoly/monoposonist position of the United States has changed over the past several decades.

In the earlier years of the postwar period, the United States possessed a high percentage of world industry and held a virtual monopolist position in a number of critical areas. First, the United States was the only nation with the capacity to produce and export advanced machine tools and sophisticated technology. In its own security and economic interests the United States re-equipped the Western European industrial plant and sought to deny modern machinery and technology to the Soviet bloc.

Second, the United States, and through the foreign holdings of American multinational oil companies, in effect controlled the noncommunist world's supply of petroleum. This monopoly of supply in fact gave the United States political leverage over its allies. Thus, when Great Britain and France launched their invasion of the Suez Canal in 1956 over the objections of the United States, the United States cut off their supply of oil forcing them to retreat in ignominy. Parenthetically, this episode has not been forgotten in either country and explains in part their reluctance to become ever again overly dependent upon the United States with respect to energy as in the case of American-proposed alternatives to the European-Soviet gas pipeline agreement.

The third source of American economic power and leverage lay in the area of international finance and investment. By the end of the Second World War, New York had replaced London as the financial center of the world and American multinational corporations had become the primary source of long-term direct investment. During this period one could have inquired regarding Chase and Citibank with little undue exaggeration what John A. Hobson remarked concerning the power of British and European finance in the latter part of the nineteenth century: "Does anyone seriously suppose that a great war could be undertaken by any European State, or a great State loan subscribed, if the house of Rothschild and its connections set their face against it?"[27] In 1956, the United States did in fact freeze the assets of Great Britain and France and in combination with the oil embargo mentioned above thereby forced the abandonment of their Suez military operations.

Fourth, and closely related to the preceding factor, the United States government possessed approximately 50 percent of the world's monetary reserves and through loans and foreign aid was the only supplier of international exchange. As a consequence of American industrial supremacy and these international reserves, the United States in effect became the world's banker and the dollar (like sterling in the nineteenth century) became the world's principal currency. Especially during the era of the "dollar shortage" (until 1959) other nations were heavily dependent upon the will of the United States for the dollars required to finance necessary imports and balance their international accounts.

Fifth, the United States set in motion and effectively dominated the two international organizations principally responsible for managing the world's monetary system and for fostering economic development: the International Monetary Fund (IMF) and the International Bank for Reconstruction and Development (World Bank). Through its virtual veto over the activities of these organizations, the United States could determine the terms on which nations in payments difficulties could get loans to balance their accounts or could get long-term loans for economic development. In short, to summarize the above three points, American private banks and corporations, the American government, and international organizations responsive to American demands had a near monopoly of international finance and development funds.

Sixth, the United States for many years following the conclusion of the Second World War was the breadbasket of the world. American foodstuffs fed devastated Europe, Japan, and much of the rest of the world. The most significant use of this food as a weapon came in response to the Soviet invasion of Afghanistan. Although the refusal to sell grain to the Soviets hurt them, it also hurt American farmers. One of the issues on which Ronald Reagan beat Jimmy Carter was the promise never to embargo the sale of grain again.

And, finally, on the monopsony side of the ledger, the United States was the world's principal market and was the single largest trading nation of the world. Although foreign trade constituted only a relatively small fraction of the American economy (about 5 percent), this trade accounted for a much larger fraction of the total world trade. Other nations required access to the American economy more than American corporations required access to their markets. The dependence of foreign exports on the American market and this asymmetrical trading relationship were a further economic leverage which the United States possessed over other nations. The termination of trade would hurt other nations more than it would hurt the United States.

Today, these former sources of American economic power either have entirely disappeared or have greatly diminished. Even in the area of food exports which some have argued should be used as a counter-weapon against the monopoly of the Organization of the Petroleum Exporting Countries (OPEC), the United States may not be able to use its continuing strong position for political ends. American farmers, as already noted, have served notice on Washington that they would not permit it, and other exporters such as Canada and Australia in wheat and Brazil in soybeans have broken the American monopoly. In all other areas where the United States once enjoyed a monopolist or monopsonist position the tables have turned. Let us consider each area in turn.

1) Although the variety and quality of American industrial machinery and advanced technology continue to be outstanding and greatly desired by other countries, America's former pre-eminence is gone and in some important areas the United States has been eclipsed by West European countries or especially Japan. In the case of machine tools and industrial technology, for example, the American share of the world market has drastically declined and in fact the United States itself has become a major importer of these technologies. More ominous for the future, a recent joint study of American and Japanese economists found that Japanese productive technology, that is, the technology that powerfully determines industrial productivity, is now generally superior to that of the United States.[28] This Japanese superiority will probably increase in the decades immediately ahead.

In a number of high technology areas where the United States once reigned supreme American corporations must now face tough international competition; these areas include computers, electronics, and other research-and-development-intensive products. Even in commercial aircraft where American producers had a virtual monopoly, the European airbus (A-300) threatens to obtain a substantial share of the market and to displace what has been (along with agricultural exports) one of America's most important sources of foreign exchange. In sophisticated military-related technology the United States certainly retains its lead but these technologies are ones sold only to "friendly" countries. Moreover, though the quality of American advance technology products usually gives them a competitive edge there are few, if any product areas, where foreign produced substitutes are not available.

Undoubtedly the most telling indication of the changed American position with respect to industrial and advanced technology is America's trade balance in this area. Although the United States continues to enjoy a surplus position with respect to certain countries and in many areas of high technology products, the United States has become a net importer in a broad range of goods. In combination with petroleum imports, these high-technology imports are a major component of America's chronic balance of payments difficulties.

2) With respect to petroleum, the transformation which has taken place since 1973 requires no emphasis. In effect, it could be argued that the control over the world petroleum market has shifted from the United States and American multinational corporations to the King of Saudi Arabia. Even in the noncommunist world the United States no longer holds its former position. Traditional foreign sources of supply outside the Middle East (principally Nigeria and Venezuela) are no longer under American control and, except for Alaska, the newest major finds—the North Sea, China, Siberia, and Mexico—are also not subject to American will.

Perhaps the most significant point that needs to be emphasized with respect to the "petro-revolution" is that for the first time in its history the United States itself is dependent upon foreign governments for a resource vital to its economic welfare and security. The United States is no longer self-sufficient and like other countries must export to obtain the foreign exchange to finance these petroleum imports. This loss of self-sufficiency has transformed the international economic and security position of the United States and has far-reaching consequences for the United States. At the least, it means that the legitimation of the use of economic pressure to obtain political objectives may no longer be in the interest of the United States. The United States itself for the first time in modern history has become vulnerable to trade boycotts.

3) In the area of money, finance, and investment the change that has taken place can be described in no lesser terms than "revolutionary." In the first place, although the dollar continues to be the basis of the international monetary system, American-held gold and other monetary reserves backing the dollar have plummeted. From a post-World War II level of 50 percent of total world monetary reserves, the United States holds less than 16 percent. Official dollar reserves of other countries are in excess of $50 billion, and private holdings total over half a trillion dollars (the so-called "dollar overhang"). In a word, potential foreign demands on American goods, services, and assets are mind-boggling.

In the area of international finance and investment, private American banks and multinational corporations still loom large on the world scene. Yet, even here a significant change has taken place. Both must now meet increased international competition abroad and in the United States. International competition in banking has in fact encouraged American and foreign banks to borrow heavily in the so-called Euro-currency market and to make highly questionable loans especially to Eastern Europe and the LDCs.* This practice in turn has led to the situation that the threat of one or another debtor country (e.g., Poland) to default gives them leverage over the banks and their respective countries. Again, what an ironic shift in economic power relations! As for American multinational corporations, while they continue to be the cutting edge of American international competitiveness their relative position has declined and there is growing concern that in order to gain access to foreign markets they must now make concessions to host countries (joint ventures and production arrangements, local sourcing of

*The Euro-currency market is composed of currencies, mainly dollars, on deposit outside the United States, principally in London. As these funds are not part of the local money supply, they are outside domestic currency regulations; nor are they subject to international regulation. These funds have been generated largely by American balance of payments deficits and the unspent funds of OPEC countries (petro-dollars).

components, buy-back arrangements, and guarantees to export a percentage of the output) that run counter to American economic interests.

Finally, the positions of the International Monetary Fund and the World Bank (and America's ability to exercise influence through them) have been transformed by the revolution in "international liquidity." Mention has already been made of this change with respect to the immense "overhang" of dollars in official and private hands and the lending propensities of international banks. More specifically, the Euro-currency market has become a competitor to the IMF and the Bank—some would say has displaced them—as a source of money and finance. This development is not only a cause of international monetary instability due to speculative shifts from currency to currency, but it means that the United States is less able to use its influence in the IMF or World Bank to bring pressure on a country as it was alleged to have done, for example, in the case of Allende's Chile.

4) The remaining potential economic lever of the United States to be considered is American monopsony power, that is, the United States as a customer. With respect to certain countries and products, this power has increased due to the fact that the United States is less self-sufficient and the foreign sector of the American economy has increased from 5 to approximately 7 percent. In the area of consumer products from Western Europe, certain developing countries, and in particular Japan, a cut-off of American imports would have a harmful impact. On the other hand, the former asymmetry has been greatly weakened. The United States itself must now export to finance petroleum imports if nothing else, and for the first time is subject to punishing retaliation. And although the foreign sector of the American economy is small relative to America's position in world markets, in aggregate the European Common Market dwarfs the United States in world trade. Thus, American monopsony power, like its monopoly power, has greatly diminished over the period since the end of the Second World War and with it the American capacity to impose its will on others through coercion.

The relative decline of American economic power has profound implications for the American world position and the capacity of the United States to pursue a sanctions policy. It is one thing to impose economic sanctions against other nations, forego the income of trading opportunities, and risk being considered an unreliable trading partner when your economy is relatively self-sufficient and lacks powerful foreign competitors. It is quite another matter when you have become increasingly dependent upon the importation of vital raw materials, particularly petroleum, and must export in a highly competitive world market to finance petroleum imports as well as other goods desired by the American consumer. Unfortunately, although the American economic position has changed dramatically, American leadership is only just beginning to realize that the United States (like Western Europe and Japan) must export to survive; the United States still tends to behave as if it were self-sufficient and can use its economic leverage to force other states to change their policies.

The recent experience of the United States in imposing sanctions against the Soviet Union and Poland in response to the imposition of martial law in the latter country dramatically illuminates the change that has taken place and the requirements for a successful sanctions policy. At this writing it is perhaps still too early to evaluate the effectiveness of these sanctions. For some, however, this episode has proven once again the ineffectiveness of economic sanctions in forcing a change in the policies of other countries. For others sanctions have not succeeded because in truth they have not really been fully applied by the Western powers. In either case, the lessons to be drawn are the same.

Although the imposition of economic sanctions by the Reagan administration has hurt both Communist countries and has served to demonstrate the disgust generated by their violation of the rights of the Polish people, the larger truth is that despite their rhetoric the administration has been unwilling and unable to take the most stringent actions available to it. It has not invoked a grain embargo lest it harm and alienate American farmers. Nor has it wished to force a default on the huge Polish debt because of the cost to American banks, its alliance with Western Europe, and the international financial system. Whether or not one agrees with the restrained actions of the American administration, the fact of its seeming impotence can not be denied.

More significant, however, has been the reaction of America's allies to the Polish situation. It is not merely that they have been reluctant to follow the lead of the United States in word and deed. What is even more striking is that during this period of crisis they concluded the most far-reaching and important accord in the history of East-West economic relations. Whatever the economic and political motives behind the European action, their gas pipeline agreement with the Soviet Union is of great moment. It completely overshadows the talk of economic sanctions and has profound implications for the future not only of East-West relations but of intra-Western relations as well. At the least it demonstrates once again that the success of economic sanctions necessitates a prior political agreement among the sanctioning powers.

CONCLUSION

The overall conclusion of this chapter is that the success of economic sanctions is dependent upon a highly restrictive set of favorable factors. Although these necessary conditions apply to any type of economy, they are less likely to exist in the case of capitalist economies which have a strong propensity to export goods. Yet, the primary reason the United States and its allies have failed to use economic sanctions effectively is more political than it is economic. The difficulty encountered by the West in imposing economic sanctions on the Soviet Union and its allies is due to the political differences among Western governments rather than to the inherent nature of their economic system. If political will and unity existed, the economic problem could be overcome, or, at least, greatly diminished. Yet, whether or not Western economic sanctions would be effective in changing the policies of other governments can only be determined on a case by case basis.

NOTES

1. This draws upon an unpublished study by Henry Bienen and the author entitled, "Evaluation of the Use of Economic Sanctions to Promote Foreign Policy Objectives," (April 2, 1979).
2. The classic study of economic warfare is Yuan-li Wu. *Economic Warfare*. New York: Prentice-Hall, Inc., 1952.
3. The effectiveness of one such strategic embargo, the Western embargo of the Soviet bloc, is the subject of Gunnar Adler-Karlsson. *Western Economic Warfare 1947–1967, A Case Study in Foreign Economic Policy*. Stockholm: Almqvist and Wiksell, 1968.
4. Andreas F. Lowenfeld. *Trade Controls for Political Ends*. New York: Matthew Bender, 1977, p. 1.
5. Peter Wallenstein. "Characteristics of Economic Sanctions." *Journal of Peace Research* 3 (1968): 248, 265.
6. Johan Galtung, "On the Effects of International Economic Sanctions, with Examples from the Case of Rhodesia," *World Politics* 19 (April 1967): 379.
7. The following discussion is based primarily on Galtung, op. cit.; Klaus Knorr. *The Power of Nations—The Political Economy of International Relations*. New York: Basic Books, Inc., 1975; Wallensteen, op. cit.; and Klaus Knorr, "International Economic Leverage and Its Uses," In Klaus Knorr and Frank Trager (eds.). *Economic Issues and National Security*, Lawrence, Kansas: Regents Press of Kansas, 1977, pp. 99–126.
8. Thucydides. *The History of the Peloponnesian War*. New York: The Modern Library, 1951, pp. 79–80.
9. Klaus Knorr. *The Power of Nations*, op. cit., p. 155.
10. Johan Galtung. op. cit., p. 385 [italics his]. It is worthwhile noting Galtung's concluding statement: "to launch economic sanctions without a careful examination of all these factors would be like launching a military campaign without military analysis."
11. For a general discussion of vulnerability, see Robert Keohane and Joseph Nye. *Power and Interdependence—World Politics in Transition*. Boston: Little, Brown and Co., 1977, pp. 11–19.
12. Klaus Knorr. *The Power of Nations*, op. cit., p. 154.
13. Klaus Knorr. "International Economic Leverage," op. cit., p. 107.
14. Ibid., p. 104.
15. Klaus Knorr. *The Power of Nations*, op. cit., p. 154.
16. Johan Galtung, op. cit., p. 389.
17. Klaus Knorr. "International Economic Leverage," op. cit., p. 109.
18. P.J.D. Wiles. *Economic Institutions Compared*. New York: John Wiley and Sons, 1977, p. 522.

19. *The Economist* (June 27, 1970): 57.

20. Both quotations from Fredrik Hoffmann. "The Functions of Economic Sanctions." *Journal of Peace Research* 2 (1967): 144.

21. Felix Gilbert. *To the Farewell Address*. Princeton: Princeton University Press, 1961.

22. Ibid., p. 131.

23. Quoted in Herbert Feis. *The Diplomacy of the Dollar, 1919–1932*. New York: W.W. Norton and Co., 1950, p. 18.

24. Ibid., p. 65.

25. Ibid., p. 64.

26. Quoted in Adler-Karlsson, op. cit., p. 39.

27. J.A. Hobson. *Imperialism: A Study*. Ann Arbor: The University of Michigan Press, 1967, p. 57. Originally published in 1902.

28. For a summary of this study by Dale Jorgenson of Harvard University and Mieko Nishimizu of Princeton University, see *New International Realities*, 3 (Winter 1978): p. 7–15.

7

Structural Constraints on Economic Leverage: Command-Type Systems

Herbert S. Levine

The objective of this chapter is to identify and analyze the influence of the systemic aspects of centrally planned economies on economic leverage: How the presence of a system of central planning affects the vulnerability of a nation to the exercise of economic leverage on it, and how central planning affects the ability of a nation to exercise economic leverage on others.

At the most general level economic "leverage" refers to the ability of one nation to affect another with regard to the achievement of certain objectives. The term may include the reduction of another nation's potential—economic, political, military—through the avoidance of actions which expand that nation's capabilities. For instance, the refusal by the United States to export state-of-the-art computers to the Soviet Union may achieve the objective of restraining Soviet military development by keeping Soviet technological capabilities below what they would be if such computers were exported to the USSR (not necessarily because the Soviets might not be able to develop comparable computers but because it would cost them time and resources to do so). In the context of this chapter, however, "leverage" will have a narrower meaning. It will refer specifically to the ability of one nation to affect the *behavior* of another. In other words, leverage here will refer to the advantage (the lever) possessed by one nation in its economic relations with another that can be used to pry noneconomic, political/military benefits or concessions from that other nation.

In examining the institutions and performance characteristics of a centrally planned economy, we will focus on the example of the Soviet Union. Given the nature of the discussion in this volume, such a focus is clearly warranted, but it does bring with it several problems. One is the perennial, rather intractable problem of separating what, in Soviet economic behavior, is the consequence of its system of central planning and what is the result of Russian culture and tradition.[1]

A second problem is that Soviet susceptibility to the exercise of economic leverage by the United States and other Western nations, and the ability to exercise economic leverage on others, is fundamentally affected by the growth and productivity performance of the Soviet economy. That is, decreasing rates of growth of Soviet output and productivity in the past and projected for the future put the Soviet Union in a position where expanded economic relations with the advanced economies of the West have been and continue to promise to be of great benefit to it. But these decreasing rates of growth of output and productivity are not the result only of the system of centralized planning in the Soviet Union. They also result from other factors, including the following:

1) exogeneous developments, such as bad weather which primarily affects Soviet agriculture, but also spills over into industry, construction and transportation; depressed economic conditions in the West after 1973 which reduced the West's demand for many Soviet exports, thus affecting Soviet ability to import Western machinery and technology; and demographic developments, the drastic reduction in the growth of the Soviet working-age population projected for the 1980s;
2) the maturing of the Soviet economy, including the depletion of raw material sources in the established industrial regions, leading to increased costs of production and transportation; decreasing marginal productivity of capital; and the aging of the Soviet capital stock, requiring substantial capital replacement especially in industry and transportation;
3) a number of strategic planning decisions made by Soviet leaders concerning such matters as the allocation of national product among consumption, investment, and defense; both the rapid growth of capital stock, in the past, with low capital retirement (high capital repair) which intensified diminishing returns to capital investment, and the recent sharp decrease in the growth of investment starting in the 10th Five Year Plan (1976-80) and continuing in the 11th Five Year Plan (1981-85) and underinvestment, in the 1960s and 1970s, in rail transportation.

While recognizing the role of these factors in the issue of economic leverage and the Soviet economy, the primary focus of this chapter will be on the *systemic elements of central planning*, how the system of central planning itself may affect the Soviet vulnerability to economic leverage and its ability to exercise economic leverage on others. We first turn, in the section below, to a discussion of the major characteristics of the Soviet centrally planned system, which will prepare the ground for the subsequent discussion of its effects on the leverage issue.

CHARACTERISTICS OF THE SOVIET CENTRALLY PLANNED ECONOMIC SYSTEM

The chief differentiating characteristic of the Soviet economic system is, of course, its centrally planned nature. Each year a detailed, operational plan is constructed and is implemented through a centralized, hierarchical administrative bureaucracy, employing a system of managerial, monetary and status incentives and disincentives. A brief description of the major characteristics of the Soviet centrally planned economic system can be provided drawing on one of the important new trends in the study of comparative economic systems—the decision-making, functional approach.[2] In this approach, attention is placed on the major functions related to decision making in an economic system, and the structures within a system for performing these functions. One way of organizing the set of functional structural categories is as follows:

the system's objective structure;
organizational structure;
information structure;
motivation and incentive structure;
economic interaction, coordination structure.

These compartments are not airtight. Their borders tend to be a bit fuzzy in the sense that the population of elements could be regrouped in other ways. Furthermore, the order in which the structures are listed should not be viewed as being unique. For, although there is some sequential or recursive sense to the ordering, there are also feedbacks and simultaneities within the analytical system.

This approach views the economic system as a set of interrelated structures for the making of decisions in regard to the economic phenomena of production, distribution, and consumption. The process of decision making is seen to involve the establishment of societal goals (the objectives structure), the distribution of authority and power to make decisions (the organizational structure), the provision of information to decision makers to enable them to make meaningful decisions (the information structure), the mechanisms by which decision makers can implement their decisions (the motivation and incentive structure), and the means for coordinating, on a system-wide basis, the decisions of individual decision makers (the coordination structure). Applied to the Soviet system of centralized economic planning, the following brief description, in a somewhat outline-like form, emerges.

Objectives Structure

A clearly outstanding feature of the Soviet system is the objectives structure. The establishment of overall societal objectives is dominated to a very significant extent by the central political leaders. From the late 1920s until the 1960s, the major objective was the rapid forced-draft industrialization and growth of the economy in order to catch up with the advanced capitalist nations of the West, to build its productive capacity with heavy emphasis on the military strength of the nation. In the more recent period, though the priority given to military production has been maintained, the additional objective of consumer welfare has been established, and is now of substantial importance to Soviet political leaders.

Organizational Structure

The distribution of decision-making authority in the Soviet Union is severely constrained by the planned nature of the system: the role of the plan and the hierarchical form of the organizational structure. On any scale, it is a highly centralized system.

Though the Soviets construct plans for various periods, presently it is still the annual plan that plays the key role in the Soviet economy.[3] For it is the data from the annual plan, not the five-year plan, that form the basis of output targets and input limits given to Soviet enterprises. And since the Soviet annual plan is promulgated in the form of a law, these targets and limits have the force of law, giving rise to the Western descriptive term *command economy*.

Soviet producing units are administered in a vertical, hierarchical structure, by branch of the economy, from the enterprises within a branch at the bottom, to intermediary branch organizations, to the branch ministry, and then up to the executive body of the government, the council of ministers. In design this is a complete hierarchy, where all lines of authority flow downward from the center, and all commands and information are to flow within the vertical hierarchy. In practice, however, there is a rather substantial set of horizontal interactions within the system, official and unofficial.[4] In the absence of an efficient system of intermediate goods distribution and in the face of supply unreliability and pressure to fulfill output plan targets, Soviet enterprises are staffed with expenditers who scour the economy in search of needed supplies, and who employ a variety of monetary and nonmonetary (including barter) means to acquire these supplies. These types of inter-enterprise relations are well detailed in the general literature on the Soviet economy; they have often been described as the grease in the machine of central planning that allows the Soviet command economy to function.

In addition, while this is not the place to discuss at length household to household relations, mention should be made of the black market, which forms a major part of the growing "second economy" existing in the Soviet Union. Suffice it to say, that it is comprised of individuals who steal state property and sell it for private profit, and of individuals who illegally produce consumer goods, usually with state property as inputs and, with use of state machinery, and sell these goods for private profit. These producing units are often quite large and well organized. It should be noted that the absence of second economy activities from official statistics leads to an understatement of output and productivity, especially in regard to consumer goods.

Information Structure

The information structure of the Soviet economy is another of those vast subjects that cannot be adequately treated here. In brief, the Soviets collect huge amounts of information for the purpose of constructing and controlling the implementation of plans (one large plant submited 17,000 pages of data for the construction of its annual plan). Partly because of its huge volume and partly because the information structure provides the data for the incentive structure (those who report the data, therefore, have a stake in the data they report), the information system is beset with problems. Information is incomplete, insufficiently accurate, largely irrelevant, and slow. Furthermore, it is expensive. In an article written over a decade ago (things have not changed dramatically since then), an important Soviet economics authority stated:[5]

> The existing system of economic information, its methods of collecting, transmitting, and processing, can barely attain even a balanced plan for an aggregate group of products. The basis of that system is data collected by the Central Statistical Agency and by means of an enormous number of telephone conversations and meetings held in organs of planning and management. Of these data, collected with a great delay, no more than 10 percent are used for purposes of planning and management. The country essentially lacks a more or less unified, scientifically based coefficient base. An enormous amount of planning-managerial information is largely subjective in character. Relying on such a system of information, the organs of planning and management often cannot formulate scientifically based plans even when using computers and modern scientific methods; and the economic organs cannot guarantee their implementation.

Basic to the entire issue of information is the absence of a meaningful price system. Since Soviet prices do not accurately reflect economic value (utility and opportunity cost), data based upon them convey at best limited information to planners and decision makers.

Motivation and Incentive Structure

The salient features of the Soviet incentive structure, well documented in the literature on the Soviet economy, concern the relativity of the Soviet managerial bonus system, its intertemporal "ratchet" nature, and its negative consequences on managerial behavior. In short, Soviet managers are rewarded for performance relative to target. Up to the mid-1960s, the major target was volume of output; since then it has been primarily a combination of volume of sales, profitability and labor productivity. But its relative nature has remained. This combined with the practice of making tomorrow's target greater than today's performance and the practice of constantly applying strong pressure on Soviet managers to increase their output has led to a number of dysfunctional consequences, that is, dysfunctional from the point of view of the growth objectives of the Soviet leaders. Primary among these is the Soviet manager's resistance to innovation in the process of production and even more in regard to the product produced. Soviet managers also produce low quality goods, wrong assortment, material intensive goods, and hoard inputs. All of which decreases the effectiveness of Soviet planning and the efficiency of the Soviet economy.

Coordination Structure

The coordination structure in the Soviet economy lies primarily in the construction of the plan. While the Soviet plan construction process does enable the political leaders to maintain the structure of resource allocation that it desires, that is, a structure aimed at high growth, it is not an effective instrument for achieving internal consistency and coordination in the economy. This is by now standard in both the Soviet and Western literature on the Soviet economy. The information-gathering and processing requirements of running a modern economy the size of the Soviet Union is far beyond the capacities of Soviet planners. In effect their plans are usually poorly coordinated, which is one of the reasons for the large set of unplanned horizontal transactions referred to above.

SYSTEM EFFECTS ON ECONOMIC LEVERAGE POTENTIAL

Factors Affecting Soviet Vulnerability to Economic Leverage

In approaching the issue of Soviet vulnerability to economic leverage and the role in it of system effects, let us return to the point raised at the beginning of the chapter, namely, the role of the growth and productivity performance of the Soviet economy. It is frequently argued that because of output and productivity growth problems, the Soviet Union has become dependent on economic relations with the advanced nations of the developed West, which makes it susceptible to the application of economic leverage by the West.

An initial problem with such an argument is the use of the word dependence. The degree of involvement of a nation in the external world economy lies on a continuous, multidimensional scale, which measures the amount of disruption that would be caused to a nation's internal economy if its external economic relations were broken. The zero point on the scale is autarky, and only the highest point should be referred to as dependence. Most developed economies, especially the large, multiresource ones, are well within the range between these two extreme points.

This concern with the use of the term dependence is not just semantic quibbling. Its use sets the wrong tone for a discussion of the vulnerability of the Soviet Union to the exercise of economic leverage by the West. The Soviet Union is not dependent for its survival on its trade with other nations. It engages in such trade because of the benefits it derives from it. As with all economic decisions, benefits are weighed against costs. The benefits derived from imports are weighed against the alternative costs of producing the imported product domestically and also against the costs of exports. When such benefit-cost calculations appear to yield net gains, decisions to trade are taken by Soviet leaders and planners. (In market economies, such results are achieved through the decisions of individual firms.)

It may well be that the Soviets do not make such decisions efficiently, but their aims are to reap the benefits that are possible from foreign trade. No longer are they the trade-minimizing, import-substituting nation that they were under Stalin. They now acknowledge the benefits that can be derived from foreign trade. This is evident, for instance, in the following statement of the Soviet Minister of Foreign Trade:[6]

> In developing economic ties with [the West], our country receives an opportunity to make fuller and more rational use of its own resources and possibilities, and at the same time to acquire, by way of commercial exchange, goods of other countries that are not produced in our country or whose production would cost more than it does to import them. Thus, foreign economic ties offer a more efficient solution to a number of problems arising in the course of economic construction.

Furthermore, while this statement rings of classical, comparative cost trade specialization theory, the kind of international specialization or division of labor that has been developing among industrialized nations and that is pursued by the Soviets involves *intra*industrial rather than *inter*industrial specialization. This means that trade between countries, especially in machinery and intermediate products at high levels of fabrication, usually entails specialization in narrow ranges of products within given industries (intraindustrial trade) rather than in the closing down of whole economic branches or industries and complete branch specialization in each of the trading countries (interindustrial trade). This clearly affects the degree of dependence of one nation on another that may be said to be represented by a given level of its imports and their ratio to national product.

In addition, the degree of Soviet dependence on foreign trade is affected by the level of economic development that it has achieved. Stalin's original objective of acquiring sufficient economic development to guarantee the national independence of the Soviet Union has been achieved. The development of economic relations with capitalist nations at this stage extends beyond this core of economic power but does not endanger it. In other words, under present conditions expanded economic relations with the West do not involve capitalist countries in the basic core of the Soviet economy (which is now sufficiently developed to guarantee the survival and national security of the Soviet Union), but operate at the margin to improve the performance of the Soviet economy.

The question then is not to what extent is the Soviet Union dependent on trade with the West for its survival, but how beneficial is this trade to the Soviet Union, and what costs are Soviet leaders willing to pay to maintain it. Any nation, let alone one at the level of industrial development and with as rich a resource base as the Soviet Union, always has alternatives when faced with an act of economic coercion by another, say in the form of an embargo. First of all, of course, it can seek supplies of the embargoed item elsewhere. If they are not available, it has the choice of producing the desired imports itself, which may involve the necessity of developing the capacity to produce the product. Or it may decide to do without the product and substitute something else which is or could be made available domestically. Whether it will comply with the attempted coercion depends on the net benefits of the imports, when compared with the alternatives, relative to the costs of compliance.[7]

The accurate measurement of the benefits from trade is extremely difficult. This is why available measures such as trade participation ratios are often resorted to. The issue, however, is not just how much trade, but of what benefit it is. Such a question requires the investigation of individual groups of imported products. While this is not the place for a detailed examination of the commodity composition of Soviet imports and their relation to domestic use,[8] let us look at two major Soviet imports and the role of systemic elements in deteminíng the benefits the Soviet Union derives from them.

Grain

One imported item which is of great benefit to the Soviet Union is, of course, grain. In the three grain-importing years (July/June) 1979/80 to 1981/82, net imports of grain have been between 14 and 21 percent of domestic grain utilization, and they are forecast at the level of 22 percent in 1982/83 (in better harvest years in the 1970s they have been in the 5 percent range).[9]

The Soviet desire for grain imports results from a combination of limited agricultural resources, a series of bad weather years, the strategic planning decision to pursue a program of rapid growth of meat production, and the Soviet system of collectivized agriculture. Soviet collectivization (different from the Hungarian) severely blunts the relationship between effort and reward, is highly centralized leaving little independent decision making to individual farms, and thus reduces the ability of Soviet agriculture to cope with the vagaries of weather, leading to great variation in grain production when weather conditions vary. In view of the heavy commitment of Soviet leaders to growth in meat production, it is desirable to prevent livestock herds from diminishing in years of low grain output. This perceived need for feed-grains, plus some need to augment the flow of bread products to the population, has led Soviet leaders to decide that it is beneficial to import massive quantities of grain in recent years. The evident benefit that the Soviet Union derives from grain imports (though it could survive without them), makes the Soviets vulnerable to the application of economic leverage in the form of a threat of grain sanctions. And the Soviet institution of collectivization, since it blurs incentives and reduces flexibility, makes a contribution to this vulnerability.

Advanced Technology

It is, however, with regard to the Soviet desire to import advanced technology from the West that systemic effects play a major role. We will first discuss this systemic role and then the benefits that the Soviet Union derives from the import of foreign machinery and technology.

Among the elements of the Soviet system of central planning that affect the ability of the economy to absorb, master, and create new technology, the one that has received primary emphasis in both Western and Russian literature on the Soviet economy is the managerial incentive mechanism, which has more or less dominated the Soviet scene since the 1930s. In the past decade the Soviet economy has been undergoing certain administrative changes but the incentive mechanism is still basically related to the fulfillment of performance targets. The relationship between such an incentive scheme and the innovation process was touched on briefly above. Let us explore it a little further.

In any situation where reward is a function of target fulfillment there are two ways of assuring success or increasing the possibility of success: performance, and keeping the target within reasonable distance. The second aspect of target-type rewarding is detrimental to the innovation process. Innovation always involves risk. The compensation for risk contained in the monetary reward for possible overplan fulfillment is reduced by the fact that success today will mean a higher target tomorrow and managerial career rewards and survival require the rather regular meeting of targets. Thus managers resist innovation and try to keep targets low.

There is much discussion in the Soviet Union on how to get around this particular problem, but nothing very effective has been introduced so far. Indeed, it can be argued that nothing very effective should be expected. Attempts to improve Soviet technology assimilation through the modification of specific forms of success indicators, profits, sales, cost sharing, and pricing devices, and the length of the plan time period against which enterprise results are evaluated will at best have limited results. For the Soviet approach to managerial incentives is fundamentally the same as the approach developed by Frederick Taylor, at the turn of the century, in regard to manual workers. The incentive problem is perceived as basically that of motivating high effort. Such motivation is best achieved by a composition of earnings which contains a high proportion of income varying in the short term with accomplishments; such accomplishments should be defined and measured objectively and simply so that the income recipient can correctly predict the financial rewards which will accompany greater accomplishments; the financial rewards should be given promptly and fully as soon as possible after the accomplishment is recorded, so that the link between the two is reinforced in the mind of the income recipient. In short, Soviet top managers in enterprises are viewed as responding to incentives in the same fashion as was predicted by Taylor for semiskilled workers.[10] This is not the approach appropriate for the encouragement of entrepreneurial initiative.

A second factor inhibiting the introduction and diffusion of advanced technology in the Soviet economy is the fact that the short run effects of innovation on the firm's fulfillment of its production target are almost always bad. Innovation interrupts the rhythm of production work. Even if the introduction of the new technology is working well, it takes time to reach rated capacity, and thus (unless this is accounted for in production plans, which rarely occurs) output, sales, and profit levels in monthly and quarterly plan fulfillment figures are down, and the manager is in trouble.

A third inhibiting factor involves the organization of research and development. Substantial effort is put forth on R and D in the Soviet Union, but to a great extent it is separated from production, and insufficient attention is paid to development in comparison with research. As a result, a fair amount of new technology is generated or foreign technology identified, but their implementation and diffusion are limited. For the reasons discussed above, the managers of industrial enterprises try to avoid incorporating new technology because it will cause problems and will not lead to sustained rewards. Furthermore, the constant pressure to meet current output targets militates against diverting resources for experimentation purposes.

Fourth, the technology transfer and diffusion process is primarily a people process. That is, technology is best transferred from firm to firm and from country to country by people (managers, engineers, sales engineers, and so on) rather than by publications (including blueprints) or products themselves. The Soviets have, in the postwar period, concentrated on the latter approaches while making minimal use of the former. Currently, however, they appear to be paying more attention to the people part of the process.

Finally, the absence of a threat of bankruptcy in the noncompetitive Soviet economy has a profound effect. In competitive economies, while the innovation process responds in a positive way to high rewards for successful innovation it also responds to the fear of being driven out of business by dynamic competitors. Indeed, the spur to innovation from the drive for survival may be more important to the system than the drive for high rewards. The absence of defensive innovation in the Soviet economy removes a fundamental incentive element in the diffusion of new technology. Though Soviet authorities might be able to improve their institutional arrangements to foster innovation, they cannot change the basic nature of their system. They cannot introduce competitive arrangements, which involve the unplanned destruction of economic units, without drastically altering the nature of the system. Thus it can be argued that a noncompetitive, centrally planned economic system will by its nature be less innovationally dynamic than a competitive economy. This is not the place to engage in a long discussion of the matter, but it should be noted that the foreign trade and leverage vulnerability implications are stronger and of a more permanent nature to the extent that the innovational lag is considered to be an intrinsic part of the Soviet system of central planning, rather than one correctable by organizational reform.

The elements discussed so far have related to specific institutions and practices in the Soviet centrally planned system. There are also consequences of the bureaucratic element itself in the Soviet system.

One such consequence concerns the creative destruction aspect of technical change, that is, when something new is introduced and it is successful, the old is destroyed. In a politicized, bureaucratized economy, those who operate the existing types of activites are much better able to protect themselves against the threat of new types of activites and new technologies. In this respect, one of the advantages of a private enterprise system is that it does not internalize within the state decision sector the destruction of the old. The price paid for new technology is absorbed by individual elements in the society rather than the society as a whole. In the Soviet Union, creative destruction has been limited by the bureaucracy; this has been an important and difficult aspect of the whole process of technical change in the Russian economy. In general, bureaucracies tend to possess a high degree of risk aversion, and ability to protect themselves against the pains of change.

In addition, established bureaucratic rules and lines of authority hamper change and experimentation with new ways of doing things. Bureaucracies tend to penalize failure more than they reward innovational success. Bureaucracies tend to favor large-scale output (this has always been true in Russia) and large-scale output itself increases the cost and risk of change. Moreover, bureaucracies establish firm lines of administration, preventing "invasion" of a stagnant branch by groups from a more dynamic branch. Such "innovation by invasion" has been a significant source of innovation and technology diffusion in the West.

Bureaucratic red tape problems are particularly virulent in the administration of Soviet technological innovation. The whole process of technological innovation takes place primarily through bureaucratic interactions between functional performers and higher ministerial authorities who serve as administrative "gatekeepers" at critical transfer points with the power to terminate an innovation project. There is little direct horizontal interplay and collaboration among actual individual and institutional performers. This makes the process inordinately long and lowers the quality of decision making by forcing decisions to be made at very high levels, far from the knowledge needed to make them.

A final key factor in the picture is that the Soviets have primarily imported foreign technology for domestic growth purposes rather than for exports that would have to be internationally competitive. Thus once the new technology is in place, there has been no pressure on those using it to keep it up to changing foreign levels, and the technology has languished. The Japanese success in developing self-sustaining technological progress through the import of technology for international competitive purposes highlights the importance of the aim of imported technology, that is, whether it is to be used only internally or also for international competitive purposes. This argument, furthermore, contributes to an explanation of why the Soviets have been much better in military technology than in civilian technology. Military equipment is by nature competitive, its performance and utility can be judged only in relation to the equipment possessed by the (potential) enemy, whereas this is not true of nonmilitary equipment.

Before closing our discussion of Soviet imports of machinery and technology from the West, a few words about the benefits that the Soviets derive from such imports. There is a fair amount of disagreement about just how beneficial these imports are. Much of the literature on the Soviet importation of foreign technology, however, is based on individual case studies and their thrust is often misdirected. They tend to stress how poorly the Soviets handle the imported technology compared with the originating country. But even though the Soviets do not handle foreign technology nearly as well as other nations do, the foreign technology imported into the Soviet Union may still be significantly more productive than the existing domestic technology and therefore may be of substantial benefit to the Soviet economy.

With the aim of deriving a quantitative estimate of the gains from imported technology by measuring the relative productivity of imported and domestic machinery in the Soviet Union, a series of calculations using the Wharton Soviet Econometric Model (SOVMOD) were conducted several years ago.[11] The model calculations showed that in the early 1970s, imported industrial machinery was approximately three times as productive as domestic industrial machinery. These quantitative results indicate a very substantial payoff to imported machinery and technology, much more than might have been assumed from the anecdotal literature. Because of this and because of widespread criticism of the methodology used in the studies, the calculations have been controversial; it is quite possible that future econometric work will yield substantially lower results.[12] On the other hand, some recent microeconomic analyses of Soviet imports of advanced technology also indicate substantial gains to the Soviet economy.[13] A generally held view, it might fairly be said, is that while the Soviets may not derive as many benefits from imported technology as the earlier SOVMOD studies indicated, they do derive significant benefit from it.[14] If this view is correct, and more importantly, if it reflects Soviet leaders' perceptions of their gains from technology transfer, then the Soviet desire for technology imports from the West can be considered to be strong.

Centralized Decision Making

The argument would appear quite forceful that the Soviet system of central planning contributes significantly to Soviet vulnerability to economic coercion through its impact on agricultural production and flexibility, and especially through the constraints it puts on the process of technological growth. In addition, the centralized nature of Soviet decision-making itself contributes to this vulnerability. First of all, it gives to the Soviet Union a centralized perception of the gains to be derived from expanded economic relations with the West (though this is modified by the problems of the Soviet information system discussed above). Secondly, the Soviet managerial incentive system and the pressure for growth put on the economy by Soviet leaders creates a situation where managers and ministers are concerned with assuring their supplies of inputs in order to meet output targets, rather than markets for their outputs. This concern with uninterrupted supplies extends to supplies from abroad.

The organization of Soviet political administration also plays a role in the leverage issue.[15] The Soviet administrative apparatus, hierarchical and centralized, receives its direction, guidance, and management from the top. The Politburo and Secretariat, through their subordinate party affiliates in all state institutions fulfill the control and feedback functions in the system. The Communist Party of the Soviet Union (CPSU), through its structure of local, provincial, republic, and central organs, monitors and measures the performance of state institutions, be they economic, scientific, military, or social in purpose and function.

With respect to the Soviet economy, the responsibility for meeting plan targets, for example, the output of an industrial concern, is borne not only by the enterprise manager and state officials, but also by the local party secretary. Indeed, one of the key principles of Soviet economic and political institutions is agent responsibility for meeting performance targets, the constant monitoring and measuring of performance, and the distribution of monetary and status rewards as a function of performance relative to targets. Thus it can be hypothesized that the party secretary in a given firm's party committee, and his superiors in the provincial secretariat, may be actively interested in methods for increasing performance, especially the utilization of proven, advanced technology from the West. This hypothesis of the active role that local party organs might play in the technology transfer process is consistent with observations made on the role local party secretaries play in other economic areas, such as reconciling problems of coordination between firms and expediting production. Party control is enhanced through its authority over the individual manager who, as an important party member, sits on the firm's party committee. Moreover, under the strict *nomenklatura* system, the career potential of any aspiring party member is dependent upon the senior party echelon's assessment of his "performance," which necessarily includes the individual's success in fulfilling and, if possible, surpassing the economic growth targets and other objectives determined by the central organs.

Certain implications can be drawn from these observations about the CPSU and the Soviet administrative system. The preeminent role played by the Politburo clearly gives the Soviet leadership the ability to resist economic coercion should it decide to do so. It is in a position to assert the primacy of political objectives over economic ones and, if necessary, to reallocate economic resources in support of its decision. However, in some interesting ways, this centralization of power also contributes to the susceptibility of the Soviets to economic leverage. Since the Politburo members are responsible for all major decisions of national policy, they have the power to deliver on agreements with Western nations should they so choose. Their authority is virtually absolute—political power is not diffused among competing governmental entities as is the case in the West. Moreover, these men sit atop a vast bureaucracy, troubled by inertia, which exhibits resistance to innovation, particularly, as has been indicated, in the economic sector. Efforts to spur the economy and heighten the efficiency of the entire administration must originate at the top—the central party organs. Thus, the Politburo is interested in maintaining the pressure for technological innovation on its own bureaucracy. Because this process appears to be effected in a highly centralized fashion, by a thin upper stratum of CPSU officialdom, there is a tendency to limit such efforts to main priorities. In the Soviet context, these main priorities often take the form of "campaigns": highly publicized projects replete with the personal identification of senior CPSU figures and thus a possible target for effective Western leverage.

Another important consideration is the Soviet leaders' penchant for "quiet" or secret negotiations. In the everyday affairs of the Soviet political administration, access to information is severely restricted and compartmentalized. This is especially true with respect to matters in the realm of national security and foreign affairs.[16] In the Soviet context, state control of mass media is absolute, and the manipulation of public opinion (insofar as it exists in the Western sense) is normal and deemed a desirable function for party *agitprop* institutions. The significance of this aspect of Soviet political behavior for possible Western attempts at economic coercion lies in the observation that the success of such attempts may be greater if they are conducted outside the scope of public scrutiny. The leaders of the USSR may prove to be more tractable over the potentially embarrassing terms of an economic leverage initiative, should these terms be kept secret.

Further, the role of middle- and lower-level Soviet party and state officials regarding a Soviet policy response to a Western leverage initiative is heightened by the systemic elements of specific agent responsibility, continuous monitoring of agent performance, and the awarding of rewards and penalties in relation to performance. To the extent that imports of Western machinery and technology help in this regard, Soviet administrators, especially at the ministerial level, may actively support the maintenance of expanded economic relations with the West, thus contributing to Soviet leverage vulnerability.

Factors Affecting Soviet Ability to Exert Economic Leverage

So far we have been discussing Soviet vulnerability to economic leverage. While this is the main issue in most discussions, there is also the issue of Soviet ability to exercise economic coercion on others—in particular, Western nations—and the role in it played by systemic elements of Soviet centralized planning. We will briefly turn to this issue and note some of its elements.

Discussions of Soviet leverage capability focus on both direct and counterleverage. The direct leverage capability refers to the denial by the Soviets of exports desired by a target nation, as for example might occur with Soviet gas after the completion of the gas pipeline to Western Europe. Counterleverage refers to the leverage ability possessed by a target nation against the nation that is attempting to exercise leverage on it. In the case at hand, this would refer to the leverage possessed by a large purchaser on individual sellers, and that possessed by a large debtor on individual creditors.

The role played by systemic elements of Soviet centralized planning in Soviet leverage capability would include, first, the supply orientation of the Soviet economy. As was described above, the growth pressures of Soviet leaders and the incentive system facing managers have led to a perennial situation of excess demand, of sellers' markets, in the Soviet economy. Soviet managers and ministers are concerned with acquiring inputs, they are not worried about being able to sell their output. Therefore, if there is a cut-off of Soviet exports to a foreign country in an attempt to exert economic coercion, the domestic producers of the export product are not greatly concerned. The internal economy can absorb the diverted exports.

Secondly, the centralized nature of Soviet decision making, operating under the principle of "democratic centralism," enhances the Soviet ability to establish a policy on the use of economic leverage and to implement it. It enables Soviet leaders to maintain the dominance of political and military considerations over economic ones. It contributes to a coordinated Soviet bloc policy (with occasional mavericks, for example, Romania). And it helps the Soviets to conduct quiet diplomacy, which is so essential to the effective exercise of economic leverage.

Finally, the systemic elements which contribute to the great benefit that the Soviets derive from imports from the West, contribute thereby to a constraint on Soviet leverage capability. That is, the Soviet willingness to apply economic coercion on the West is limited by their need to earn hard currency with which to finance the imports they derive from the West. This, for example, is important in the analysis of the Soviet leverage potential in the gas pipeline arrangement.

CONCLUSIONS

The argument of this chapter has been that Soviet foreign trade is based upon the calculation of benefit and comparative advantage. That is, the Soviet Union imports from the West because of the benefits it derives from these imports rather than because it is dependent upon them for its survival. Systemic elements of Soviet centralized planning, particularly in agriculture and Soviet managerial practices, lead to significant Soviet benefit from the import of grain and advanced Western machinery and technology. Soviet leaders, the driving force in pressuring the economy to grow, recognize the benefits that can be derived from these imports, and under the conditions of centralized decision making in the Soviet system have the power, if they deem the benefits outweigh the costs, to trade noneconomic benefits sought by the West in return for these imports of grain and advanced technology.

This chapter has been concerned with the systemic factors which contribute to economic leverage potential. The actual exercise of leverage by the United States or by the Soviet Union may, for a variety of reasons, fall far short of realizing this potential. Though it is beyond the scope of the chapter, let me make a few concluding remarks about the elements of an effective U.S. economic leverage policy.[17]

To begin, since what is at issue are Soviet benefits from imports rather than dependence on them for survival, we do not have a stranglehold on the Soviet Union and, therefore, our goals in a leverage program must be moderate and realistic. We have the possibility of affecting Soviet cost-benefit calculations to some extent and this can yield us some returns. But much of the confusion in the debates on leverage arises from the failure to delineate reasonable U.S.

objectives and from the often-made implicit assumption that if U.S. political policy objectives of greatest importance cannot be achieved, then the development of an economic leverage program is not worth pursuing. On the contrary, a well formulated, balanced foreign policy involves instruments to achieve a range of different objectives.

Second, if the application of leverage is to be effective, it must consider certain salient Soviet sensitivities. Soviet leaders are concerned with issues of political legitimacy; therefore, they are particularly sensitive to any threats to the sovereignty of the Communist government. Thus the tactic of a quiet, diplomatic application of leverage is preferable to a declaratory, overt application of leverage.

It follows from this that threats of sanctions are better than the application of sanctions. Yet these threats have to be credible, which may require the occasional actual application of sanctions. Consequently, the public record of the effectiveness of economic coercion may be misleading. What is usually observable is the effect of overt sanctions; this effect being most often negligible. What one would want to measure is the effect of the overt sanction on the next round of secret negotiations. Thus, the Afghanistan grain sanctions have not led to the removal of Soviet troops from Afghanistan, but they may have contributed to the decision not to send troops into Poland.

Third, as discussed above, the fact that major policy decisions in the Soviet Union are made by a small group of party leaders in the Politburo contributes to their ability to resist economic coercion, but it also offers some advantages to the exercise of leverage by the United States. Since the Politburo is responsible for all major policy decisions, it has the power to deliver on agreements, including unpublicized agreements, with the United States. Moreover, since the Soviet economic bureaucracy resists change and innovation, the Soviet political leaders—if they are to maintain national power parity with the United States—must exert pressure from above to introduce and spread new methods and new technology. Thus their commitment to the import of advanced foreign technology is great. Operating as they do in the political sector, these pressures take the form of high priorities and campaigns usually focused on a few major projects that receive substantial public attention and become identified with senior party officials. As a consequence, Soviet leaders would be vulnerable to a U.S. leverage effort directed toward such major projects.

Fourth, in choosing a leverage instrument, it would be good if it were possible to vary its application, to increase or decrease its scale quickly and easily. For example, this is true of credit, especially if the credit is being provided by a U.S. government agency (such as the Eximbank). On the other hand, it is not true of MFN status. In addition, leverage instruments should be capable of responding to the interests of different groups in the United States. For example, if grain exports are to be used in a leverage program the government must have the means of maintaining U.S. farm income if it intends to reduce such exports.

The usual view is that the way to exercise economic coercion is to threaten to cut off the flow of specific exports to the target nation. However, leverage can also be applied by threatening not to buy exports from the target nation. It could be argued that the first type is appropriate for leverage applied on a centrally planned economy and the second type for leverage applied on a market economy, because of the supply driven nature of the former and the demand driven nature of the latter. But the more the Soviet Union gets involved in economic relations with the West, the more vulnerable it becomes to threats of refusals to buy its exports. For the hard currency it earns from its exports is needed to finance its purchases from the West and to repay its debts.

Fifth, the objectives and policies of different agencies within the U.S. government and of the public and private sectors in the United States must be coordinated in order to operate an effective leverage program.

And finally, it should by now be clear to all, that multilateral coordination between the United States and its allies regarding policy toward economic relations with the USSR is of crucial importance. Since in many areas the USSR can substitute relations with other developed industrial nations for those with the United States, it is vital that the United States pursue coordinated policies with other Western countries in order for there to be any chance of an effective U.S. leverage policy.

NOTES

1. This problem is well illustrated by the Soviet anecdote:

Question: Why is it that the East German economy with a system of central planning similar to that of the Soviet Union is so efficient and the Soviet economy is so inefficient?

Answer: No one has yet devised an economic system that can prevent Germans from working hard.

2. See, e.g., David Conn, "Economic Theory and Comparative Economic Systems," *Journal of Comparative Economics* Vol. 2, No. 4, December 1978, pp. 355-381; Egon Neuberger and William Duffy, *Comparative Economic Systems: A Decision-Making Approach*, Boston, Allyn & Bacon, 1976; John M. Montias, *The Structure of Economic Systems*, New Haven, Yale University Press, 1976.

3. The recent July 29, 1979 Resolution of the Council of Ministers and the CPSU on Improving Methods of Planning called for an increase in the role and importance of the five year plan. Its effect in this direction remains to be seen.

4. See the article by Aron Katsenelinboigen, "Coloured Markets in the Soviet Union," *Soviet Studies*, Vol. XXIX, No. 1 (1977), pp. 62-85; and the two articles by Aron Katsenelinboigen and Herbert S. Levine: "Market and Plan, Plan and Market: The Soviet Case," *American Economic Review, Papers and Proceedings*, 1977, and "Some Observations on the Plan-Market Relationship in Centrally Planned Economies," *The Annals* (of the American Academy of Political and Social Science), November 1977.

5. N.P. FED. Fedorenko, cited in the chapter by Richard Judy in John P. Hardt et al., *Mathematics and Computers in Soviet Economic Planning*, New Haven, Yale University Press, 1976.

6. N.S. Patolichev in *Pravda*, December 27, 1973, p. 4 [Translation in *Current Digest of the Soviet Press*, 25:52, January 23, 1974].

7. The costs of compliance include the perceived disutility of the policy the coercing nation is demanding, and the costs of appearing to give in to the coercive action of the other nation. More on this below. See also the discussion by Klaus Knorr in this volume.

8. For such a study, see Michael R. Dohan, "*Export Specialization and Import Dependence in the Soviet Economy, 1970-77,*" in U.S. Congress, Joint Economic Committee, *Soviet Economy in a Time of Change,* Vol. 2 (Washington, D.C.: U.S. Government Printing Office, 1979), pp. 342-395.

9. U.S. Department of Agriculture, *Foreign Agriculture Circular (Grains),* Washington, D.C. July 15, 1982, p. 20.

10. This analysis derives from David Granick, "Soviet Introduction of New Technology: A Depiction of the Process," (Washington, D.C.: SRI/Strategic Studies Center, 1974).

11. Donald W. Green and Herbert S. Levine, "Macroeconometric Evidence of the Value of Machinery Imports to the Soviet Union," in John R. Thomas and Ursula M. Kruse-Vaucienne, eds., *Soviet Science and Technology,* George Washington University (Washington, D.C.: National Science Foundation, 1977), pp. 394-424 (reprinted in *Survey 23,* no. 2 [Spring 1977/78]: 112-126). See also the earlier paper: Green and Levine, "Implications of Technonlogy Transfers for the U.S.S.R. *East-West Technological Cooperation* (Brussels, 1976).

12. See, for example, the articles by Martin Weitzman, Yasushi Toda, and Donald W. Green in *Journal of Comparative Economics,* Vol. 3, No. 2 (June 1979); also, Padma Desai, "The Rate of Return on Foreign Capital Inflow to the Soviet Economy," in U.S. Congress, Joint Economic Committee, *Soviet Economy in a Time of Change,* Vol. 2, Washington, D.C.: GPO, 1979, pp. 396-413.

13. See Philip Hanson, "The Impact of Western Technology: A Case Study of the Soviet Mineral Fertilizer Industry," in Paul Marer and John M. Montias, eds., *East European Integration and East-West Trade,* Bloomington: Indiana University Press, 1980.

14. See Philip Hanson, *Trade and Technology in Soviet-Western Relations,* New York: Columbia University Press, 1981, chapter 9.

15. This section draws heavily on Herbert S. Levine, Francis W. Rushing, Charles R. Movit, "The Potential for U.S. Economic Leverage on the USSR," *Comparative Strategy,* Vol. 1, No. 4, pp. 371-404.

16. This was strikingly revealed in the SALT negotiations. Here Soviet representatives appeared to have incomplete information on their own nation's strategic weapons systems and often had to refer to higher authority for both access and jurisdiction.

17. See the article by Levine, Rushing and Movit, cited in Note 15, above.

8

The Vulnerability of Modern Economies

David Deese

For at least the past century, economic and financial capabilities have been a vital element of national power. Nations' diplomatic and military strategies have frequently exploited these capabilities in the projection of power worldwide. During peace and war economic diplomacy has included everything from subtle implicit threats to intensive strategic bombing.

As we learned long ago, however, power projection anywhere in peace or war requires political support at home and sometimes in allied nations.[1] The result is a complex blend of requirements and objectives for economic diplomacy distributed across domestic, foreign, and international audiences. Often the blend changes over time. So the problem for scholars involves not only seeking out the unstated, at times central objectives of diplomatic or wartime action but also plotting changes in national objectives as events unfold. Such analysis is frequently difficult for years, if not decades, after the event takes place. Even with recent revelations, for example, we still do not seem to understand all the key motives and elements of information influencing President Roosevelt in the weeks prior to the attack on Pearl Harbor in 1941.

Such problems in research are reflected in the associated literatures. While some important analysis and findings exist on sanctions, coercive diplomacy, and economic warfare, there is still a high level of disagreement over some fundamental questions. Work in this area should therefore proceed cautiously, watching for new cases and evidence and trying out new approaches and methods to reinterpret all relevant historical materials. It is crucial to establish a reasonably consistent framework for developing and presenting new cases in this area so that findings are comparable.

This chapter offers a framework for defining and measuring vulnerability to foreign economic coercion. Wherever possible it attempts to focus on the special and difficult case of comparative vulnerability of centrally planned, or command economies, especially the Soviet Union and Eastern Europe, and market economies, especially the Western industrial nations. It will also apply to many cases involving third world nations, but here the dividing line between command and market economies is frequently more difficult to discern, although many third world nations' styles of macroeconomic management have more in common with centrally planned economies.

The focus is economic diplomacy under steady state, and to some extent, crisis and wartime conditions. Most relevant past cases, including both quantitative and qualitative analyses, involve economies that were not mobilized for war. In some cases these studies of peacetime economic diplomacy may reveal findings relevant to economic warfare. In cases of international crises or limited conflicts, such as the Korean War, the Suez crisis of 1956-1957, the Vietnam War, and the oil crises of 1973-1974 and 1979, results may be even more easily extrapolated to general wartime conditions. Finally, a more comprehensive literature is beginning to be available on the importance of supply restrictions, mobilization, and battlefield logistics during war. Two important contributions to this literature are offered in the chapters by Milward and van Creveld in this volume.

My working hypothesis runs against much of the conventional wisdom that economic coercion has almost always failed as a diplomatic measure. Much of the existing literature makes two heroic and dubious assumptions (or assertions) concerning the objectives of sanctions. First, it is assumed that the initiating nation aims its action primarily at the target nation. This misses or underemphasizes objectives involving international markets and domestic politics, both at home and in other nations. Second, most sanctions are said to be intended to change the target nation's policy, rather than to punish, discredit, or embarrass. Yet the primary objective can be even more subtle—simply to avoid what might be interpreted as a reward soon after a specific action or event. President Carter's denial of additional options for grain sales to the Soviets after their invasion of Afghanistan in 1979 appears to fit best into this latter category. Futhermore, this action may have been aimed more at domestic audiences worldwide, including Afghanistan, than at Soviet political elites. Until we have better specified what a nation intended to accomplish with economic coercion, it makes little sense to focus on what it failed to do.

I expect economic coercion to be a potentially effective element of foreign policy and grand strategy, if it is carefully planned, timed, and executed. Yet, if used too often or hastily—which is frequently the case—it may accelerate or even precipitate damaging instability in international political-economic and military relations. Instead of substituting for military coercion, economic diplomacy might endanger important arms control negotiations, escalate superpower conflict, and undercut the longer term power position of the initiating state. Manipulating the Soviet and Polish vulnerability in international finance may, for example, be more effective for the West than refusing or drastically curtailing all future access to Western liquidity, including other nations in Eastern Europe. It is therefore necessary to apply a carefully structured framework for defining and assessing both vulnerability to economic diplomacy and the implications of its use.

Economic sanctions are hypothesized to be increasingly effective as conditions approach crisis and even wartime proportions. This is a result of greater control over domestic political institutions and increased cooperation among nations involved in initiating action when confronted with a real and tangible threat. There are, however, offsetting effects since the target nation must, at least to some extent, also be assumed to be able to rally domestic support and counteraction more effectively when immediate and clear threats exist. There may also be some important exceptions, such as Soviet needs to worry about consumer unrest and official opposition from East European nations under wartime situations. We will therefore explore questions such as how compressible economies seem to be under severe pressure, up to and including limited wars.

Central to the analysis are the concepts of dependence, or the degree of actual physical reliance of a country on external sources of trade, finance, investment, aid or high technology, and vulnerability, or the liability to actual damage resulting from such dependence. These definitions are intended to emphasize that a nation can be highly dependent on another without necessarily incurring significant vulnerability, or only marginally dependent on another nation and yet highly vulnerable, depending on conditions at home, in international markets, and in other nations.[2]

Finally, the analysis focuses on finance, investment, foreign aid and trade in high technology as much as all other trade. While levels of trade, financial flows, activity by multinational corporations, and foreign aid are related, they differ significantly in their roles in economic diplomacy and warfare. Each must be included in any general analysis of vulnerability. Since data is limited and less is known generally about Soviet and East European financial flows, there is a continuing tendency to focus on trade. This may distort results in any context, but especially here since the United States may well retain more independent leverage in international finance than in trade, where other Western nations can increasingly replace most U.S. exports.

A FRAMEWORK FOR COMPARISON

Despite the difficulties created by continuing controversy over sanctions and confusion in the literature, understanding the use of economic diplomacy seems more urgent than ever. Relatively unique circumstances have emerged over the past decade, where two competitive, and at times still hostile, blocs of nations find themselves interlocked in an economic web presenting serious vulnerabilities and opportunities. At least U.S. officials now seem increasingly prone to resort to economic coercion, even under conditions which sometimes stress alliance cohesion and defy clear understanding of likely implications.

The past work in economic diplomacy relies too heavily on the declared policy objectives of the initiating state. The result: a broad consensus in much of the literature that economic diplomacy is usually ineffectual, or even counterproductive. In this environment it is difficult to assess comparative vulnerabilities of command and market economies.

The literature on economic diplomacy overflows with supposed examples of failure. Practitioners, interest groups, and academics join ranks in condemning economics as an effectual tool of diplomacy. Yet, have we carefully explained why leaders resort to economic diplomacy or warfare? Do we really have a reliable measure of success or failure? We frequently evaluate economic sanctions in economic terms when their purpose is overwhelmingly political, sometimes as much domestic as diplomatic and as much to change attitudes as behavior. Careful analysis of even strategic bombing in World War II reveals that severe effects on attitudes, such as among Japanese and German populations, can result in negligible behavioral change towards governments.[3]

Too frequently in the past, analysts failed to specify carefully the objectives of the initiating state and the intentions and outcomes for the target state. Economic diplomacy can be initiated by one, two, or more states independently, on an alliance basis, such as the EEC sanctions against Argentina during the Falklands War, or even on a broad multilateral basis, such as through the United Nations. Cooperation by allied or friendly nations can involve agreement not to impede another nation's sanctions, for example, by not taking offsetting action, diplomatic support without parallel action, and complete involvement in the full set of sanctions urged by the initiating nation. Economic sanctions may be directed primarily at the domestic audience of the initiating state, the target state, and/or international markets. They may have economic effects at any of these levels, with or without political consequences, such as policy shifts by governments. They may be directed at certain leaders, the elite generally, specific interest groups, or consumers and the population at large.

The political objectives of an initiating state may thus be classified as primary, if aimed mainly at the target nation; secondary, if focused on local and allied audiences; and tertiary, if intended for international markets. It is the interactions and combinations of these three objectives that are most useful in attempting to explain state behavior since there will frequently be multiple and changing purposes. Several cases, such as Carter's feedgrain embargo of the Soviet Union in response to the Afghanistan invasion in 1979, seem to start with the secondary objective as most important and then shift emphasis to the primary objective. At times the secondary objective may be focused on interest groups in allied nations as much or more than on local political coalitions.

Under conditions imposed by increased complex interdependence in the post-World War II period, effectiveness in foreign policy often demands at least minimal domestic political consensus. We may therefore more often find that foreign policy elites use sanctions for secondary objectives. They seek to help mobilize domestic political groups at home and in allied nations, and perhaps to express condemnation internationally, as much or more than (or at least prior to) other objectives. They may also be focused on international markets, or tertiary objectives, as well as target nations, thus requiring secrecy and careful timing. Thus publicly declared objectives frequently cannot be taken literally, or as the complete explanation. In fact, public statements are sometimes specifically designed to mislead other nations, especially to help mask actual behavior.

The ultimate test of statesmanship lies in finding a delicate balance between the dramatic public use of economic diplomacy to rally public support against an external enemy and the maintenance of prudence in not announcing unattainable goals, which may well come back to haunt the government later. This is especially the case for Western nations facing a skeptical media and powerful public interest groups. Overall failure is as likely to result from lack of early public support in initiating sanctions as it is from lack of continuing public acceptance as costs are felt at home and declared objectives seem elusive.

If the initial or most important purpose is a firm demonstration of opposition to egregious behavior by another nation, including moral condemnation, then other objectives, such as restricting supplies to the opponent's market, should be either carefully qualified or unannounced. In this case the costs may be particularly difficult to explain to the domestic audience. In all cases it is important that the government expected hardship at home in advance and make every attempt to distribute the domestic costs equitably across government, industrial, and consumer sectors.

While action focused on primary and tertiary objectives is usually initiated with a dramatic public statement, this is unlikely to be the case for the secondary objective. Support at home must be generated by rallying public opinion against the external threat. The publicly stated purposes of economic diplomacy must therefore always be expected to be directed outwards, regardless of the actual intentions of foreign policy elites. If in fact much economic diplomacy is partially directed at domestic groups at home and in allied nations, then it is impossible to explain such action on the basis of stated objectives. The literatures in this area, especially in the East-West context, must be carefully screened for their treatment of declaratory policy objectives. It thus also becomes essential to sort out carefully the ends of economic diplomacy from the means in each case.

Economic sanctions may also be intended for short term or longer term effects, and objectives may well change over time. Sanctions are frequently most effective, at least in economic terms, in the first few weeks and months before offsetting action in international markets or target nations takes effect. Surprise and deception can therefore clearly be important. The rallying of domestic support at home or changing policies in target nations are likely to require short term effects, while restructuring international markets may take much longer. Probable risks must also be calculated since longer term losses can outweigh short term gains. This means that such events are not always amenable to the type of analysis conducted in the past, which focused on the longer term results. In *Force Without War*, Blechman and Kaplan found that the objectives of an initiating state may well be met in the short term, although the situation is likely to return to the earlier status quo over several months or years.

It is also absolutely essential to evaluate how the target nation may react to economic diplomacy. Rapid and careless action can be counterproductive, both to the domestic and alliance politics of the initiating nation. Rapid adaptation and restructuring may occur in the target nation, possibly even allowing the authorities to generate new public support for their policies on the basis of a highly visible external threat.[4]

Furthermore, comparative vulnerability of command and market economies, and in the Eastern and Western blocs specifically, must be assessed in a broad framework. Trade, finance, and aid relationships with many countries are all important, especially for the West. Action taken against one nation or group of nations must be viewed in light of overall economic relationships with nations worldwide. This includes, for example, Western and Eastern vulnerability to disruption of oil imports, especially from the Persian Gulf, and U.S.-Soviet competition for influence over third world regions.

It is certainly possible that economic diplomacy does in fact make an important difference, during peace as well as war. Negative or positive sanctions can demonstrate a state's economic, political, or military resolve, or perhaps even the capacity, of a nation to act forcefully, thus capturing domestic support at home. They focus public and press attention on international events, perhaps causing another nation to carefully assess its earlier actions. They can also influence allies through public opinion or reinforce a specific coalition in the target state.

A nation's international financial position may frequently be even more vulnerable than its trade posture. Decreasing access to foreign exchange, or especially the loss of access to financial assets in foreign countries, can rapidly threaten national access to vital imports, thus creating public displeasure or even panic and slowing industrial activity. Whereas most traded items, or even high technology and foreign aid may be available from various sources, larger scale international liquidity and investment or aid on concessional terms may more frequently not be readily replaceable. Before any such action is taken, however, it is essential to assess carefully the probable political consequences at home and in the target state, as well as in international markets.

When action is primary, or taken with the explicit intention of affecting another state, the steps may be negative, that is to embarrass, punish, or restrain; or positive, to give credit, reward, or encourage. These objectives may be targeted at specific decision makers, the entire regime, or the broader political community. The specific group or groups that are targeted may be as important as the nature of the sanctions. Effects are both economic and political, with the latter often lagging economic change by weeks or months, or not following at all if decision makers can hold out against economic discomfort to the economy generally, or to specific consumers or industries. It is frequently very difficult to achieve direct political effects on the target state, and great care must be taken not to provide its regime with a means of mobilizing strong domestic support.[5] Yet economic effects can flow from even subtle pressure or threats short of coercive action. Panic flights of capital from a country or commodity hoarding, for example, can cause crises without warning.

The tertiary objective of affecting international markets may also be difficult to accomplish. It frequently requires some degree of coordinated action by national and international suppliers, and sometimes a degree of skill and good luck with weather and international market conditions. Yet success certainly does not require verifiable impacts on domestic audiences at home and allied nations, target nations, and international markets. Positive results in any one of these areas could certainly be adequate, as long as they are not offset by equal or greater negative effects in other areas.

Crude oil and petroleum products provide one important example of such results, at least in economic terms, in both individual countries and international markets. Oil has some unique characteristics and Arab nations certainly have not been completely successful in meeting their objectives.[6] Yet here it is possible to document important and consistent effects of disrupted international flows.

First, a crisis for leaders at all levels of government need not involve an actual shortage of supply. When adequate future supplies for at least several months are not guaranteed, surge demand by consumers and industry at all levels of distribution and consumption creates most of the same effects as an actual shortfall. Leaders must act on the basis of their best estimates of future supply and these are necessarily conservative. Furthermore, government actions taken in anticipation of supply shortages can actually aggravate, or even cause, a shortfall.

Consumers and businesses do not generally wait to be punished by action in the initiating state. Evasive action will be taken in advance, usually by massive hoarding of the good or service (where possible) in question. Stockpiles may be increased at all levels, from the tankers or freighters at sea, through primary, secondary, and tertiary (consumer) points in the processing and distribution system. This action can make extremely serious what would otherwise be only a slight or moderate supply shortfall. The crisis therefore can be caused by a surge in *demand* rather than a significant restriction in supply.

Finally, when shortages do strike as a result of surges in demand or restrictions in supply, they affect individual countries, companies, regions, and consumers unevenly. A crisis in one limited region of a country or for one company can readily become national in scope. There is a time lag while the market balances demand and supply. The political system, even in a command economy, frequently has to treat a shortage anywhere as a serious problem. Furthermore, short term effects like these may disrupt the prior pattern of companies and markets and induce longer term price and supply effects for many consumers. International spot markets for crude oil and petroleum products, for example, serve as one important indicator of future price paths for longer term contracts. Companies frequently are forced out of business or out of a particular regional market as a result of such crises.

Indices of Vulnerability

Comparative vulnerability should be measured with qualitative and quantitative indices of a nation's power position, economic resiliency, and political will and capacity in each given case. Power position is defined on the basis of measureable factors such as military force, projection capacity, and economic resources, and intangible factors such as perceived morality of foreign policy and control over multinational corporations. Economic resiliency includes a longer list of more specific factors in trade, aid, or finance related to the given economic sanction, such as elasticities of demand for the product or substitution possibilities. Some measureable and many intangible factors make up political will and capacity. These include, for example, unitary or federal political system, number of political parties and active interest groups, willingness of consumers to make short term sacrifices, and consistency of leadership and planning.

The process for assessing comparative vulnerability in each case should include at least four steps. The power position, economic resiliency, and political capacity of the initiating nation must first be analyzed to determine the extent to which the sanction can be carried out domestically. Is it possible, over the short and longer terms to prevent export or import of the product or service, at least from national borders? Next comes the analysis of the same three elements for the initiating and target states, and of the involved international market to determine if the sanction can be executed internationally. Is it possible over short and longer terms to deny the product or export to the target nation? Third, even if the product or export is denied, will any of the intended economic effects occur in the target nation? Or, to what extent can the national government offset the macro- and microeconomic effects of the sanction? Finally and most difficult, does the economic diplomacy have a reasonable probability of affecting national policy in the direction intended by the initiating state? While all steps should be completed, it is important to reiterate that success at any level may well fulfill original objectives. It is clearly not necessary to be successful at every level in all cases.

Power Position

A nation's overall economic, political, and military posture internationally is obviously crucial to economic diplomacy and warfare. Despite the continuing dispersion of significant economic and military capabilities to small and medium powers worldwide, many essential resources remain highly centralized on an absolute scale. U.S. food production includes roughly 40 percent of all wheat, 75 percent of corn, and 80 percent of soybeans that are traded internationally. Oil and natural gas reserves are concentrated in the Middle East, North America, and the Soviet Union. The Soviets command a particularly powerful position in future international natural gas markets. About two-thirds of all bauxite reserves are found in Guinea, Jamaica, Australia, and Suriname. Four-fifths of world copper reserves are in Chile, Peru, Zambia, and Zaire. And many strategic minerals are concentrated in a relatively small number of countries, especially the Soviet Union and South Africa. At the same time there is instability in the shifting of relative power, such as the decline in the U.S. share of world GNP from 34 percent in 1960 to 17 percent in 1976.

A nation's power position is made up of economic, political, and military factors, but military and sometimes even diplomatic resources are not always convertible to leverage in economic diplomacy short of conflict and war. Thus while military force projection capabilities, size of defense budget, and ability to act decisively, for example, are important, we must weigh them carefully for each specific case. How large and well diversified is the economy? What is the capacity for short term technological innovation or adaptation? Which key natural resources does it produce or have secure access to, and in what percentages of consumption? How important is trade to the GNP, and to economically and politically sensitive sectors of the economy? Is the national currency convertible? If so, what leverage is available over international liquidity, from commercial banks and public financial institutions, for itself or other countries? What is the trend in balance and terms of trade? How available are alternative buyers for national exports, and suppliers for imports? Is there any significant control over multinational banks or corporations? How much and what kind of foreign aid is given or received? How is it used? How vulnerable is the economy to attack and how fast could it recover from given levels of warfare?

Economic Resiliency

Here we determine a more specific level of national economic capacity. If foreign purchasers of national exports or suppliers of national imports, international liquidity, or foreign aid abruptly end most or all transactions, are there other sources? Some analysts conclude that the most effective measure of trade warfare is the refusal to buy a nation's goods, which restricts its foreign exchange or strains the balance of payments and thus reduces the ability to import critical commodities. If this is the case, the ability *on relatively short notice* to sell exports to, or gain access to foreign exchange from at least several different sources is extremely important.

It matters, of course, whether resiliency is based on flexibility over short, as opposed to longer periods of time. Short and longer term costs of and opportunities to mitigate disruptions must be assessed. Costs should be estimated as direct, indirect, opportunities forgone, and capital effects.[7] Opportunities for mitigating effects can be assessed at the microeconomic, macroeconomic and international levels. What are the short-term price elasticities of demand and supply? What type of product, service, or foreign aid is likely to be disrupted? Is it technologically important to the economy? How important is it to national outputs, or what percentage of output would be disrupted? How easily and quickly can substitutes be made or found? Are prices of forgone goods or services set by the market, the government, or limited by the government? Are there stockpiles? If so, are they ready to be used? How geographically dispersed (or hardened) are major industrial complexes? Do recent U.S. population migration trends into more rural areas beyond metropolitan concentrations build in greater industrial resiliency to economic warfare?

International factors are equally important. They include the level of dependence on a specific product, service, or foreign aid program, and of diversification in foreign suppliers. Diversification includes the number of suppliers, their relative location, especially distance away, and a qualitative measure of reliability. Closely related is the availability of replacements or substitutes from neighbors, allies or international institutions, including both public organizations and the private sector. This can involve specific agreements at the bilateral level, such as the U.S. guarantee of oil supplies to Israel, or multilateral level, such as the emergency oil sharing agreement of the International Energy Agency. During economic warfare this involves the degree of a nation's access to vital industrial and military production in other nations.

It is extremely important to assess the fungibility of international markets. If many suppliers are involved in providing the good or service, there are probably excellent prospects for finding alternative supply channels at each step in the production and delivery process, perhaps even on a timely basis. While grain and crude oil are relatively easy to replace, international liquidity is frequently difficult to find quickly. Furthermore, turbulence in currency flows, especially a rapid withdrawal of funds from the economy or depreciation in the currency, is frequently politically destabilizing.

Political Will and Capability

Indices of political will and capacity can be categorized in terms of the political structure and functioning of the government, relationships between consumers and the government, and relations among domestic and foreign actors. For both initiating and target states, the legitimacy of the government, level of commitment in government and among consumers, and urgency of the issue are extremely important. A decentralized governing system with several active political parties and interest groups must generate confidence on the part of citizens and consumers that clear and reasonable demands have been set, that the government is committed to them, and that effective decisions and management will follow. This holds for either position: the state being acted against or the initiating state.

Also critical is the ability of government to pass sacrifices on to consumers through either coercion or legitimacy based on perceived equitable distribution of the costs. For wartime strategy, command economies as well as market oriented ones must carefully consider how much hardship consumers are willing to bear before they begin to question basic national objectives. While command economies will generally have more control over public groups in peacetime conditions, crisis and war may make it more difficult for central authorities to maintain tight discipline.

Even if domestic support is mustered and a government can act quickly and sometimes secretly in its foreign policy, success is not guaranteed. Frequently direct support from allies and at least minimal international support is necessary, both to manipulate international markets and to maintain domestic acceptance. This demands flexibility and a strong sense of timing in modifying objectives and policies as events unfold. Nations handicapped by ideological rigidity or paralysis of decision-making mechanisms are at a distinct disadvantage in negotiating economic sanctions. At times a reputation for irrational behavior may also serve as an advantage, at least in short-term crisis bargaining over economic sanctions.

It also may be useful to divide target nations into three general categories based on administrative capacity and some measure of political strength. Nations with strong capabilities in each area may frequently be able to weather, or even ignore sanctions without serious consequences. Those lacking in both areas may not be easy to influence politically, even under economic hardship, due to their inability to comply with the initiating state's demands. If carried far enough, however, it may be possible to overthrow certain officials or even a government in this type of target nation. Finally, if a nation is administratively competent, but highly vulnerable to domestic political pressures, it may be relatively easy to cause panic and even favorable shifts in government policies.[8] Some such individual shifts may have occurred in oil-importing Western nations during the Arab oil embargo and production cutback of 1973-1974, although this is difficult to ascertain due to the lack of clear Arab objectives. Under economic warfare, command economies may begin to lose some of their administrative advantages and come under greater domestic political pressure.

Most important perhaps are measures of the precise nature of demands by, and the degree of seriousness in, the initiating state. Even if demands are limited, precisely defined, and carefully communicated, it is necessary to carefully assess how they are to be transmitted to, and what they actually expect of, the target state. In most cases some measure of success in changing the target's policies will be much more likely if demands are communicated secretly, thus relieving the government from obvious embarrassment if it negotiates or complies. Covert communications allow both sides to negotiate and compromise objectives more readily, as long as they stay within the legal limits of their foreign policy authority. No matter how committed and persuasive the initiating state, it is extremely difficult for a target nation to give in once demands are made public.

Blechman and Kaplan categorize demands from the most to the least difficult to obtain: to induce an action, to compel a state to act, to deter action, and to assure a state of your adherence to a particular position.[9] Assurance may be the only one which could be assisted by making demands public, as a means of making a commitment more obviously binding. Deterrence is of course also relatively easy to perform since the target state need not actually change its behavior, unless it has already announced its intention to carry out a given action. The political will and capacity of the initiating state is tested most rigorously by the attempt to compel or induce a state to act. Particularly in the East-West context it is difficult to find examples of successful economic diplomacy in these categories. This is further complicated if the initiating state is trying to induce behavior on the part of one nation, through pressure on another, such as U.S. action against the Soviets as a means to change policy in Poland or Soviet action against a West European nation in pursuit of shifts in U.S. foreign policy.

Since domestic actors and national governments vary widely in their degree of actual or perceived commitment to such coercive diplomacy, writers have stressed the critical nature of seriousness of purpose. Clear correlations can be established between the level of commitment before and during a crisis and the likelihood of some measure of success. Not only target states but also allied or friendly nations seem to be much more willing to support economic diplomacy if they assess the initiating nation as strongly committed and willing to take further action as necessary.

ASSESSING COMPARATIVE VULNERABILITY

Context is the central element in analysis of the comparative vulnerability of modern economies. It is first essential to define general conditions in the international arena. Are conclusions being drawn from experiences before the 1800s, before World War I, during or between the World Wars, during the cold war or détente, or the early 1980s? For useful direct comparison of command economy-market economy and East-West vulnerabilities, it may be imperative to focus on experience from the past decade when there were trade and financial flows among the blocs which approached the levels existing today. Yet it is obviously important that we draw upon all possible earlier experience to assess the resilience of command and market economies under crisis and wartime conditions, and the possibility of drawing inferences from similar or analogous situations.

The comparative assessment of vulnerability in command and market economies, especially in the context of East-West power, remains elusive. Complexity and controversy defy reasonably complete description, classification, and explanation of how overall economic leverage balances out. The literature to date fails to define and analyze carefully the purposes, contexts, and outcomes of economic diplomacy, and the explanatory power of the associated East-West literature tends to be especially diluted by advocacy. With very few exceptions, these literatures concentrate on a relatively small number of the most publicly visible and highly controversial cases, usually involving only trade, and almost always in a North-South rather than East-West context.

This results from the post-World War II evolution of two almost entirely separate economic systems. In the 1950s there was very little interchange between the blocs in trade or finance. The growth of two largely separate post-World War II economic systems was reinforced by the U.S.-led effort, especially through the COCOM, to enforce relatively tight restrictions on technology transfer to the East.

Things began to change in the 1960s. By 1969, in response to external and internal pressure, the Brandt government formally instituted Ostpolitik. A long term trade agreement of July 1972 between Bonn and Moscow led to the lifting of restrictions on 84 percent of all goods traded. Over the period 1970 to 1976, when West German trade doubled overall, trade with the Soviets increased in value by 400 percent. For the first three quarters of 1979, West German exports to the Soviet Union exceeded those to the United States.

While the overall volumes of economic transactions continue to be predominantly within the separate blocs, the rate of change and qualitative significance of relatively limited inter-bloc flows have been dramatic. In annual debt service, for example, Table 8.3 shows an eightfold increase for the Soviet bloc and a tenfold increase for the U.S.S.R. between 1972 and 1979. Highly aggregated data also miss the large proportions of total official export credits to the CMEA, for example, from West Germany, France, and the United Kingdom, including especially high levels from West Germany to East Germany and from France and West Germany to the Soviet Union.

Yet even this grand opening and rapid development of economic relations in the late 1960s and early 1970s, which is both recent and unprecedented in the overall history of East-West relations since 1945, did not usher in an entirely new era of behavior by either superpower. In 1967 and 1968, for example, the U.S. Congress explicitly linked the granting of access to U.S. markets to Soviet behavior towards the Vietnam War. Nixon and Kissinger decreased trade concessions during 1971 and 1972 in attempts to punish, deter, or induce specific Soviet actions, from the immigration of Jews to steps in Vietnam and other third world areas.[10] Even by 1974, concessions in the major U.S. trade act were again explicitly linked to the immigration of Jews from the Soviet Union.

The heyday of détente from 1975 to 1978 reduced the use of such economic diplomacy, but the Soviet invasion of Afghanistan in 1979 triggered an even more intense reliance by the Carter administration on sanctions as frontline elements of foreign policy. The Reagan administration has gone even further in erecting economic sanctions as a fundamental premise of its East-West policies. These have become a central instrument not only in crisis conditions, such as those surrounding martial law in Poland, but also steady state relations. When progress on forcing the allies to back down on the East-West natural gas pipeline deals appeared impossible, the administration shifted its campaign toward building a common policy to restrict official export credits in East-West trade. In place of selective manipulation of concessions that are important to the Soviets, the administration seems to have adopted the assumption that everything from scientific exchanges to commercial loans provide unwise degrees of assistance to the East's economic and military development.

In the early 1980s, the members of each bloc were searching for a new equilibrium somewhere between the old restrictions of the cold war and the heyday of détente. There will clearly be some levelling off in the rates of increase in East-West transactions, but given the depth of commitment to what started with Brandt's Ostpolitik in 1969 for West Germany and is paralleled in the rest of Western Europe, there will certainly be no returning to the days of isolated blocs.

One specific example of the limits of drawing on most post-World War II experience is provided by energy. Only since the early 1970s has the Western bloc been heavily reliant on oil supplies from far beyond its own national borders, and only since the late 1970s have Eastern European nations been significantly reliant on oil from external sources at full world market prices. As shown in Table 8.4, about 11 percent of total oil use was imported in 1979, and the prices paid and foreign exchange consumed for this oil were escalating rapidly. Furthermore, the Soviet Union is now providing smaller increases in oil exports to Eastern Europe each year. It now appears, for example, that Czechoslovakia, as well as Poland, Romania, and Hungary, face energy shortages and direct economic and financial repercussions.

Under wartime or even crisis conditions, this now means that much imported oil, especially the 35 to 40 percent of Western oil from the Persian Gulf, may well not be available. This puts definite limits, for example, on the potential duration of a conventional war in Europe or even in the Persian Gulf, and leads to the earlier than otherwise consideration of using nuclear weapons by Western nations. It also gives tremendous potential economic and strategic leverage to oil-producing nations which maintain the capacity to export during crises or war.

Short of war, the Soviet Union, for example, could become a much more critical source of petroleum and natural gas to Western Europe. Concerted action by the Western Alliance under such conditions, especially beyond the formal NATO operating boundaries, could become extremely difficult. Only under a clear and present danger of war would the Alliance be likely to pull together and act decisively. Yet East-West economic flows are much deeper than energy alone. The Soviets and Eastern Europe stand to lose access to a wide variety of manufactured equipment, and machinery, and tremendous financial resources if all ties are cut when conflict starts.

The second essential element in defining context for economic diplomacy and warfare is the paradox inherent in the current web interlocking economies in the East and West. If we hold the crucial Western vulnerability in oil and gas supplies constant for a moment, we can establish a rough qualitative measure of comparative U.S.-Soviet economic leverage. The United States appears to hold some net advantage under both peace and wartime conditions due to some important degrees of control over international liquidity, high technology exports, world foodgrain exports, and world phosphate exports. Yet any such attempted coercion will involve reciprocal costs for the United States.

The East-West context may make objectives particularly difficult to assess. While it is quite true that the Soviet Union has carefully minimized its vulnerability, if not always its dependence in economic relations with the West,[11] the nation is not immune.[12] Certainly the loss of control over and need for domestic political support of foreign economic policy in the West[13] do not affect the Soviets as strongly. Yet there are indications that there is considerable bureaucratic maneuvering and domestic political sensitivity involved in Soviet macroeconomic decisions.

Beyond their vulnerability to fluctuations in Western business cycles, weather, and the market prices for gold and oil, the Soviets may also have some important direct vulnerabilities to the West. In energy they seem to be gradually losing not the ability to satisfy their own needs but rather the capability to continue exports at current levels. Table 8.4 focuses on the increasing need for East European nations to import OPEC oil at prices much higher than those paid to the Soviets. Since exports to third world nations such as Cuba, Vietnam, and India remain relatively small, the key problem is how to balance the critical need for exports to the West for hard currency and technology with exports to Eastern Europe for economic and political stability. This will be discussed in some detail below.

The Soviets are also vulnerable to some extent in international finance, since Western loans are essential to their ability to import needed goods and carry out large scale projects such as the Yamal natural gas pipline. Foreign exchange is their central limiting factor since their export markets are unstable: By far the most important and fastest growing source of export earnings—oil—may gradually decline if no further near-term disruptions occur in world oil markets. At least during 1982-1983 the Soviets increased the volume of oil exports to the West in order to maintain their level of foreign exchange earnings during a period of declining world oil prices. The key question for Soviet energy exports is whether natural gas exports will increase at a rate which is rapid enough to replace decreasing crude oil exports.

The areas of continuing discussion, such as high technology for industrial and military uses and foodgrain and phosphates, are also vulnerabilities, although of highly controversial significance. These are highlighted in Tables 8.5 and 8.6. Most of these potential vulnerabilities are, however, vis-à-vis the West in a collective sense much more than the United States alone. Coordinated action by at least the three or four most involved nations is necessary to carry out any real threat or use of economic coercion against the Soviets. This problem is central to later sections of this chapter.

Even more important, of course, to Soviet vulnerability are indirect threats through Eastern Europe. The political compressibility of Poland, Romania, Hungary, and even East Germany may be considerably less than the Soviet Union. Economic effects of Western sanctions or CMEA decisions may be translated into political problems much more rapidly in Eastern Europe. Their behavior on these measures appears to be much more European than Soviet. The Soviet Union already faces serious and heavy economic costs through bloc economies, opposition from bloc leaders to economically costly steps, or political breakdown in the bloc which is sparked by Western economic diplomacy. Compared to the West, the Soviets have much greater economic, political and military leverage over Eastern Europe, yet Western support is critical to the Soviet ability to keep Eastern economies, and thus political systems, functioning. While Soviet diplomatic action or reaction may therefore not be contingent on public support, the range and duration of measures may be seriously constrained. Major Western governments must generate support for embargoing grain, computers, or high technology projects, while Eastern European governments must at least be careful not to exceed consumer tolerance.

East-West economic relations also present a special situation with respect to ideology and the flow of information. Responses in the East to Western economic threats must be tailored within the constraints of established dogma on the goals of multinational corporations and Western governments, thus leaving little room for admitting harmful effects from Western economic diplomacy. It is difficult to understand actual results of past cases both because information is frequently not published or unavailable, and because real economic effects can be at least partially masked. This may create a situation where positive sanctions are particularly relevant since a communist regime can tolerate public knowledge of trade-offs with a Western government much more readily than of concessions due to diplomatic pressure.

It is important, however, to emphasize that the overwhelming elements of leverage available to each superpower beyond their own borders apply primarily through influence over the behavior of the other nations in the opposing bloc. The United States and several Western nations can readily exert much more leverage over individual Eastern European nations such as Poland, Romania, and Hungary than over the Soviet Union. Similarly, individual West European nations are much more vulnerable than the United States to Soviet leverage.

Table 8.1 shows the relatively minor overall U.S. position in East-West trade. Soviet imports from the United States were steady at only 2 percent of their total imports and total bloc imports from the United States averaged only about 4 percent for 1978-1980. The United States averaged only 16 percent of all Western exports to the Soviets, and about 13 percent to the bloc for 1978-1980. These are very small proportions given that total U.S. exports in this period were about one-third of total European NATO exports.

Table 8.2 shows that, with the exception of Turkey and perhaps also Greece and Iceland, trade by individual NATO countries with the Eastern bloc nations remains a small fraction of total trade. While only exports are shown, Western imports from the bloc are generally even a smaller fraction. For the United States, only an average of 2.4 percent of total exports in 1979-1980 went to European CMEA countries.

Although the financial data in Table 8.3 are only estimated, they illustrate that the Soviets have also been cautious. Their almost $5 billion annual debt service to the West is important, but still relatively small when compared to the other major CMEA members. Soviet debt service in 1979 was about 28 percent of the total for CMEA, or under 40 percent of the total for non-Soviet CMEA. This is relatively low considering the size of the Soviet economy compared to the rest of CMEA. It also reflects the generally greater caution of the Soviets in trade with the West.

The superpowers are also generally less reliant on international trade than their allies. By the late 1970s, for example, Soviet foreign trade contributed only 5 percent of GNP. This contrasts sharply with about 12 percent for Poland, 15 percent for East Germany, over 15 percent for Hungary, Czechoslovakia, and Yugoslavia, and over 20 percent for Bulgaria and Romania. While Bulgaria and Yugoslavia were deeply involved in international trade throughout the 1970s, all the others made a rapid transition during the

TABLE 8.1: Total East-West Trade: 1978–1980

	1978			1979			1980		
	U.S.	*Total*	*U.S. as % of total*	*U.S.*	*Total*	*U.S. as % of total*	*U.S.*	*Total*	*U.S. as % of total*
Eastern Imports (millions $)									
Poland	439	3,849	11	427	4,475	10	417	5,029	8
USSR	254	11,347	2	324	16,184	2	453	20,027	2
Soviet Bloc	1,256	24,583	5	1,355	32,975	4	1,424	39,298	4
Western Exports (millions $)									
Poland	677	5,251	13	786	5,669	14	710	6,012	12
USSR	2,249	13,331	17	3,604	16,528	22	1,510	16,902	9
Soviet Bloc	3,698	28,505	13	5,731	37,027	15	3,975	39,298	10

Sources (Tables 8.1 and 8.2): UN, OECD, U.S. Census Bureau, F.R.G.—Statistical Office 1977–1981.

TABLE 8.2: Trade of NATO Countries with European CMEA Countries,* 1979 and 1980 Exports (million $, f.o.b.)

Country/Area of Origin	*Exports to European CMEA Countries*		*Exports to European CMEA as percent of Total Exports*	
	1979	*1980*	*1979*	*1980*
Belgium-Luxembourg	1,059	1,308	1.9	2.0
Denmark	377	391	2.6	2.3
France	4,027	4,646	4.1	4.0
F.R.G.	11,270	12,671	6.5	6.5
Greece	361	525	9.3	10.1
Iceland	64	83	8.1	8.9
Italy	2,633	2,736	3.7	3.5
Netherlands	1,144	1,420	1.8	1.9
Norway	246	266	1.8	1.4
Portugal	100	92	2.9	2.0
Turkey	325	463	13.1	16.8
U.K.	2,058	2,628	2.3	2.3
Total European NATO	23,663	27,228	4.0	4.0
Canada	991	1,776	1.8	2.7
United States	5,674	3,853	3.1	1.7
Total NATO	30,328	32,857	3.6	3.4

*Bulgaria, Czechoslovakia, G.D.R., Hungary, Poland, Romania, and USSR.

TABLE 8.3: Soviet Block Dependence on Western Loans and Credits (millions $) (annual debt service payment)

	1972	*1973*	*1975*	*1977*	*1979*
Soviet Union	476	729	1773	3115	4754
Bulgaria	182	217	313	572	885
Czechoslovakia	134	202	324	458	785
GDR	301	435	775	1,302	2,475
Hungary	140	224	324	548	1,236
Poland	274	487	1,219	2,887	5,800
Romania	337	447	667	699	1,174
Total	1,844	2,012	3,622	6,466	12,355
Total pact	2,320	2,741	5,395	9,581	17,109

Source (Tables 8.3 and 8.4): Adapted from NFAC *Estimating Soviet & East European Hard Currency Debt.*

TABLE 8.4: Patterns in East European Oil Imports: 1971–1978 (thousand B/D)[1]

Year	*Total Oil Consumption*	*Oil Imports as a Percent of Total*	*Oil Imports from the USSR*	*Oil Imports from the USSR as a Percent of Consumption*	*Oil Imports from Non-Communist Sources*	*Oil Imports from Non-Communist States as Percent of Total Consumption*	*Equivalent Cost of E. European Oil Imports from Non-Communist States at OPEC Price ($ Million)*
1971[2]	1217	71	895	74	25	2.0	$ 27
1973	1539	77	1100	71	83	5.4	$ 155
1975	1676	79	1269	75	63	3.8	$ 278
1977	1943	81	1420	73	159	8.2	$ 747
1978	2063	83	1490	72	228	11.0	$1076
1979	2125	89	1559	73	235	11.0	$1601[3]

[1]Adapted from CIA ER IESR 81-004 (U) 28 April 1981 pp. 25, 27, 28 and DOE International Energy Indicators. Excludes Yugoslavia.

[2]There is a discrepancy in data involving oil imports and oil imports from the USSR.

[3]If East European oil imports from non-Communist countries were maintained at the 1979 levels, the import cost would be $2.6 billion in 1980, and $3.0 billion plus in 1981.

TABLE 8.5: USSR Sources of High-Technology Products from the Western Industrialized Nations (millions of $)

	1972		1977		1979		
Country	*High-Tech Exports To USSR*	*As Percent of Total*	*High-Tech Exports To USSR*	*As Percent of Total*	*High-Tech Exports To USSR*	*As Percent of Total*	*As Percent of I.W. Country's Exports to USSR*
Canada	0.7	0.2	7.2	0.3	11.3	0.5	1.7
U.S.	26.8	8.1	184.3	8.8	154.7	6.5	4.4
Japan	41.8	12.7	343.5	16.5	398.9	16.8	16.2
Bel-Lux	4.3	1.3	18.6	0.9	21.1	0.9	4.5
Denmark	4.6	1.4	14.6	0.7	17.1	0.7	18.1
France	38.0	11.5	232.9	11.2	376.8	15.9	18.8
West Germany	79.4	24.1	677.0	32.5	668.3	28.2	18.5
Ireland	—	—	1.2	0.1	1.3	0.1	2.9
Italy	51.1	15.5	233.1	10.7	257.2	10.8	21.1
Netherlands	3.2	1.0	19.1	0.9	16.7	0.7	5.5
U.K.	43.4	13.2	46.1	2.2	94.0	4.0	10.5
Austria	4.8	1.5	73.0	3.5	43.7	1.8	8.5
Finland	5.4	1.7	67.0	3.2	70.9	3.0	4.6
Norway	0.2	0.1	1.4	0.1	8.2	0.3	9.4
Sweden	9.0	2.7	76.6	3.7	119.9	5.1	35.3
Switzerland	16.3	5.0	99.8	4.8	111.3	4.7	41.9
Total	329.2	100.0	2085.4	100.1	2371.3	100.0	13.1

Source: Adapted from John A. Martens, "Quantification of Western Exports of High Technology Products to Communist Countries," ITA, Project D-41, Dept. of Commerce, January 1981.

TABLE 8.6: Soviet Dependence on Grain Imports (total grain incl. wheat, coarse grains and misc.)

	1971	*1972*	*1973*	*1974*	*1975*	*1976*	*1977*	*1978*	*1979*
Domestic production									
Actual (million tons)	171.4	158.4	210.7	181.6	132.0	211.8	184.7	226.1	171.3
Imports									
Total (million tons)	7.8	22.5	10.9	5.2	25.6	10.1	18.4	15.0	30.5
From U.S. (million tons)	2.9	13.6	7.9	2.3	13.9	7.5	12.5	11.1	15.3
U.S. as percent of total	37	60	72	44	54	73	68	74	50
Total consumption (million tons)	169.5	177.1	201.8	193.9	171.1	208.1	215.0	219.7	217.3
Imports as percent of total consumption	5	13	5	3	15	5	9	7	14
Cost of grain imports									
Estimated $ cost of imports (millions $)	72.5	652.5	1264.0	676.0	2073.3	1977.6	1232.8	1965.0	4483.5
$ Cost of imports as percent of total Soviet imports	.7	4	6	3	6	5	3	4	

Note: 1971 MT Grain = $9.3; 1972 MT Grain = $29; 1973 MT Grain = $116; 1974 MT Grain = $130; 1975 MT Grain = $81; 1976 MT Grain = $192; 1977 MT Grain = $67; 1978 MT Grain = $131; 1979 MT Grain = $147.

Source: Adapted from USDA *Agricultural Situation: USSR: Review of 1979 and Outlook for 1980*; USDA *Statistical Report USSR*; and CIA *Handbook of Economic Statistics*.

decade. Over the period 1970 to 1978, the trade as a percentage of GNP indicator roughly doubled for Romania and the Soviet Union, and increased by 50 percent for Poland.

The two superpowers are thus relatively immune from direct economic attack, even though selected U.S. high technology and grain exports and international financial support may, at least temporarily, be important to the Soviets. A complex and vital question thus arises: How does each bloc gain or lose the most from the potential exploitation of this economic web?

The answer to this question for each specific case must reflect the fact that both superpowers lack major direct leverage over each other, and therefore need the support of their own trading bloc. There are at least two important results of this situation. First, it is increasingly difficult for the United States to make use of its potential leverage, especially with negative sanctions. West European nations are reluctant to take action against Eastern Europe because of the importance of existing trade and financial relations and their view that this is an inappropriate, if not ineffectual means of leverage over the Soviets. Furthermore, U.S. unilateral action against Eastern Europe in conditions short of war is considerably less effective than joint Western efforts.

Finally, even if Eastern Europe is affected by U.S. action, the results could be counterproductive. It is usually not Eastern Europe that we want to influence as much as the Soviet Union, and this of course provides Soviet and East European regimes with a clear excuse and scapegoat for harsh domestic countermeasures such as strict rationing. Yet there are some conditions such as in the transfer of high technology with military applications where it may be not only appropriate but essential to act against Eastern Europe in order to affect the Soviet Union.

The second result includes the relatively greater leverage available to the Soviet Union through unilateral negative action against Western Europe. The West may in some cases be unable, short of war, to effectively impose negative sanctions on Eastern Europe in order to get at the Soviets. Yet while the Soviet Union may be able to constrain or punish the United States through action, or at least implied threats against Western Europe, we must carefully assess the limits on such potential Soviet leverage.

In oil and gas supplies, for example, the difference between war and all other situations may be important. While we must assume the loss of Soviet supplies to Western Europe during war, under most other circumstances the Soviets would be reluctant to stop, or even explicitly threaten to stop, energy flows. This is because of short term losses in foreign exchange earnings (which, in the case of gas do not start until the 1990s), if Western exporters are careful to make payment arrangements only on a quarterly or biannual basis, and in important imports from the West, especially from Western Europe, and longer term loss of high technology, private investment capital, and credibility as a reliable business partner.

If, as the Reagan administration has argued strongly, these exports and imports are crucial to the Soviets, then it must also follow that they will be extremely reluctant to forego them. There remains, however, at least one important possibility—that the Soviets gain an immediate bargaining advantage by threatening to cut off energy supplies to Western Europe, whereas the West only gains offsetting leverage in an intermediate to longer term context.

An absolutely crucial response for this case may be available in the West: emergency preparedness. Offsetting domestic and international measures can be taken in advance. For example, natural gas pipeline networks can be designed to allow regional and international diversion of supplies. Dual use burners can be installed in major plants, where consumption may also be concentrated for ease in fuel switching. Stockpiling of supplies beyond normal operational levels is also feasible in some regions.[14]

The most interesting case may therefore be potential modification of behavior by West European nations as a result of implicit or very subtle threats from the Soviet Union (and the use of positive sanctions through bloc nations). When Soviet deliveries of energy supplies to West European nations slow or even stop at times in the winter, for example, it is never possible to be sure of Soviet motives. It has already been suggested within the Reagan administration that the stoppages in 1980-1981 were related to Western attempts to sanction the Soviets after the invasion of Afghanistan.

Is some form of intimidation of West European nations at all probable? Or is it likely that Western nations will gain offsetting leverage against the Soviets under nonwartime conditions? If structured carefully, it is clearly possible that flows of foreign exchange, high technology, and private investment from Western Europe will be as important to the Soviets as the exchanged gas supplies will be to the Allies. There may also be offsetting energy options available to the West since Austria may export increasing supplies of electricity to the Eastern bloc and the Soviets may face decreasing foreign exchange earnings from energy exports. Under wartime conditions, furthermore, most energy flows to Western Europe must be assumed to be disrupted so the specific source of imports may not be overly important.

Resisting implicit or very subtle Soviet threats may demand common action by Western nations. Offsetting Western power in East-West relations is monitored carefully in the Soviet Union. The Soviets seem to be increasingly skillful at playing off nations bidding for business ventures in the East, keeping negotiations secret, and insuring that trade and foreign exchange balances are maintained within safe limits. Western Europe in particular may therefore have to carefully seek terms for maintaining control over flows of foreign exchange, energy, and technology. Their position is greatly strengthened if they can interrupt these flows, including any increased electricity exports, assistance in nuclear power, and all other important high technology exports to Eastern Europe as well as the Soviet Union. The challenge, of course, lies in establishing at least a minimal degree of coordination, if not cooperation, in Western deals with the Soviet bloc. Without serious and continuing consultation and coordination, the temptation could be overwhelming for individual nations to quietly accept Soviet conditions in order to gain special treatment, especially under ambiguous circumstances. It turns out for example, that France did indeed reap positive benefits, in the form of increased oil imports, during the critical months of the oil embargo of 1973-1974 and the Iranian crisis in 1979.

The analysis gets more complex if we relax the assumption that the West must obtain large quantities of oil and gas supplies from imports and consider the possibly greater resilience of market economies in the West to wartime conditions (van Creveld, Chapter 2). Under extreme crisis, conflict, or wartime conditions, the Soviet Union can certainly cause at least temporary interruptions in oil tanker routes, thus making Western governments highly uncertain about their oil and natural gas supplies from overseas. In a crisis a simple overflight of the Straits of Hormuz by Soviet aircraft capable of laying mines could cause panic in the West and freeze tanker traffic if the major shipping insurance companies revoke coverage of vessels in these waters.

Under any such scenario, conventional war fighting capabilities could be seriously restricted.[15] U.S. and NATO war reserves of crude oil and petroleum products, in addition to other basics such as ammunition, are not capable of supporting major engagements beyond several weeks (probably less than three or four and perhaps less than two). Almost independent of the specific circumstances that developed, it would be essential to maintain access to Persian Gulf oil. If Japan and Western Europe could not count on these oil flows, the crisis or wartime bargaining balance would be shifted heavily towards the Soviet Union.

The exact form and degree of economic diplomacy stands out as an important third element of context. Is the action a positive or negative sanction? Is it an implicit or explicit threat, partial restraint or encouragement, complete economic assistance or embargo, a blockade, or strategic bombing? Are there unintentional or "chaotic" events as well as intentional ones that may be important? Does the action cover finance, investment, foreign aid, high technology, or other foreign trade? How many and which suppliers participate, to what degree, and for how long? How many nations are targeted by the action? Finally, once the action is taken, is it available for future use? Or are international markets likely to be permanently restructured in a way that would be damaging to the initiating state? The answers to these questions must be specified as precisely as possible in order to assess the relevance of past cases or to make estimates concerning future economic diplomacy.

Positive sanctions capture much less public attention, but they merit considerably more assessment. This is especially the case in the East-West context since both superpowers are much more vulnerable to pressure through their blocs than they are to direct sanctions, but where neither wants to jeopardize longer term diplomatic relations with at least key members of the opposing bloc. Negative U.S. action against Eastern Europe or Soviet action against Western Europe could certainly backfire. Increasing interdependence between the West and Eastern Europe, especially if managed carefully by Western nations, could therefore even lead to favorable asymmetries.

Soviet political leaders certainly understand that they gain strong potential leverage from control over energy and other raw material imports essential to Western neighbors. They establish both direct and indirect leverage, a reputation as a reliable business partner, and a serious and continuing source of contention between the United States and Western Europe. Two crucial questions for future investigation and analysis are whether the Soviets have ever actually used energy exports against Western nations and, specifically, what were the reasons for sharply reduced Soviet oil exports to Western Europe after the invasion of Afghanistan and during U.S. attempts to gain wide support for sanctions against the Soviets.

Comparative Vulnerability to Economic Warfare

Throughout the analysis in this volume we find that the basic elements of economic diplomacy can change radically during war. It is, however, extremely difficult to draw operational distinctions between conditions of peace, crisis, short war, and long war, for each overlaps significantly with others. We must still, for analytical purposes, attempt to isolate the relative advantages and disadvantages inherent in command and market economies during war, when economies are mobilized and emergency powers have been invoked by political systems.

Many of the overall structural economic and political-economic advantages of command economies during peacetime and even crisis conditions may swing to market economies during war. In market and semimarket economies, such as those in most of Western Europe, parts of East Asia, and a relatively small number of third world nations, there is a continual tension between private sector activity and government behavior that directly affects the economy. Even in countries such as Japan and West Germany, where strong free markets coexist with active direct and indirect government intervention, there is tremendous opposition to any major new encroachment of public policy on traditional private sector roles. The result is reluctance to invoke government war powers in anything short of national emergencies. This reluctance and the relative inexperience of market economies with the operation of crisis/war powers make the transition to war status awkward and slow.

Prior to this transition, command economies will frequently enjoy greater ability to manipulate their economies to political and military advantage. Despite administrative inefficiencies and frequently poorly managed agricultural sectors, they can work closely in foreign economic policy with allies and use private corporations to their diplomatic advantage. With adroit management, they can play off one corporation against another to their economic and military advantage. Their economies can be prepared for conflict or war, even to the point of matching production lines, specific weapons systems, and mobilization plans to the capabilities of a primary competitor. What they sacrifice in longer term economic strength they make up in short term readiness to manipulate the economy for political purposes.

Without mobilization, or at least emergency status, market economies respond to a different set of signals, with much more emphasis on decentralized and dispersed decision making. Short term political and diplomatic gain is frequently sacrificed for economic efficiency. Economic management in government and private companies responds to its own interpretation of public interest, profit maximization, and corporate/national objectives. The result is a constant struggle to protect sensitive information, minimize friction among allied governments, and reduce tensions from unemployment, inflation, and other macroeconomic variables. Preparation for crisis or wartime economic diplomacy must take place within the context of multiple competing goals, frequently as defined by the legislative as well as the executive branch of government. Secondary objectives of economic diplomacy focused on domestic audiences at home and in allied states may take on more importance than in command economies, especially in the sense that the political structure must at least tolerate executive decisions.

The peacetime government budgetary process in the United States, and to some extent in other market economies, places strict limits on readiness for crises and war. Expenditures for low visibility items such as training and readiness, or war reserves of ammunition, fuel, and prepositioned supplies of water, food, and clothing, are extremely difficult to maintain on a consistent basis. Production lines for critical equipment or weapons, such as primary naval torpedoes, may number one or two, or in some cases none. Where cooperation and coordination is required on these issues, such as in NATO, it is even more difficult to ensure that each individual nation expends the funds necessary to maintain readiness. Finally, prepositioning or especially the establishment of bases overseas quickly escalate into major domestic or alliance political debates over the reliability of the host nation, and the possibility that our actions will increase the political instability of an important ally in the third world.

Market economies have also been stressed by crisis and wartime experiences of the 1960s and 1970s. The longer term economic effects of the Vietnam War on the United States, for example, are still not fully understood. We can estimate that the increasingly high and persistent levels of inflation faced in the mid-1970s were partially the result of U.S. attempts to fight the war without mobilization and maintain consistently high government expenditures in all, or most, nondefense sectors. In defense spending, we generally drew down weapons and supplies from other theaters, especially Western Europe, to support our efforts in Vietnam. The result was an accumulated drag on both the economy and our fighting forces which is yet to be fully repaid.

As the Vietnam War was winding down, the oil embargo and production reduction of 1973 and 1974 caught all the major market economies by surprise. Throughout the early 1970s, the OECD nations were growing at, and consuming energy at, rates that were higher than ever before. Even before U.S. oil production peaked in 1971, the capacity to produce extra oil in emergencies was fading to insignificant levels. The loss of surge production capacity placed the United States in a position of vulnerability similar to that of its allies. Under the pressure of embargo many nations emphasized unilateral responses, often scrambling frantically to gain access to crude oil and petroleum products.

Yet when the smoke cleared, the Vietnam War, the embargo, and the foodgrain crises of the mid-1970s had not damaged the major market economies as badly as expected. Individually and as a group these nations were much more resilient than predicted. Certainly U.S. force projection needs for the Persian Gulf increased, but domestic and international structural resiliency was surprising. First, in the very short term the oil companies were able to shift and balance world oil markets to the extent that no nation endured significant oil shortages. Second, international financial flows were equilibrated relatively rapidly and none of the predicted dire failures occurred. Private sector lending increased rapidly and filled the gap that could not be covered by individual governments and public international institutions. Third, while oil-importing nations ran huge balance of payments deficits, as OPEC surpluses began to decrease in the mid-1970s, OECD deficits also decreased. The overall losers have been oil-importing third world nations, but even here aggregate growth rates were not slashed as badly as expected.

Comparative resiliency to the 1973-1974 embargo and the international economic shocks from the Iran crisis of 1979 are difficult to assess, but at least some trends have emerged. When individual major market nations scramble in panic during a crisis, their behavior has ripple effects throughout all other linked economies. Beggar thy neighbor steps hurt in the short term, when less of a given commodity or financial asset is available for common use, and in the longer term, when international markets are restructured in favor of supplier nations.

Overall, however, the major market economies which proved most resilient absorbed the shocks through rapid adjustment to price and supply changes, allowing market forces to work. Germany, for example, passed through almost all price increases directly to consumers and the nation overall experienced relatively low price increases, few problems with shortages, and less damage as measured by most macroeconomic indicators. Market signals worked more rapidly than government allocation programs and seemed to allocate petroleum products more equitably than the complex U.S. system of price controls and allocation.

Third world oil-importing nations faced, and continue to face, accumulated structural economic problems both domestically and internationally. Yet those which chose to adjust to the shocks as rapidly as possible, rather than to borrow their way through, did considerably better. Countries such as Brazil and Turkey suffered severe decreases in growth rates by the late 1970s after trying to borrow as much as possible in the mid-1970s, without slowing down their economies. Command economies, with structural barriers to changing macroeconomic policy relatively rapidly, fared poorly. It was essential, for example, in many countries to shift tremendous effort to increasing exports as a means of offsetting much larger oil import bills and demands on foreign exchange.

The Soviet Union reaped a huge windfall from increased oil prices since, at least in the short term, petroleum exports were worth much more. Even with tremendous increases in purchasing power in energy exports, however, foodgrain imports and energy needs in Eastern Europe neutralized this gain. All the command economies of Eastern Europe confronted many of the same problems encountered throughout the third world. Slowed growth in the major market economies slashed their export markets and strained a common pool of international financial liquidity. Their transformation in the 1970s to significant interaction with the Western international economic system could not be turned back suddenly, and growth rates had to be trimmed back. Structural problems began to emerge, such as the beginning of East European dependence on OPEC oil supplies at world prices, as opposed to the subsidized rates provided by the Soviets.

The 1970s left severe scars on most nations worldwide. The conventional assumption of efficiency advantages in command economies did not hold up in many cases. Flexibility and speed of adjustment seemed to be highest in the relatively open and unfettered markets, both domestically and internationally. Counter examples can certainly be cited, but it is clear that the private banks and corporations command an even more important role in economic coercion and warfare in the 1980s than they did in the 1970s.

While these trends are important to comparative resiliency in short or longer conventional and nuclear warfare, they must be augmented by analysis of wartime cases. During World War II the Soviets and Western nations both mobilized and recovered rapidly. Yet both experienced dangerous points when major campaigns were working against them. Nazi submarine warfare against the Allies in the Atlantic came perilously close to crippling the war effort. With better access to wartime intelligence on allied ship losses for the Nazis, or on effects of strategic bombing in Germany for the allies, either side could have changed outcomes, especially the timing of otherwise slow results. Under such long war conditions, command economies seemed to work surprisingly well up to a point where severe pressure pushed the systems rapidly towards collapse. Of course command economies of this period did not have the current Soviet capacity for mobilization in depth as well as breadth.

In a prolonged conventional war and or limited nuclear exchange in the 1980s, strategic planners face many new vulnerabilities on top of the same ones encountered in the 1910s and 1940s. Both command and market economies are constrained by relatively heavy reliance on international markets generally, and on flows within their principal economic blocs specifically. Relative power positions, economic resiliency and political capacity would more than ever before depend on the degree of cohesion maintained among allies. Argentina's relative isolation, for example, as compared to British access to international resources during the Falklands War proved extremely important. If Argentina had been able to maintain immediate resupply channels for key equipment and weapons, the war would at least have been greatly prolonged and extremely burdensome for the long British logistic lines. This also holds in the negative case, where concerted action will be necessary to deny enemy access to critical materials and technologies from any individual supplier nations, especially major Western market nations which may be tempted to negotiate separately with the Soviets.

Short war scenarios present a more favorable situation for command economies which have capitalized on their relative advantages in peacetime preparedness for mobilization. While market economies are struggling with the awkward process of transferring economic management to the public sector, prepared command economies can bargain on the basis of more advanced civil defense programs, hardened industrial complexes, and at least short-term bloc cohesion. Emerging advantages for some market economies, such as the U.S. population and employment shift into more rural areas, are probably offset in many cases by the shorter warning time which could accompany short wars. The first few days and weeks of warfare, at least at conventional levels, present market economies with major vulnerabilities in coordinating policies among allies, establishing critical logistics lines at sea and in the air, and operating communications and intelligence systems among a relatively large number of allies with different procedures and equipment.

The strength in depth provided by market systems' combined capabilities in economic resiliency and political capacity would take hold after the first few days of warfare. Technological advantages, such as are apparent for the Israelis in Middle East combat, would begin to make a difference in electronic warfare and antisubmarine warfare. Market economies' tremendous potential in airlift capacity through takeover of commercial airlines would be triggered if conflict was clearly underway. Some breakdown of alliance systems among command economies, especially those of Eastern Europe, would be likely, with a streamlining of Soviet efforts around a few core bloc countries and combat divisions.

The immediate result in any clear wartime situation would be a drastically segmented world economy, with only remnants of the prior links that connected large markets. Depending on the location of conflict, oil, for example, would become available only in certain regions of the world and large segments of world production capacity could soon become unavailable due to sabotage, lack of equipment or personnel, and war damage. Market economies would gain tremendous advantages from the gradual availability of unemployed labor and production facilities, but this would not be relevant in a short war. They would certainly be in a better position to isolate and lay seige to international markets which would be important to enemy command economies. Soviet economic vulnerabilties in peace and crisis could be magnified significantly under longer war conditions.

CONCLUSION

The process of assessing and using economic diplomacy and warfare is complex and dynamic. Vulnerabilities of modern economies must be measured on a case by case basis, using financial, aid, corporate investment, and high technology data as well as the traditional indicators from trade statistics. When testing or searching for specific vulnerabilities through case studies, it is essential to uncover the objectives behind national actions. This means being careful not to impute complex motives where they do not exist, but also not stopping with public statements of national objectives. Many cases reveal multiple and changing objectives, especially when diplomatic action is taken publicly. In the context of comparative vulnerability of command and market economies, the additional complication of East-West or North-South ideology and rhetoric further complicate the analysis. Here it is especially important to go beyond the few most visible cases and the press coverage which dies out as events drag out over months or even years.

A multiple stage process with assessment of power positions, economic resiliency, and political capacity provides some support for the working hypothesis that economic sanctions may have been more effective than suspected in past analyses. This results from disaggregation of objectives, giving careful attention to what both initiating state(s) and target nations were trying to do, and specification of which objectives failed, and why. Often it may turn out that economic diplomacy or warfare may have failed on some measures, but for international market reasons rather than as a result of any specific counter action taken by the target nation. In other cases it may have worked, but the results were covered up or distorted by the target nation.

We must also look increasingly to domestic objectives of economic diplomacy, especially among market economies, to explain national behavior. This may be occurring at the same time that command economies are focusing more attention on how to protect themselves from, and gain all possible advantages from, international markets that are increasingly important to them. One pertinent example may be provided by the recent U.S. Department of Commerce statement, based on a study of Soviet prices and trade, that the Soviet Union is far more vulnerable to economic sanctions than assumed in the past. This is obviously at least indirectly connected to President Reagan's campaign, at home and in allied nations, to clamp down on economic relations with the Soviet bloc, especially the natural gas pipeline deal with Western Europe and the granting of government credits by Western nations.

Under wartime mobilization conditions in the 1980s, it is difficult to specify consistent advantages and disadvantages for command and market economies. Market economies may be most vulnerable in the early stages of conflict, especially if warning time is short. Yet their disadvantage here is not as large as under nonmobilized war conditions such as the Vietnam War. Alliance cohesion and transition to mobilized status are critical variables that are likely to be troublesome for market economies in the first days of any future war.

Market economies may begin to gain leverage after several days from alliance cohesion and control over international markets, if recent events in the 1970s provide reliable indicators of future behavior. External shocks seem to be most effectively handled by passing effects through to consumers rather than protecting the economy in the expectation that the crisis will pass quickly. While oil flows stand out as the greatest Western vulnerability, the Soviets must gain access to foodgrain needs and foreign exchange. In the most unlikely case—a war that continues for months or years—the Soviets could begin to confront shortages of many imported basic goods, such as transportation equipment and electric motors, unless large stockpiles are built. Most important, of course, for comparative vulnerability of command and market economies even during war is the degree of flexibility of each key sector to anticipate and respond to rapidly changing markets and shortages.

NOTES

1. Kissinger, Henry A. *A World Restored: Metternich, Castlereagh and the Problems of Peace 1812-22*. Boston: Houghton and Mifflin, 1972. Also, Howard, Michael. "The Forgotten Dimensions of Strategy." *Foreign Affairs*, Summer 1979, pp. 856-875.

2. Deese, David A. and Nye, Joseph S. *Energy and Security*. Cambridge, Massachusetts: Ballinger Publishing Company, with Harper & Row, 1981.

3. Brodie, Bernard. *Strategy in the Missile Age*. Princton: Princeton University Press, 1959, pp. 131-144.

4. Galtung, Johan. "On the Effects of International Economic Sanctions, with Examples from the Case of Rhodesia." *World Politics* 19 (April 1967): 378-416.

5. Galtung, Johan. "Economic Sanctions." Also, Green, Jerrold D. "An Analysis of Galtung's General Theory of Economic Sanctions," for the Annual Convention of the International Studies Convention, 1982.

6. Licklider, Roy E. "The Failure of the Arab Oil Embargo of 1973-74." *Comparative Strategy* (forthcoming).

7. Losman, Donald. "International Boycotts: An Appraisal." *Politics* 37 (Spring 1973): 648-671.

8. Licklider, "The Failure of the Arab Oil Embargo of 1973-74."

9. Blechman, Barry M., and Kaplan, Stephen S., eds. *Force Without War: U.S. Armed Forces as a Political Instrument.* Washington, D.C.: Brookings Institution, 1978.

10. Kissinger, Henry. *White House Years*, Boston: Little, Brown, 1979, pp. 152-55, 840, 1134, and 1271-1273.

11. Finlayson, Jock and Marantz, Paul. "Interdependence and East-West Relations." *ORBIS*, Spring 1982, pp. 173-194.

12. Portes, Richard. "East Europe's Debt to the West: Interdependence Is a Two Way Street." *Foreign Affairs*, 1976/77, pp. 749-782. Also, Goldman, Marshal I., *Détente and Dollars: Doing Business with the Soviets*. New York: Basic Books, 1975; "Will the Soviet Union Be an Autarky in 1984?." *International Security*, Spring 1979, pp. 18-36.

13. Destler, I.M. *Making Foreign Economic Policy*. Washington, D.C.: Brookings Institution, 1980. Also, Katzenstein, Peter J., ed. "Between Power and Plenty." *International Organization*, Fall 1977; and Kohl, Wilfrid L., *Economic Foreign Policies of Industrial States*. Lexington, Massachusetts: Lexington Books, 1977.

14. Deese and Nye. *Energy and Security*.

15. Deese, David A. "Oil, War, and Grand Strategy." *ORBIS*, Fall 1981, pp. 525-555.

III

Strategy, Policy, and Economic Instruments

9

Economic Relations as an Instrument of National Power

Klaus Knorr

Economic instruments have been used with great frequency in exerting power internationally even though the results in promoting national interests make up a checkered history, and substantial payoffs have seldom been achieved when economic coercion has been attempted in cases of high diplomacy in which the stakes at issue are political and of a high order. There is no way to know whether bungling and failure have been more frequent in these cases than where other forms of pressure, including military force, have been brought into play. But I have the impression that the employment of economic instruments has often been hasty or ill-considered, or both, and that relevant statecraft is shallow. The question raised by the record is not whether economic means, especially when used to coerce, should remain in the repertory of statecraft. It is rather whether resort to them should not be considered only when the opportunities and likely outcomes have been studied with great care.

ECONOMIC INSTRUMENTS AS POWER RESOURCES

One conceptual problem merits brief attention before we examine the several uses of international economic relations for purposes of projecting power abroad. There are different ways of defining power.[1] In the following, I adhere to the position that power resides in the intended effects produced in the outside world, and not in the means which are employed to produce them. The means are power resources whose application may succeed or fail depending on the contextual circumstances of each case. This holds true even when a country attempts to strengthen or weaken a foreign country, and the distinction is especially crucial when economic or military resources are used in making threats for the purpose of influencing the behavior of a foreign government. The attempt may succeed or fail, or partly succeed. Power is exercised only to the extent that the attempt achieves its purpose.

Using foreign economic relations as a power resource means denying or giving things of economic value to some other state or to nonstate actors such as rebels. These things of economic value are many in kind, such as the supply of goods and services (including arms and military assistance), granting markets for goods and services; extending loans (whether hard or soft), financial gifts, and transfer of technology. It is also possible to deny foreigners the use of their own assets (for example, bank deposits that are under control of the sanctioning state). All that is required in this respect is an appropriate foreign demand for an economic value.

The mere possession of economic values—assets belonging to a state or its citizens—does not necessarily mean that they are at a government's disposal and to be used at its discretion internationally. If a government wants to give foreign economic aid, it must normally tax or borrow from its citizens. If it wants to withhold high technology from a foreign country, it may have to seek the cooperation of business firms or assume control over their commercial activities. If it wants to give a country preferential access to the national market, it must be free to discriminate against other exporting states. All of these limitations are on top of the possibility that national governments themselves are divided on the issue, that parliaments refuse authority to the executive, and that division within executive bureaucracies presents serious obstacles. Clearly, international differences in the political and economic constitution of countries have an important bearing on the extent and ease with which economic relations can be used as an instrument of national power.[2]

Authoritarian states face fewer constraints than pluralist democratic countries, and centrally administered economies, whether socialist or not, face fewer constraints than do capitalist free market countries. These differences are especially significant regarding foreign trade, foreign investments, and technology transfer. In the state-trading Soviet Union, for instance, the government has immediate control over exports and imports, foreign investment, and technology transfer. In the United States, in contrast, the government must ordinarily seek special authority for securing a degree of control. A political burden is precipitated to the extent that governments must persuade or offend private owners of economic assets in order to release them for national foreign-policy purposes. Of course, impediments stemming from divided governments are, in principle, generic to all systems.

In the matter of using trade as a power resource, capitalist free-market states labor under an additional handicap because they have established and operate in a liberal international economic order intended to promote freedom of trade and minimize government interference with that freedom. These countries subscribe to GATT (General Agreement on Tariffs and Trade), including the most-favored-nation clause, and are therefore largely constrained not to accord special access to their markets to individual exporting states.

The degree of government control over the nation's economic assets for international application is, however, only one determinant of the supply of assets that can be used as power resources. The other determinant, of course, is the level and kinds of assets in the possession of nations. And while countries adhering to relatively free-market economics suffer from more institutional restraints in using economic values for projecting power than countries with centrally directed economies, and especially communist states do, it happens that the former are by and large much richer than the latter in the possession of economic assets. Historically speaking, the capitalist societies have been far more creative in producing wealth than have the communist states or nonsocialist countries with authoritarian economic systems. But the incidence of gifts of nature is another important variable. Oil has made Saudi Arabia at present very rich although it hardly features a free-market economy.

The use of economic values as power resources must be conceptually distinguished from their use for serving material interests by means of exchange. Exchange is evidently one mode of using national economic assets internationally in order to further national interests. Examples are the procurement of imports or making foreign investment by means of exports, tariff bargaining, or giving economic aid for naval bases abroad. Strictly speaking, this mode is beyond the scope of this chapter, and is therefore only briefly mentioned. As long as things of equal value are freely exchanged, economic assets are not used as instruments of national power. There is a mutual exchange of "purchasing power" of one kind or another. To be sure, rich nations can obtain from abroad more things they value than can poor countries. They can import more goods and services, including arms, secure more naval facilities in the outside world (provided money can buy them), and so on, and some of the things procured redound to a nation's international power, whether in the form of military strength or diplomatic influence. As in domestic contexts, the wealthier actors will be better off. But the economic assets in these cases do not figure as instruments of national power.

When the use of economic assets as international power resources is under discussion, attention is often focused excessively on purposes of coercion. Although this chapter as well will devote more examination to this use than to others, because it raises more complex analytic problems, this focus fails to do justice to the entire range of uses. National economic values can be employed in six principal ways to promote national interests abroad:

Structural power
Support of foreign countries
Weakening of foreign countries
Coercion
Positive sanctions
Pseudo-sanctions

In analyzing these uses, we are interested mainly in the conditions for effective employment and in attendant costs of application. Whether employment yields net benefits depends on the cost-effectiveness of the means. How do the various disadvantages associated with such employment compare with resulting achievements?

The five applications of national economic assets as power resources are distinguished by the purposes they are meant to serve (although this purpose is imminent rather than operating on the surface in our second mode) and/or by the mode of employment. Before proceeding to our analysis, three further methodological problems must be noted.

SOME METHODOLOGICAL DIFFICULTIES

First, while the foregoing distinctions in terms of purposes are conceptually clear, it is often difficult to subsume historical cases under this choice of concepts. This happens either because government references are ambiguous (possibly because the policy makers are ambivalent) or because the same act is intended to serve more than one purpose. Thus, it may be impossible to tell with confidence whether an economic favor is meant to strengthen a foreign actor or constitutes a positive sanction intended to influence his behavior, or both. And whatever the intention, the act may actually achieve both. Similarly, it is not always clear whether withholding an economic good is meant to weaken or to coerce a foreign actor. To give an example: In 1960 the United States imposed an embargo on trade with Cuba following Castro's accession to power and the anti-American direction of his foreign policy. I have read much of the documentation, but is not clear to me whether this policy was intended to weaken Castro's Cuba or to coerce the Cuban leadership to establish foreign policies more amenable to American interests. Note that if the American objective was one of coercion, the embargo failed to achieve its purpose. On the other hand, if the embargo was to weaken Cuba, a case can be made to the effect that the policy had considerable success because it made Cuba economically extremely dependent on Soviet subsidies (and such dependence entails substantial disadvantages) and probably stifled Cuba's economic and especially industrial development.

Second, empirical information on the uses of economic assets as international power resources, and on the effects of their uses, is exceedingly fragmentary in many cases. These uses receive plenty of public attention when they occur in transports of high diplomacy in the course of a serious international crisis, although even then collection of data suffers because attention flags after a time or because government documents remain classified. However, a much larger number of cases (we do not really know how many!) occur, often routinely, without public notice, as when the act is consumed in a word or two by or to an embassy official or in a letter that remains secret.

Third, the effectiveness of the uses of national economic means as power resources often remains obscure because the particular action takes place and leads to certain results in the context of other factors that impinge on effectiveness. Thus, a foreign country may receive economic support intended to strengthen an ally which nevertheless grows weaker for domestic reasons. More generally, an economic power play may be enacted in a context featuring multiple dimensions of power and counterpower. In 1956, when Britain and France proceeded to intervene militarily against Egypt in order to restore their control over the Suez Canal, the Eisenhower administration sharply denounced this action and—as the British pound had begun to fall in international value—declared that it would not support Britain's currency in the foreign-exchange market. At the same time, Khrushchev threatened military action in support of Egypt. The interventionary attempt—which had been executed in a bungling fashion to begin with—was stopped. The case has often been regarded as one demonstrating the efficiency of coercive economic threats in high diplomacy. For the United States to announce that it would not support a sagging pound sterling was indeed no mean threat. Yet it is far from clear that it was this economic threat that induced Britain and France to desist. The very fact that Washington, a key and trusted ally, emphatically denounced the intervention shocked the British government and public which had been in any case very divided on the wisdom of the policy. (The Soviet military threat had little effect because it was met immediately by a U.S. counterthreat against the Soviet Union.) I am personally convinced that the economic threat had only a subsidiary effect in this instance. In 1973, when the war between Israel and its main Arab neighbors had broken out, the Arab members of OPEC imposed a partial embargo on oil exports to the United States, its West European allies, and Japan, and demanded that the Middle-Eastern policies of those countries turn more favorably toward the Arab case against Israel. Japan and the West European countries (except the Netherlands) complied by declaring their support for UN Resolution 242 which, among other things, required Israel to return Arab territories occupied in the course of the war. These countries were evidently coerced by economic means. It remains, however, to my mind an open question whether the United States was similarly coerced. It did not join in the chorus approving of Resolution 242, but it became suddenly far more active in diplomatic attempts to solve the Arab-Israeli conflict. The reason why I am skeptical in this case is that the United States, having become recently and growingly dependent on OPEC oil, had plenty of other grounds for revising its previous Middle-Eastern policy. The Arab embargo may have had a subsidiary effect, but I have found it impossible to pin this down empirically.

STRUCTURAL POWER

The concept of *structural power* has only recently come into general usage.[3] Its roots stem from dependency theories that address international economic relations as they affect the poorer countries of the world. Structural power enables a state or group of states to fix the rules by which international economic transactions are governed. During the nineteenth century, the United Kingdom gradually introduced an international regime of relatively free trade—free, that is, from governments. This order largely collapsed after World War I but was resurrected in more elaborate form by the United States and its Western allies after World War II. Great Britain had been the world's leading financial, commercial, industrial, as well as colonial and naval power. After World War II, the United States was the world's premier state in economic wealth and military strength and, together with the other capitalist states now associated in the OECD, accounted for the vast bulk of world trade and international capital movements. Such were the assets that allowed these powers to structure international economic relationships and impose that order on the rest of the world. In each instance, their governments declared and probably assumed that the liberal order they had fashioned also benefited the less developed parts of the world. However, adherents to dependency theories contend that the structural power of the rich enables them to exploit the world's poor and keep them in economic bondage. One may be skeptical of either assertion or both, but it is beyond question that the leading economic countries were able to employ their economic assets, perhaps with an assist from military strength, in placing the bulk of the world's international economic relations under a design of their choosing. Supported by communist states, the countries of the third world are incessantly active in pressing for substantial and, ultimately perhaps, radical changes in the existing regime, but they cannot succeed, except marginally by persuasion, unless the world's leading economic and trading countries become disunited on the issue. The latter's structural power will become dissipated if this happens.

The crucial constituents of structural economic power, that is, a large share in global output, trade, and foreign investment, the consensus among leading states on the type of international economic order that best serves their economic systems, and the supportive military strength of like-minded societies, have evidently evolved over long periods of time and not for the express purpose of bringing about structural power. But unless it is under the control of a single state, this power can wane and shatter if the states in possession become disunited on its uses, as happened between World Wars I and II. Unlike the structure of economic interdependence between particular countries, structural power over the global economic system does not lend itself to tactical manipulation.

SUPPORTING FOREIGN COUNTRIES

Most economically advanced or relatively rich states give foreign economic aid to less developed countires, whether through such UN institutions as the World Bank and the IMF or ad-hoc consortia, or on a bilateral basis. Such aid is beyond the scope of this chapter as long as it does not serve purposes of international power and influence. Our focus is on the use of economic assets to support foreign countries (not necessarily poor or economically underdeveloped) or nongovernment actors (for example, rebel movements) in order to strengthen them economically or militarily because doing so is in the specific political or military interest of the donor country. But the dividing line between purposes is often fuzzy in the real world where mixed motives are apt to be at work. Aid may be given for a combination of humanitarian, commerical and power purposes.

To give money to allies or to enemies of one's enemy has been a time-honored practice among states. When waging war against France in the New World, Great Britain extended subsidies to Frederick the Great of Prussia who was fighting the French on the European continent. In modern times, such support is often given in the form of arms. But whatever the form, as long as it consists of, or embodies, economic resources, support is given frequently in time of peace as well as war.

In many instances, the intention behind these practices is not to influence the behavior of the recipient who is normally already committed to doing things of which the donor approves. The purpose is to enable the recipient to survive or to do these things better. Yet while these different purposes are conceptually distinct, they can be combined in practice.

When the Soviet Union extends aid to India, Syria, Ethiopia, or Angola, it presumably not only wants to strengthen the recipients but also to keep them in the Soviet sphere of influence. But the Soviet Union has repeatedly given economic aid to Poland, when that country's economy experienced serious distress, not for influencing its government but in order to keep a strongly pro-Moscow regime domestically in power. It is likely that most of the time the USSR subsidizes Cuba simply to strengthen it, since Castro usually pursues, without prompting, policies in line with Moscow's interests. The Marshall Plan is the most renowned American example of applying economic resources in an internationally supportive mode. Its purpose was not to influence recipient governments but—at a time when these countries still suffered from the ravages of war—to bolster them internally against radical political forces. Similarly, when the wealthier NATO countries join in an attempt to succor the frail Turkish economy, it is not for purposes of influencing a country that has been a staunch ally. On the other hand, large-scale American aid to Israel has at times served the purpose of influencing Israeli policy as well as that of keeping this country militarily strong. The planned sale of AWACS planes to Saudi Arabia—which involves support by giving access to a new military technology—is presumably induced by mixed motives.

The historical record suggests that policies of giving economic support to foreign actors often, and perhaps usually, serve the intended purpose. But it is an international use of economic assets that can fail. It can do so because contrary circumstances continue to weaken the recipient country. The Turkish economy is still in bad shape. It can also fail because, though strengthened, the recipient shifts course and begins to pursue policies harmful to the donor's interests. Following years of Soviet support to Nasser's Egypt, Sadat reversed course and assumed a firm anti-Soviet position. But there is no way to generalize usefully about the prospects of success or failure. Contextual factors can remain favorable or turn unfavorable. Whether—or to the extent that—giving economic support to a foreign actor achieves its purpose is an empirical question.

WEAKENING FOREIGN COUNTRIES

Foreign countries can be weakened by withholding goods and services or finance from them, or by freezing their foreign assets. The purpose is not to coerce, that is, to influence the behavior of governments, although both objectives can be and sometimes are pursued simultaneously by such denials. The specific purpose is either to make the economy of the target state function less efficiently than it would with uninhibited economic access to the denying country or to restrict or altogether prevent the import by the target state of particular goods it is unable to produce at home and which would enhance its strength.

The prototype of such acts of denial is found in the economic warfare practiced in time of hostilities. In World Wars I and II, for instance, Germany's enemies not only embargoed all trade with their opponent but also restricted its imports of essential supplies by means of preemptive buying in neutral states and by limiting exports to neutral countries that were trading with Germany. The aim was to weaken the German war economy.

This mode of using economic relations as an instrument of power is also cultivated in the absence of war. Four different applications can be distinguished: First, the total embargo on trade (or on exports which is an act of economic warfare); second, universal export restrictions regarding one specific commodity; third, sequestering foreign assets of a country; fourth, partial embargoes against a particular country. The United States has been the major practitioner since World War I. It imposed an embargo on all trade with the Soviet Union until the early 1930s. In 1960, it embargoed exports to Cuba and maintained trade embargoes against North Korea and Vietnam after the cessation of hostilities. No doubt, such acts of economic warfare by even a single trading country, especially an important one, hurt the target state to some extent but the damage is usually quite limited and soon diminishes progressively with time as that country readjusts its commerce with the rest of the world. Sources of imports can be found elsewhere. The embargoing state does not escape some economic costs from such interference with the normal course of international trade and may also incur political disadvantages, if only because its government may find it difficult to terminate the policy of denial when it has become ineffective, either because it detests the symbolic act of reversal or because of sheer inertia. Withholding of economic values by a single state for purposes of weakening another in time of formal peace does not commend itself as an exercise of realistic statecraft unless exceptional circumstances clearly promise appreciable cost-effectiveness. Target states normally trade with many countries and can adjust to an embargo even if transitional difficulties are experienced, as with spare parts for machinery imported from the embargoing state. Problems of transition are more severe when arms supplies to a customer of long standing are cut off. But, generally speaking, target countries cannot be substantially weakened by total embargoes imposed by one state. Economic warfare by means of a total embargo would naturally be much more effective if all major trading partners of a target state of suitable vulnerability joined against it, severely limited evasion through third countries and continued economic denial for a long period of time. But such an alliance against an international pariah is obviously hard to bring about and maintain, for it calls for an exceptional identity of national interests.

Restricting exports of nuclear materials, processes, and plants, as under the U.S. Nuclear Proliferation Act of 1978, is the most prominent example of an embargo on specific exports of widespread or universal application.[4] The purpose of preventing or slowing down the development of nuclear weapons roughly fits our category of denying goods in order to weaken foreign countries. The intention is to prevent them from adding to their military potential and strength. Effectiveness depends on the degree to which other exporting countries follow identical policies. The United States has experienced considerable difficulties with somewhat conflicting export policies on the part of France and West Germany. Over the longer run, there is also the question of whether such controls will not increase the incentive of target states to become self-sufficient in the nuclear industry even if their capability to do so is impaired. To the denying state there are also economic costs in terms of removing export markets to commercial firms in the field.

In 1950, during the Korean War, Washington blocked economic assets owned by North Korea and the PRC and, in 1962, Cuban assets in the United States. These acts of economic warfare were of doubtful efficiency because the values involved were very small. They were also costly because the sequestered assets were in each case a very small fraction of American assets in the target states that naturally retaliated.

Partial embargoes imposed on particular countries have been used chiefly with the objective of withholding high technology from opponent states. The prime example has been the American attempt to deny the Soviet Union (since 1947) and China (from 1950 to 1971) imports of products, installations, and industrial designs that would foster their military development and, less clearly, perhaps also retard their industrial growth.[5] The motivation is attractive. Why strengthen one's foreign adversaries? The effectiveness of such measures, however, is subject to doubt, and the difficulties and costs associated with them have been formidable.

Despite the denial of high technology from abroad, the Soviet Union has certainly achieved high rates of industrial growth and has not been prevented from becoming an awesome military power. (If China's experience has been more checkered, this is probably the result mainly of self-stultifying policies, for example, the "Great Leap Forward" and the "Cultural Revolution.") It can be argued, of course that the achievements of the USSR would have been still greater or come yet faster without denials of technology transfer. But this is a very speculative hypothesis. It is at least equally arguable that the embargo made Soviet governments more determined to attain self-sufficiency in armament production and any deleterious effects were deflected onto the civilian economy. It can be contended with more confidence that Soviet industrial and military growth would have been substantially retarded if the denial of foreign technology had been more complete. But this was not a feasible option. One must nevertheless accept that the enacted policy of denial entailed some harm to the functioning of the national economies concerned. But whether these results of uncertain or readily absorbed impact have been worth the attendant difficulties and costs of the embargo policy remains an open question.

The embargoed state has three choices of response. It can do without, develop its own production of desired imports, or purchase them somewhere else. Deprivation or delays and high costs are attached to the first two remedies. The third option is free of costs except to the often tolerable extent that the country will perhaps pay a little more or must sometimes be satisfied with the second-best if the best is produced exclusively in the embargoing state. Therefore, the effectiveness of denying technology transfer depends on the degree of control over world supply enjoyed by the denying state. If this sort of economic blockade is not tight, it risks being close to useless. Yet a high degree of control over supply by one state is relatively rare in the contemporary world. A number of countries beside the United States produce sophisticated technology.

In the late 1940s and early 1950s, the United States mangaged to organize supporting sanctions by its European allies and Japan. More dependent on international trade than the United States, these countries were reluctant and, initially, it required American threats to suspend economic aid to them to obtain grudging collaboration. Two international coordinating committees—the COCOM vis-à-vis the USSR and CHINCOM vis-à-vis China—were set up to ensure parallel action. In order to secure agreements, however, American embargo proposals were often and increasingly watered down. Moreover, as these foreign partners ceased to need American economic support and could no longer be pressured, and the coordinating committees lacked power of enforcement, the application of controls grew more leaky as time went on. Embargo power eroded. Not only was effectiveness jeopardized, but continuous frictions between the United States and its allies also became an appreciable disadvantage incurred by the policy.

The major problem both in the United States and in the coordinating committees naturally turned on the definition of strategic goods. Denying the exports of weapons technology presented no problem. But many items, for example, trucks, computers, communications equipment, have military as well as civilian uses and, in principle, even industrial goods for the civilian market could be considered for the embargo list because production factors freed by the availability of imports can be shifted to production in the military sector of the target state's economy. Although the United States at first pressed for a very broad definition of strategic goods, the resistance of its partners soon compelled retrenchment to critical technologies directly suitable to armament production or clearly capable of dual use. Yet the United States and its allies often disagreed on criticality and, from the late 1950s on, Washington withheld technology which the Soviet Union was able to procure elsewhere. The technological blockade of the Soviet Union thus became increasingly less effective.

In the meantime, the costs of the program—aside from continually generating irritants between allies—became more and more apparent. First, the embargoing country or countries lose the productivity-raising effects normally associated with free international trade. Second, the loss of exports was especially burdensome for the United States when foreign supplying countries replaced the exports foregone by the United States; and this burden became particularly onerous when the denying country experienced a large trade deficit, as has happened to the United States in recent years. Third, American business firms obviously lost customers, and American workers jobs, often to foreign competitors. Fourth, the administrative costs were extremely high. It became necessary to maintain a sizeable bureaucracy for this purpose which, furthermore, operating in the usual bureaucratic manner, labored slowly and caused lengthy delays in deciding whether particular exports should be prohibited or receive the green light. In 1979, for example, the Office of Export Administration in the Department of Commerce expected to receive 70,000 license applications from American firms, which amounted to 300 per working day.[6] Not seldom these firms lost sales that would have been approved eventually because the Russians would have faced a delay of many months while able to buy the same or very similar goods much more quickly in Europe or Japan.

It is fairly clear from this record that even a country with an economy as large and advanced as that of the United States has little opportunity to withhold technology from an opponent unless it can secure full cooperation from other exporting states. Without such support, the denial of technology can be effective only for key items regarding which this country enjoys a monopoly or near-monopoly of supply. Even in such cases, the monopolist advantage is apt to be temporary because other countries will catch up. But when the exporting state has significant lead time in the development of new and strategically critical technology, it can hope to enforce a delay on its acquisition by adversaries; and the associated economic and administrative costs will be more modest when the application of this mode to weaken a foreign country is accordingly very selective. It hardly needs saying that any resorting to this way of using economic power internationally must also consider the possibility of political costs.

COERCION BY ECONOMIC MEANS

A state can threaten to withhold things of economic value from another and, if necessary, execute the threat in order to influence its behavior in a favorable direction.[7] Whether the things of value involve trade, finance, or whatever does not matter analytically. What matters is the chance which the attempt at coercion has to succeed and whether, in view of associated disadvantages, the attempt at coercion is worthwhile. The following theorems explain these problems: first, country A is the more likely to succeed in compelling desirable behavior by B, the greater A's control over the global supply of economic value X, the greater B's need for X, and the lower B's costs of compliance with A's demands. B's costs of compliance have two components: the disutility of the behavior A wants B to adopt and, very importantly the political costs of being observed, at home and abroad, in bowing to a foreign economic threat. Many historical cases suggest that yielding to an economic threat is widely regarded as more ignominious than yielding to a military threat. Second, the expected cost-effectiveness of A's attempt at coercion is the greater, the less are the various disadvantages or costs of mounting the attempt, and the higher is the probability that B will comply. Cost-effectiveness is, of course, zero if it turns out that B successfully defies A's coercive act.

My research has convinced me that, in terms of the stated goals, attempts at international economic coercion succeed often only under two conditions, although it is admittedly impossible to verify this thesis empirically. One such condition prevails when one state threatens another with economic reprisals in order to obtain a concession in trade policy as, for example, when the United States threatens to impose restrictions on the import of Japanese automobiles in the event the Japanese do not do so themselves, or when the United States threatens to limit imports of West European steel, whose production is subsidized by governments, unless these imports are reduced by European action. Such threats or actual reprisals often succeed because the large American market is important to foreign producers and the political costs of compliance tend to be low because the use of economic threats in international economic bargaining—that is, in the same issue area—has been traditionally accepted as a routine practice. Results are seen simply as reflections of the different bargaining power of the actors. They involve no political onus. The second condition that tends to make economic threats successful is when the stakes of conflict are small for both countries, and the threat is kept secret or is expressed in so low key a fashion as to cause little or no publicity. This is the case for instance, when a foreign-aid official tells an official of the recipient state that the prospects of receiving further economic aid would brighten provided the recipient country puts its financial house in order, or mitigates restrictive tax policies on foreign multinational corporations, or mutes its criticisms of the donor country at the United Nations. In such instances, the costs of compliance are ordinarily low because not much is demanded substantively and the threatened government is not seen or barely seen by the eyes of the public as complying with a foreign threat. Incidentally, it is precisely because no or very little public information is precipitated in these instances that numerical empirical assessment is so difficult. The statistical universe of cases at this level has not been explored.

The prospects of successful international economic blackmail are, however, much less favorable when it is attempted in conflicts of high diplomacy, that is, when crisis conditions attract abundant publicity, when the stakes involved and the costs of compliance are very high, and when stake and means belong to different issue areas, as when the means are economic and the objective is political. I do not suggest that there is in these applications a clear dichotomy between cases of high and low diplomacy. One assumes the existence of a continuum and there are some cases that fall in between. However, I believe that there is a considerable tendency toward polarization with the large majority of cases remote from one another on the continuum. Again, I see no way of testing this hypothesis because the necessary empirical data have not been collected.

It seems useful at this point to look at some examples of high diplomacy in which coercion by economic means was attempted. First, a little known case. Spain ceded Gibraltar to Great Britain in the peace treaty of Utrecht (1713).[8] For some decades, Spain has pressed Britain in vain to return this parcel of its territory. In 1964, Spain restricted movements of goods from Spain to Gibraltar and, in 1966, closed the frontier entirely with the effect of preventing Spanish labor from working in Gibraltar, removing the colony's principal source of food, and blocking the main market for its industrial output. The policy amounted to an economic siege. The purpose of coercing Britain was not achieved.[9] The British government was adamant not to yield to this pressure, especially since the large majority of Gibraltarians had voted in a referendum in favor of the status quo. It helped the colony by increasing local defense expenditures and developing the tourist industry, food was imported from other sources, and Spanish workers were replaced by Moroccans. Gibraltar, to be sure, needs food imports, export markets, and foreign workers, but Spain's control over supplying these needed things were obviously much too small to bring about coercion. The British government regarded the costs of compliance unacceptable even though it had earlier offered to return the colony to Spain provided the latter would guarantee the personal rights of the Gibraltarians and Great Britain continued use of the naval base. The costs to Spain of this abortive attempt at coercion were substantial. Spanish workers lost jobs and the Spanish government felt induced to provide public funds for the development of the impoverished region adjacent to Gibraltar. The Spanish government also suffered from the sheer fact that its coercion policy had publicly failed.

The Peruvian government announced in 1968 its intention to purchase sophisticated military aircraft from France. Washington, which previously had refused to sell American planes to Peru, was displeased, cut aid commitments and suspended export credits to Peru in order to make it abandon its plans. The Peruvians were infuriated and went through with the purchase without hesitation. It had turned out that American economic leverage was insufficient because Peru was little dependent on American aid and credits which had been of modest volume. On the other hand, Peru felt that its sovereignty had been infringed upon. The costs of backing down were unacceptable.

In October 1973, when the cold war had yielded to détente, the Soviet Union and the United States came to an agreement on greatly expanding mutual trade, in part through the extension of American credits. Yet when the enabling act was voted, the Congress attached the Jackson-Vanik amendment which prohibited the granting of export credits and of most-favored-nation treatment to nonmarket economies whose governments imposed unreasonable restrictions on emigration. This stipulation was an attempt at coercing the Soviet Union into liberalizing the emigration of Soviet Jews. In response, Moscow quashed the agreement. Although it was eager to expand trade with the United States, it had been able to do without it and it regarded the Jackson-Vanik amendment as an outrageous interference in its domestic affairs. It was out of the question that a great power would let itself be coerced and humiliated in so demeaning a fashion.

Following the Soviet invasion of Afghanistan, the United States imposed an embargo on grain exports of about 17 millions tons to the USSR (excepting several million tons covered by previous contracts). It was a decision made in great haste.[10] If this was part of an attempt at coercing Moscow to withdraw its troops from Afghanistan, the policy failed. Having suffered a poor grain harvest, the Soviet Union was in dire need of large grain imports. Yet although Washington tried with only limited success to organize support from other grain-exporting countries, the Russians were able to obtain unexpectedly big imports from elsewhere, especially Argentina, and to make other adjustments that moderated the impact of the American embargo. They ended up importing a record 31.5 million tons of grain, vastly more than the Carter administration had estimated. No doubt, the embargo had caused some concern in Moscow. But it was unimaginable that the Soviet Union would desist for this reason from its operation in Afghanistan even though it incurred other disadvantages as well, for example, the expressed disapproval of many other states, including a large majority of the nonaligned countries, and even though the military task of pacifying Afghanistan by force proved very difficult. Although the United States is by far the world's premier grain exporter, its control over the market was wholly insufficient to afford exceptional economic leverage. More important, Moscow would hardly permit itself to be coerced by economic pressure especially publicly, in so vital a matter. At the same time, the action caused considerable costs to the Carter administration, economic costs in terms of exports foregone, domestic political costs in terms of irritating the farm vote in an election year, and international political costs in terms of engaging in a power play that went down in defeat. Washington could have made the bite of the embargo more effective if it had engaged in preemptive buying of Argentinian and Canadian grain. But this would have meant additional costs, still unhappier farmers and it would have remained improbable, in my opinion, that the Soviet Union would have abandoned its military intervention in Afghanistan.

It has been by no means only the United States that has used economic pressure for coercive purposes in vain. When Communist Yugoslavia asserted its independence from Moscow's control, the Soviet government in 1948 cut off trade and economic aid, and induced the other Communist states in eastern Europe to follow suit, in order to compel Belgrade to return to the fold. More than half of the country's trade was affected and all of its receipts of economic aid. Yet Yugoslavia staunchly resisted. It was able quickly to expand trade with the noncommunist world and to secure aid from willing capitalist countries. Moscow's sanctions, though disruptive temporarily, caused no damage that could not be repaired and Tito was stoutly unprepared to give up sovereign independence. After a period of reconciliation and resumed economic relations, Moscow tried it again in 1956 with the same means and the same results. It also placed Albania under similar economic pressure in 1961 in order to curb its government's recalcitrance, only to see Albania defiantly turn to China for trade and aid.

Many more cases of failure can be culled from the historical record, while the number of clear successes is minuscule. Indeed, after searching as far back as the end of the eighteenth century, I found only four such cases[11], and one or two others in which the results were ambiguous. In all these cases of evident success, it took exceptional combinations of circumstances to make the attempt at coercion by economic means effective. One of these cases is the aforementioned coercion by Arab members of OPEC to extract from West European governments and Japan declarations favoring the Arab cause against Israel. At the time, these target states were virtually dependent on oil imports from the Middle East, and the shock of the partial embargo was correspondingly profound. Without oil, the economies of these industrial target countries were bound to become paralyzed. No other economic threat would have proved effective. Even so, it must also be noted that the costs of compliance were quite low, for these oil-importing countries had already come close to, some in fact were getting ready to, announce support for UN Resolution 242. The cost was primarily in the public humiliation of having been compelled to do so.

One more case may serve to illuminate the problems of this type of international sanction. Ten days after the Iranians took 52 American hostages in 1979, President Carter froze all Iranian assets, that is, about $12 billion in bank deposits and gold, in American banks, including those overseas, and cut off most exports to the country.[12] While the Shah had been in power, commercial transactions, including arms transfers, had reached a very high level and Iran seemed therefore vulnerable to U.S. economic reprisals. No doubt, they gradually deprived Iran of critical supplies, especially spare parts, and compelled it to obtain some of these through expensive deals with middlemen. Still, for a year or so, these economic pressures did not work, even though American allies reduced their trade with Iran in response to Washington's demands. This ineffectiveness is not difficult to explain. On the one hand, the revolutionary leaders of Iran were little interested in their country's economy and its development. Religious and political issues exhausted their agenda. Nor were they much interested in Iran's modernized armed services. And the country continued to earn foreign exchange even if on a substantially reduced scale. On the other hand, Khomeini and his cohorts had proclaimed the United States as their arch enemy and the costs of yielding to American pressure were therefore prohibitive.

And yet, when the agreement for the release of the hostages was negotiated 14 months after their seizure, the blocked assets figured as a key bargaining chip. Did the economic sanctions finally work after all? We lack information to give a clear answer to this question. The Iranians had other reasons to let the American captives go. The issue diverted Iranian leaders from other business and had isolated Iran diplomatically, even from most third-world countries. Nonetheless, it is highly probable that the pressure of the American sanctions contributed to the eventual denouncement. But they did so only by dint of a new intervening factor, namely the outbreak of war between Iran and Iraq in September 1980. This fortuitous event not only increased Iran's needs for military supplies, but also caused its receipts from oil exports to dwindle to a trickle. It is unlikely that American economic leverage would have exerted sufficient impact without the eruption of this war. The example shows once again that attempts at economic coercion in crises of high diplomacy succeed only if extraordinary circumstances favor them.

It needs also pointing out that the sanctions generated considerable costs for the United States. In this instance, to be sure, American business firms did not resist. There was no business to be done with Iran, and many of them attached claims for previous losses to the frozen Iranian assets. But the United States strongly reinforced its reputation for breaking economic contracts for political reasons. As the USSR had done before, OPEC countries now revised their practices in investing surplus funds abroad. Since 1980, the proportion entrusted to American banks has substantially declined.

The reasons for the dismal record of attempts at international coercion by resorting to economic leverage in conflicts of high diplomacy are plain. Sometimes the need for the economic good withheld was modest (for example, Peru in 1968). In the large majority of cases, the need was vital but the state threatening or impairing economic sanctions lacked sufficient control over the global supply of whatever was denied. Target countries, although suffering temporary costs of adjustment, were able to turn elsewhere for relief. Other countries are ususally eager to offer it, for to do so is good economic business and sometimes also politically attractive. The Soviet Union often stands ready to assist when the United States plays the game, and vice versa.

Even large-scale collective attempts at coercion by economic reprisals—organized by the League of Nations against Italy when it had invaded Ethiopia in 1935, and the UN-established boycott of Rhodesia in 1966—were ineffective because enough states and traders did not cooperate. Rhodesia in fact experienced an economic boom despite the UN's sanction. Given the usually inadequate leverage at the disposal of the sanctioning state and the usually high costs of compliance to the target country, it is not at all surprising that successful defiance rather than abject surrender is the rule. Even when economic denial hurt, defiant governments have in virtually all instances received strong public support on the issue. Being subjected to economic denial in conflicts of high diplomacy tends to have a politically unifying effect on the target country.

Even when coercive sanctions do not achieve their declared aim, they do hurt the target state more or less at least for a time until the denied economic values are procured elsewhere, possibly at a somewhat higher price. They may therefore induce the target country to be marginally more reluctant to cross the interests of the sanctioning state in the future. If this happens, there is a delayed coercive effect even though it is unobservable.

To achieve this sort of delayed coercive effect may indeed be the actual purpose, or one of the actual purposes, of resorting to attempts at economic coercion in crisis confrontation. The verbal statements by which such attempts are introduced do not always make the purpose unambiguously clear. As I mentioned above, there is some doubt about whether the American embargo against Cuba was meant to coerce or to weaken Castro. The objective pursued by means of the grain embargo against the Soviet Union in 1980 also was expressed with some ambiguity. The intent may have been, and probably was, to pressure Moscow into pulling back from its intervention in Afghanistan. But it may also have been to register United States displeasure regarding the type of aggressive move represented by the Soviet invasion of Afghanistan. In any event, in some cases, attempts at coercion probably followed this purpose in addition to that of affecting the behavior of the target state on the immediate issue that precipitated action. The grain embargo of 1981 could have been intended to compel Moscow to consider in the future all disadvantages to be expected before again taking aggressive action similar to the Afghanistan intervention. Of course, such emphatic recording of displeasure—a strong act of warning—also is meant to coerce, but the attempt is then to influence the opponent's conduct in the indefinite future. If that was the intent of the Carter administration, then it is impossible now to conclude whether the attempt will achieve positive results. Indeed, it may also be impossible to conclude so later because we will not know if, at some future time when the Soviet Union considered the merits of a similar resort to force, Moscow took account of the grain embargo of 1980 (recently canceled by the Reagan administration) in making a decision. And, for this very reason incidentally, the expression of displeasure by punitive economic reprisals is apt to have a better chance to succeed than attempts at coercing a foreign power immediately and visibly in the full publicity of a crisis. Should the opponent be persuaded to desist from some future action by the known displeasure of another state, and its proven readiness to have recourse to economic sanctions, that effect will materialize in secrecy. The costs of compliance would therefore be appreciably less.

Even though delayed coercive effects may be generated by an international use of economic leverage that fails in its directly stated purpose, this result cannot be counted on. Not only might such feedback fail to materialize, also the opposite feedback might occur. Having experienced successful defiance, the target state's resistance to future pressures could be reinforced, and it might take special measures to render itself less vulnerable the next time round.

Two further points are worth noting. First, as in applications of military power, international economic power is realized at lower costs when the threat of economic deprivation is effective, because the costs of its execution, or of having the threat revealed as a bluff, are saved. Second, the form of threat also affects results. Distinguishing between explicit ultimatum-type threats, as in the cases of the grain embargo against the USSR or the freezing of Iranian assets, and vague inferential threats that raise the possibility of economic sanctions, we may infer that the former are less likely to work, because costs of compliance to the target state are higher than the latter in which the nexus between threat and compliance is less clear. Of course, the inferential threat must be credible to be heeded. The target government must take it seriously. If it is credible, however, the dangling threat is apt to be more effective, and more cost-effective, than the economic threat embodied in an explicit ultimatum. Thus, in February 1982, when the Reagan administration considered declaring Poland in default on its debts to the West, in order to put pressure on General Jaruzelski to relax martial law in his attempt to repress the Solidarity movement, the question had to be faced as to which option would likely be more effective, executing the threat or leaving it dangling.

POSITIVE ECONOMIC SANCTIONS

Governments can also influence the behavior of a foreign country by giving it something of economic value or by promising to do so. This practice has been fairly widespread, but I am unaware of a systematic collection of cases. For example, Saudi Arabia has made massive and regular financial contributions to Jordan and, until recently, to Egypt. I am sure it is understood by the King of Jordan that he owes Saudi Arabia close support in its policy on the Arab-Israeli dispute. The Saudis eventually stopped subsidizing Egypt after Sadat signed the Camp David Agreement. Other states in the Persian Gulf and Libya have also engaged in this practice. After the Sandinistas came to power in Nicaragua, the Carter administration gave economic aid in the expressed expectation that this grant would persuade the new rulers to maintain a pluralist political system. (The Reagan administration suspended this aid when the Nicaraguan radicals squeezed their domestic opposition and lent support to the left-wing rebels in Salvador.) Indeed, much of the extension of foreign economic and military aid contains, at least potentially, an element of the positive economic sanctions.

We have clearly a use of international economic relations as instruments of power in these cases. To be sure, if A gives a fat soft loan to B on the understanding that B will refrain from acting in a fashion detrimental to A's interests or, more positively, will act in ways pleasing to A, and B behaves accordingly, we have what looks like the sort of exchange transaction discussed above. Despite this appearance, however, I find it analytically more accurate to regard the resort to economic rewards as an act of conditional coercion because it is implicit in these transactions that the reward will be withdrawn in the event B's behavior ceases to please A. In effect, we have the use of the carrot and the stick.

The effectiveness of positive sanctions, like all international applications of economic power resources, raises in each instance an empirical question. Much depends upon context. There is no lack of cases in which the gift of the carrot failed to achieve its intended purpose, even if it did so for a time. The example of Sadat is to the point. The prospects of success hinge analytically on the very same factors that tend to determine outcome in cases when the punitive coercion mode is used. The sanctioning state's control over the supply of the economic benefit in question, the degree to which the recipient needs it, and the costs of complying with implicit or explicit demands determine outcomes. Sadat's action was undoubtedly facilitated by the expectation that the Camp David Agreement would lead to substantial aid from the United States. It can also be assumed that, at the initiation of the process culminating in Camp David, Sadat strongly preferred this policy to the Saudi scheme for settling the Arab-Israeli conflict.

Yet, compared with the straightforward attempt to coerce punitively by threats or execution of economic reprisal in crises of high diplomacy, there are some differences in the cost-effectiveness equation. For the state employing positive sanctions, canceling a reward is economically beneficial rather than harmful, and the political costs—domestic and international—of having the recipient of rewards turn fractious is ordinarily less damaging than is successful defiance of a punitive attempt at economic blackmail, especially because the act of defiance receives high publicity while in the case of positive sanctions, fractious behavior often occurs gradually and is less observable and salient. Finally, the recipient of a reward is better off even if it restricts his conduct than the target of punitive economic confrontation, that is, the costs of compliance are of a different order. As a result, positive sanctions more often achieve their objective than do negative ones. Finally, it is worth noting that a positive sanction may still be working even when the recipient has turned fractious. The carrot may have kept him from becoming even more obstreperous, and so he will become once the stick swings into action. It is not certain, for instance, that by suspending aid to the Sandinistas, the United States was serving its purposes better than by leaving the carrot dangling. Withholding the withdrawal of reward is in effect like the dangling inferential threat of denial discussed above.

PSEUDO-SANCTIONS

In view of the overwhelming frequency with which the employment of negative economic sanctions in crises of high diplomacy has proved abortive, one naturally wonders why it has been tried so often. Faulty intelligence, hasty and careless planning, and sanguine expectations no doubt account, at least in part, for many ill-fated attempts. Indeed, it stands to reason that inept statecraft has its way more often when confrontation leads to economic reprisals than when an appeal to military force is chosen because the consequences of failure tend to be less destructive. Yet one suspects the presence of still other sources of apparent miscalculation. Degradations of rationality, common enough in all kinds of policymaking, will scarcely stop when it comes to making economic threats and executing them. Such lapses can be engendered by various motivations.

Three additional kinds of motivations seem to me hypothetically to have been at work in misfiring attempts at effecting coercion by economic means in matters of high diplomacy. One is sheer desire for vengeance. A has been hurt by B and, enraged, seeks emotional relief by hitting out at B. In this event, it does not matter, or matter much, if the supposed coercive purpose of the economic power play fails to succeed. The reward is internal and is consumed in the act. The second motivation thrives on the need, usually domestic but in some cases also international, of governments to do *something* and to be seen doing something, when the country has suffered an affront at the hands of a foreign actor. Lacking effective means of reprisal, the government cannot, without a loss of prestige, limit itself to vain verbal protest and complaint. It wants to look forceful, and economic sanctions may be available when military are not. In this case again it does not matter whether the explicit attempt at coercion works or not. The payoff is of a different nature and may be considerable. Third, a government may resort to economic reprisals for recording displeasure with the behavior of another, not in order to coerce as discussed above, but for the purpose of symbolizing its strong disapproval. In this case, the payoff is a sense of, and a reputation for, rectitude. Finally, economic sanctions, though not likely to achieve their immediately stated effect, may have the additional, and perhaps principal, objective of generating delayed effects, as discussed above, or—if the sanctions are mild—to put the opponent on notice that more severe threats may be dangling.

I suspect that perhaps one, or two, or all three of these motivations were at work when President Reagan, in December 1981, enacted economic sanctions against the Soviet Union for its presumed responsibility in the curbing or repression of the Solidarity movement by the Polish government. The sanctions—canceling two flights to the United States by Soviet airliners, ending scientific exchanges, closing Soviet purchasing agencies in the country and halting exports of high-technology goods—were too minor to cause the Kremlin more than inconvenience. Their imposition by themselves could not possibly be assumed by any knowledgeable official to compel a change in its policy on a matter as vitally important to it as the future constitution of Poland. I submit that they were probably, wholly or for the most part, pseudo-sanctions, that is, measures pretending to attempt coercion but actually serving other ends. Analysis of cost-effectiveness ceases to apply when the various costs of the sanctions are capable of measurement but the payoffs are not, even if they are not entirely subjective. That does not mean, however, that a government resorting to pseudo-sanctions should not estimate the economic costs and other disadvantages before it decides to act. To do otherwise would be irrational. And above all, it should be regarded as indispensable that such a government sort out its purposes in order to be clear about them.

One disadvantage associated with all resorts to coercive sanctions, as also with economic denials meant to weaken an adversary, is the difficulty of terminating them when the measures have proven ineffective or have ceased to be so. In the case of attempts at coercion at least, it would seem prudent to attach a renewable time limit such as one year. To do so would facilitate abandonment of an ineffective policy while the renewability of economic pressure would act in the manner of an inferential threat.

CONVERGENCE THEORY

Before concluding, we must note one additional manipulation of international economic relations for achieving important political ends, if not exactly power. During the 1960s, fashionable theories of international economic interdependence gave birth to convergence theory with particular reference to the Soviet Union. It was suggested that, by opening the Soviet Union to vastly increased trade with the West, its economy would experience pervasive modernization and that, as that economy grew more similar to Western economies, and ever more interdependent with them, Communist ideology would become eroded, Soviet political culture transformed, and Soviet political behavior moderated and more pacific. This notion attracted a remarkable following during the heyday of détente. It promised the use of expanded trade, facilitated by credits, to subvert the Soviet system and thereby achieve revolutionary changes in an opponent country.

These expectations were, however, based on illusion.[13] Not only would the Soviet ruling class and government have paced the evolution of foreign trade in strict line with perceived utility, they would also have resisted any tendency of increasing trade to affect the politics of their country, and they would have been in possession of the political means to do so effectively. Nor is it in keeping with Soviet economic doctrine to let the USSR become vitally dependent on the capitalist world when doing so is a matter of choice. Convergence theory of the 1960s did not in fact advance original ideas. Around the middle of the nineteenth century, the Manchester School in Great Britain, which advocated absolutely free trade, had predicted that, once this condition was achieved, the extreme economic interdependence of countries would make war unfeasible and that, by breeding a universal cosmopolitanism, would make it also undesirable. By the end of the century, an approximation to free trade had in fact come into being in the capitalist countries of Europe. World War I occurred nevertheless.

CONCLUSIONS

This chapter is not concerned with the morality of using economic resources for power purposes, although it may be said in passing that, given the prevailing international system, that use can no more be regarded as objectionable on moral grounds than the resorting to military force. Our question is rather whether, to what extent, and under which circumstances, this use has utility.

All uses of international economic relations as instruments of power present difficulties, incur costs, and can fail, wholly or in part, to serve their purpose. Economic values are always scarce relative to demands made upon them. Because of these opportunity costs, economic power resources should be employed only when the probability of cost-effective use is reasonably high. This chapter has discussed the conditions which in general determine this probability. Yet prospective cost-effectiveness is difficult to estimate in particular international contexts because our knowledge of contextual structure and processes tends to be fragmentary and obsolescent, and because faulty assumptions about the properties of a particular scenario can easily distort perceptions. Given the normal problems of estimating future events, probabilities of outcome are more difficult to estimate when the object is to weaken than when it is to strengthen a foreign country by economic means, just as it is also more difficult to foresee outcomes when negative economic sanctions rather than positive sanctions are brought into play. The difference lies in the fact that, in the former modes, the target state is apt to be cooperative while in the latter it is apt to resist the manipulations of the sanctioning state, and this adds a dimension of complexity.

The historical record suggests that, in approaching the possible use of economic values as international power resources, governments have tended to exercise policy choices with less care than they have bestowed on analyzing options of resorting to military force. Even if the consequences of failure are less severe in the use of economic than of military instruments, they are far from negligible, not only because economic values are wasted but also because policy failure precipitates unfavorable political impressions, especially abroad, on the capacity and competence of the government concerned. The need to act prudently should be obvious.

Two more specific problems seem to account for the poor performance of governments in these matters. First, unlike with experiences of military conflict, statecraft appears to be inadequately familiar with the historical record of frequent failure when economic values are used as power resources, especially when they are used for purposes of punitive coercion. Not enough has been learned from history in this functional area. But where in the institutions of modern governments should an appropriate memory be cultivated? This question leads directly to the second problem. Employing economic instruments for projections of international power is an enterprise that requires complex analyses of policy options, and this can be done properly only if political and economic analysis are closely integrated. In modern governments, however, political and economic expertise tend to be dispersed over separate bureaucracies. In the United States, for example, economic expertise regarding our subject, is largely cultivated in the Treasury and Commerce departments while political expertise is cultivated in the Department of State and the staff of the National Security Council. And even to the limited extent that both types of expertise are to a degree present in all these bureaucracies, they are represented by disciplinary specialists rather than by people who have multidisciplinary competence. This situation entails that policy analyses on the use of economic power plays tend to be less rigorous and sophisticated than they ought to be; and this defect is compounded by the fact that top leaders, that is, the consumers of policy analysis, usually also lack full comprehension of the complex interaction of economic and political factors in the outside world. It is because of this institutional dispersal of relevant lines of expertise and educated judgment that it is hard to assign an institutional memory of historical precedents to a proper bureaucratic location. Performance of statecraft in attempts at using things of economic value for projecting international power will not improve unless these weaknesses are remedied.

Finally, it is clear that American presidents have resorted to economic sanctions in crises of high diplomacy much more often in recent years than have the leaders of other prominent countries. This has happened perhaps because the country's relative international political influence and military strength have diminished, and perhaps because more states than before in this turbulent world cross American interests, or American perceptions of interest, in situations to which an appeal to force is not germane. If, or to the extent, these economic power plays were meant to coerce, they usually failed because even this rich country's control over economic values is insufficiently commanding and because allies have been reluctant to give support or enough of it. But it has probably been considerations leading to the adoption of what I called pseudo-sanctions that have accounted for much of this behavior, especially the felt need to do *something*, and to be seen doing something, when other states pursue offensive policies and we have no other means to counter them.[14] I do not deny the legitimacy of such resorts to international economic reprisals. They deserve a place in the armory of states. But I have the impression that Washington turns to these sometimes, and perhaps often, without being clear what exactly it is after and without taking the associated disadvantages, whether political or economic, fully into account. There is a definite need for statecraft to become more competent in this area.

NOTES

1. On these conceptual problems, see Klaus Knorr, *The Power of Nations*, New York, Basic Books, 1975, chapter l; and David A. Baldwin, "Power Analysis and World Politics; New Trends versus Old Tendencies," *World Politics*, 31, January 1979, pp. 161-194. The latter, a superbly penetrating article, is critical of some of my own formulations of the problem.

2. See Stephen D. Krasner, "Domestic Constraints on International Economic Leverage," in Klaus Knorr and Frank N. Trager (eds.), *Economic Issues and National Security*, Lawrence, Kansas, The Regents Press of Kansas, 1977, ch. 6.

3. For a good discussion see Cheryl Christensen, "Structural Power and National Security" in Knorr and Trager, *Economic Issues and National Security*. ch. 5.

4. See Joseph A. Yager (ed.), *Nonproliferation and U.S. Foreign Policy*, Washington, D.C., Brookings, 1980; and Albert Wohlstetter et al., *Nuclear Policies: Fuel without the Bomb*, Cambridge, Mass., Ballinger, 1978.

5. For more detailed discussion see Gunnar Adler-Karlsson, *Western Economic Warfare: 1947-1967*, Stockholm, Almquist and Wicksell, 1968; Jonathan B. Bingham and Victor C. Johnson, "A Rational Approach to Export Controls," *Foreign Affairs*, v. 57, Spring 1979, pp. 894-920; Knorr, *The Power of Nations*, pp. 138-146.

6. Bingham and Johnson, op. cit., p. 902.

7. For a more extensive analysis of coercion see Knorr, *The Power of Nations*, chs. 4, 6 and 7.

8. Martin Edmonds, "Gibraltar—Where Two Monologues Do Not Make a Dialogue," *Review of International Studies*, v. 7, vol. 1981, pp. 217-225.

9. The Spanish government has recently resumed negotiations with the United Kingdom. According to an agreement reached in April 1981, Spain will regain the frontier sometime in 1982 and then the two governments will negotiate to solve the problem of Gibraltar.

10. See Joseph Hajda, "The Soviet Grain Embargo," *Survival*, v. 22, Nov./Dec. 1980, pp. 253-258. This is an excellent analysis.

11. Knorr, *The Power of Nations*, p. 152.

12. For an incisive account and analysis see Robert Carswell, "Economic Sanctions and Iran," *Foreign Affairs*, v. 60, Winter 1981/82, pp. 247-265. The author served as deputy secretary of the Treasury at the time.

13. See Howard M. Katchen, "Interdependence, Convergence and the Economic Basis of Détente," *The Jerusalem Journal of International Relations*, v. 4, no. 4, 1980, pp. 13-30.

14. See Carswell, op: cit., pp. 264-265.

10

Strategic Purpose and the International Economy

Martin Shubik and Paul Bracken

The world debt crisis of the early 1980s has sparked considerable interest in the international economic system. Lesser developed countries (LDCs) have accumulated debts of approximately $700 billion and East European states have about $85 billion outstanding. (See Table 10.1 for sample estimates.) The fears—some might even call them threats—associated with such large borrowing are that a debt default by one large borrower, perhaps Mexico or Brazil, might precipitate a chain reaction among the others, causing a deep and permanent contraction in world trade and finance. While most prudent observers doubt the likelihood of such a scenario, and we agree, the mere fact that the world economic system could get into such a position so quickly, along with the demonstrated inability of most major governments to shape the events that led to this crisis, should cause concern.[1]

Derivative scenarios play on slightly different fears. Borrowing nations might form a debt cartel to enhance their bargaining power in renegotiations with lending nations. Or debtor states might not "take their economic medicine" as prescribed by the International Monetary Fund (IMF) and lending banks, leading to a sharp decline in international liquidity and resultant slower world economic growth.

These and other fears have been addressed in several forums and are among the vital concerns of most governments. But another aspect of the debt crisis has received little attention and thought. How long can questions of strategic purpose be divorced from major international economic developments such as the debt crisis? The conventional wisdom for managing the debt crisis is symptomatic of the limited conception of economic security relationships, and as such the debt crisis is a useful example of just how narrow some of these

TABLE 10.1: Foreign Debt of Selected Countries—December 1982 (in $ billions)

Country	*Debt*
Mexico	80.1
Brazil	85.5
Venezuela	29.5
South Korea	36.0
Argentina	38.0
Chile	17.2
Philippines	16.6
Taiwan	9.3
Colombia	10.3
Yugoslavia	19.3

Sources: Federal Reserve Board and the Morgan Guaranty Trust Company.

policy conceptions really are. By defining policy variables only in terms of economic growth rates, wage increases, and investment targets, more important foreign policy and security interests are pushed under the rug, where they remain in a limbo-like existence. The ideas and questions offered in this chapter are meant to bring some of these neglected economic and security relationships into the open for more direct discussion and analysis.

Whether or not it is generally recognized, policies concerning trade, investment, debt, markets, and multinational corporations are established in a framework that is almost exclusively economic. Especially in the United States, the style of "free market-government hands off" economics has more of a grounding in the hyperbole of business leaders than it does in the real world. At best the free market covers a specialized segment of the economy. To pretend that the supply and demand for defense permits the same level of discourse as the supply and demand for ice cream cones verges on the suicidal. The lip service paid to free markets, lack of government interference, and unconstrained private enterprise, even where it impinges directly upon defense is at best naive and is, in all likelihood, parochially self-serving and nationally dangerous.

The United States needs to recreate at least the infrastructure of institutions that can coordinate the information gathering and control needed between the Departments of Treasury, Defense, and State and the private sector in order to make sure that U.S. private enterprise acts in concert with U.S. public goals and needs. With the exception of a periodic determination to impose a strategic embargo on the East-bloc nations, political and economic questions are usually viewed as entirely separate.

The debt crisis is only an illustrative example of the deep disjunction that has arisen between the formulation of strategic purpose and international economic policy. In the 1970s, at the height of the energy crisis, plans and forces were organized to seize Middle Eastern oil installations in the event it became necessary. In addition to the formation of the Rapid Deployment Force (RDF), a strategic petroleum reserve (SPR) was constructed at considerable expense. Both the RDF and the SPR dominated security analyses of the oil crisis. Yet one of the most obvious features of the world financial system tended to be overlooked in these analyses; if one wanted to coerce OPEC, a better target than the oil fields would be the Swiss banks where their wealth is stored. In 1981 OPEC had more than $354 billion invested in Western economies.[2] While the image of landing RDF parachutists on top of Swiss banks may be absurd, the lack of consideration given to freezing these assets compared to the attention and resources devoted to creating the RDF and the SPR is striking.

The strategic implications of a complex world economic system, where enormous resources are stored in financial as well as commodity holdings, has not received the attention it deserves. Some of the trends and ideas discussed here are unpleasant, but they are nonetheless important to examine. For the next few years it is likely that there will be considerably slower economic growth in the developing world (a consequence in part of the debt situation); at the same time there will be an era of intense strain in Soviet-U.S. relations. The possibility of political upheaval therefore is potentially greater than in previous decades. While Soviet-U.S. relations may not revert to the cold war status of the 1950s, the added component of numerous unstable LDCs increases the chances of igniting the feared spark of confrontation.

DEBT, AID, AND FINANCE IN A LARGE AND DECENTRALIZED WORLD ECONOMY

The U.S. conception of interrelated military and economic security was formed in the 1950s and 1960s, at which time the world was divided into East and West. The advent of nuclear weapons seemed both to reinforce this division and to lessen the importance of nonmilitary variables in defining it. The division was reinforced because only the Soviet Union and the United States could mount the diversified technological programs necessary to build effective nuclear forces. Economic factors contributed to these bipolar security regimes in a number of ways, but they were deemphasized in comparison to more direct military considerations. The bombs, overseas bases, and the Strategic Air Command made up the core of U.S. security policy. Foreign aid, economic stockpiles, and trade embargoes against the Soviet bloc were all judged important, but less so than the tools of nuclear deterrence themselves.

Another way of looking at this period is through the evolution of what has come to be widely known as the American military-industrial complex. The cold war is often dated from the immediate postwar years when the U.S.

military rapidly demobilized, but the Soviet military did not. Throughout the late 1940s, large standing Soviet armies induced grave fears in the West about the security of Western Europe. Not until the Korean War of 1950 did the United States build up its nuclear and conventional military forces to meet this perceived threat. It is much less widely recognized that the American demobilization that occurred in 1946 was both military and economic.[3] The nation dismantled its industrial military base with dedicated efficiency. Equally important, it eliminated the elaborate bureaucracy used by the public sector to administer the wartime economy. Whole organizations, with names that are today unfamiliar to most contemporary students of security policy, were disbanded. The Office of Export Controls, the Board of Economic Warfare, the Office of the Alien Property Custodian, the U.S. Commercial Company (used for preemptive buying of strategic goods overseas), the Foreign Funds Control Office, and other similar agencies had been directed to serve U.S. security policy during the war. Their legitimacy arose from the grand tradition of a nation immersed in total war in which all of the resources of the state were brought together in an integrated geopolitical expression of strategic purpose. Identical control systems had been set up by the enemy and allies alike as an accepted way of conducting security policy.

Of course, this system was abolished following the war, so that U.S. security demobilization was both military and economic. When the Korean mobilization came in 1950, only the most feeble attempt was made to reestablish this control system, largely in the form of the Defense Production Act. Some limited standby legislation was passed to permit more extensive public-sector control of the economy for security purposes, but the sense of much of this legislation pointed to a national emergency (such as recovery following atomic attack) and not to the day-to-day conduct of security affairs.

Throughout the 1950s interest in the relationship between economics and security narrowed further, never disappearing but confining itself to a smaller set of relevant subjects. With the Vietnam War in the 1960s there was an attempt to divorce the two subjects completely, by fighting a war without any vestige of military mobilization or consequent economic controls. Seen in this light, it appears that the United States has the very opposite of an all-encompassing military-industrial complex. What has evolved is a highly specialized collection of weapons suppliers and consumers, with little or no overall geopolitical integration of the nation's many sources of power, like those manifested in the economic control system set up during World War II. With its state-controlled economy, of course, the Soviet Union has chosen a very different evolutionary path.

The strategic implications of debt, finance, and markets are today almost considered to be relics of a bygone era, an age when leaders saw an intimate connection among these subjects. One of the primary reasons for this development is that the bipolar world of the 1950s and 1960s no longer exists. The world has become far more pluralistic in political and economic terms. Yet the bipolar security regime lingers, obliged by strategic technology to involve all nations should the ultimate showdown ever occur. A curious mismatch exists between the pluralistic world economy on the one hand and the bipolar security regime on the other. Security, which in a more geopolitical age was thought to incorporate economic subjects, has appeared to go its own way and have little or nothing to do with the regulation of corporate behavior, trade, and finance.

Markets take up the coordination that once would have been conducted between bipolar powers, using an elaborate public-sector control system. The public-sector economic control apparatus described earlier has its counterpart today in a largely private-sector economic control system that relies on international markets, instant communications, and business-to-business contacts to coordinate international economic affairs. In a pluralistic world, markets have become more rather than less important.

The growth and dimensions of international market and business activity are not evident to most people. Although most people are aware that world population is growing rapidly, which necessarily stimulates an increased level of exports and imports, the growth in international economic activity far exceeds that needed merely to serve a growing volume of world trade. For example, on an average business day the amount of international trade among all countries approximates $10 billion when the world is not in recession. On the other hand, international financial flows on a typical day average around $210 billion. What is all of this money doing? Much of it is in the foreign exchange market; some is used to underwrite trade or balance the books of multinational corporations; and in recent years some has been lent to developing countries on the syndicated loan market. The point is that international economic activity and markets, especially financial activity, have become enormously important.

The combination of a governmental "hands off" attitude toward security aspects of economic affairs, especially international financial affairs, and the increasing importance of markets and associated business issues has led to a strange situation. The strength of a modern democratic country such as the United States is also partially a measure of its weakness. Instinctively, we wish to keep politics and economics separate, even when it is painfully obvious that it is logically and technologically not feasible to do so. There are many areas of policy where this separation mainly serves artificially to distort fundamental issues.[4]

One such example is in the relative shares of public versus private capital flows and their effect on U.S. foreign aid. U.S. aid programs were conceptualized in the 1950s when most countries had virtually no other alternative but to turn to the United States.[5] At that time the problem in the world economy was viewed primarily as consisting of barriers to international capital mobility. The reason for establishing a World Bank was to create capital flows to developing nations that were denied access to most private investment areas. Academic studies of this period emphasized the higher returns available on overseas investments, which encouraged U.S. companies to operate abroad.

The situation has changed dramatically since that time. In today's international economy, private capital flows vastly outdistance public-sector flows. In 1982, syndicated loans from European, Japanese, and U.S. banks amounted to $82 billion. Direct corporate investment, short-term interbank loans, Eurobonds, and other mechanisms all reinforce this basic trend.

With little difficulty, a country such as Argentina was able to amass $33 billion in incremental debt between 1978 and 1982, about $5 billion of which went to army purchases. Compared to a foreign-aid grant or a public-sector loan, the funds came with few strings attached to their use. Unlike many aid grants or public-sector loans, syndicated private bank loans can be executed in a very short period of time, without the lengthy bureaucratic approvals of the former. No wonder the Carter administration's attempt to employ economic and trade sanctions against Argentina in the late 1970s over human rights and nuclear proliferation matters proved so ineffective! As international bankers are so fond of saying, money is fungible. It has been argued that attempts at economic coercion may produce behavior directly opposite to that desired. But economic leverage is bound to be even more ineffective when the object of coercion can raise huge sums from a decentralized world market whose private-sector control apparatus is indifferent to strategic purpose.

The Argentine case is an example of the effects of the shifting balance between public- and private-sector capital flows. For the 35-year period between 1945 and 1980, U.S. foreign and military assistance to all the nationals of Latin America amounted to $15.3 billion, or about $450 million per year on average.[6] Between 1977 and 1981, U.S. private banks alone lent approximately $80 billion to these countries. Over the same period, aggregate loans from all banks to Latin America amounted to $278 billion. Private capital flows have come to dwarf public-sector flows, and with this imbalance comes a corresponding and inevitable decline in the possibility for using economic resources to achieve strategic purposes. In the late 1970s and early 1980s many of the most important developing countries (from a U.S. security perspective) were benefiting from the private international loan market, a market that ignored strategic considerations in determining the supply of capital.

In the summer of 1982 a precipitous change in this pattern occurred. A sudden withdrawal of credit to the major borrowing countries of Mexico, Brazil, and Argentina led to severe liquidity and debt problems in these countries. The unexpectedly long recession in the United States and the world, the oil glut, the maintenance of greatly overvalued currencies in some nations, and the psychological fears produced by the Falklands War came together to dry up the international loan market for those developing countries most in need of further loans to service their existing debt. The result was the world debt crisis.

The major borrowing nations needed financing at a time when private financial resources were sharply cut back. The immediate reaction to this state of affairs was that national governments intervened to forestall a potential collapse of the world financial system. This was done through central banks and through an agreement whereby the IMF directed private banks in the ratification of new loans to borrowing nations. The IMF itself could not possibly finance the needed amounts, but relied instead on the private sector to lend greater amounts through approval of the reform programs of the indebted countries.

The world financial system worked remarkably well in averting an immediate financial collapse following the partial suspension of repayments by major debtors. The logistics involved in coordinating the emergency loans of hundreds of private banks are considerable, and the private sector reacted very quickly to the crisis. However, two features of the debt problem deserve attention. A boom-bust cycle in private international capital flows had developed, and governments expressed little interest in the cycle until a sharp downswing took place. During the late 1970s and early 1980s, when loan activity was increasing to the major debtors, the governments of the United States and most other members of the Organization for Economic Cooperation and Development (OECD) adopted a hands-off attitude. This was done with benign interest, not ignorance; it was thought to be a good thing to recycle petrodollars, and it was also regarded as desirable to have strong capital flows going to rapidly growing third world countries. Of equal importance in this hands-off governmental policy, however, was the simple assumption that the international financial market was exclusively an economic creature with which governments had no business meddling.

While we cannot offer ready answers for such complicated issues, we note that important questions were never asked about the political consequences of a liquidity crisis in developing countries, the intervention into private capital for strategic purposes, or the possible behavior of these markets in an international political crisis. It is very curious that as world finance, trade, and debt grew to unprecedented historical levels, there was virtually no interest in addressing the strategic consequences of these trends.

One especially glaring example of the tendency to divorce economic and security issues took place in 1975 during hearings before the Senate Foreign Relations Committee. Following the first oil shock of 1974, massive OPEC funds were flowing into U.S. and European money-center banks. Senate legislation was proposed to require U.S. banks to make detailed disclosures about these deposits. One prescient fear was that OPEC countries with large deposits in U.S. banks might suddenly withdraw them, causing chaos in U.S. financial markets. Merely the threat of such action could prove catastrophic; it would not be necessary to carry out such an extreme measure. A strong lobbying effort by the banking community, however, arguing that the possibility of sudden withdrawals was so remote as to preclude any need for financial disclosures, worked against any such legislation.[7] Eventually, a much watered-down reporting system was put into effect that preserved the secrecy of the holdings of individual banks.

The bankers' need for secrecy is understandable, as it is crucial to their conduct of business. What is remarkable about these circumstances, however, is not that the bankers were proven wrong about the remote threat of sudden withdrawals (as Iran had demonstrated in 1979), but that they saw no connection between this issue and the RDF and the SPR. Effectively, the private sector made the case that business is somehow above the concerns of national security. The core argument advanced—and accepted—was not that the United States and its allies should refrain from freezing OPEC assets in an emergency, but that nations should not even collect basic data necessary to think about this question. All this hypothesizing was taking place at a time when elaborate and dangerous military contingency plans were being developed to take over the oil fields. Freezing financial assets is provocative, but it is certainly less dangerous than mounting a full-scale invasion of a nation.

A second observation on the debt crisis is that there has been little other than an economic definitions of what actually constitutes the crisis. Broadly speaking, the sense one gets from most discussions is that when for one reason or another the major lending banks do not get paid, this leads to some kind of major liquidity and trade collapse in the international economy. But this way of thinking about the debt situation, while certainly not wrong, implies that the crisis takes place only when banks do not get their money or when there is a major shock to the world financial system.

We would make a different point. The real debt crisis is political and has already occurred. Unlike the business and economic aspects of the debt situation, the political debt crisis has been poorly managed; indeed, it has been ignored by the private-sector control apparatus designed to manage the purely financial aspects of the problem. The really important debt crisis is the partial surrender of sovereignty by nations like Brazil and Mexico, an acceptance of foreign dictates about how they should run their countries. This loss of power is an interesting reversal of the increased independence given these countries during the upswing in international lending during the late 1970s. At that time, Brazil, Mexico, and others could use the international markets to increase their own economic maneuverability. Now they have to do the reverse, following the directions of an IMF-led consortium of private banks in order to secure needed financing to pay off their old debt.

To look at the world debt crisis in this way suggests a new set of questions which we only touch on. Economic stability is seen as dependent on political stability, rather than the other way around. Signing a rescheduling agreement that carries with it severe penalties for domestic growth and improved quality of life may not be as bad as signing a military surrender treaty, but the two documents have much in common. Instead of focusing on whether or not banks are repaid, we should instead look to the literature on war termination and strategic surrender to understand the debt crisis.[8] The tendency for coalitions to be seen domestically as "patriots" or "traitors," depending on their willingness to uphold national sovereignty or to cooperate with foreign adversaries, makes a distinction that already applies to political dynamics in some debtor countries. What will be the political fate of those who sign such submissive agreements? If these signers are removed from the scene, what validity can the agreement have?

THE WORLD ECONOMY IS INTERDEPENDENT, BUT NOT MONOLITHIC

The various debtor nations do not have identical problems, nor did they get into their current situations by any common failures of policy. It is important to understand the differences that exist among the different nations in debt.[9] Brazil borrowed heavily for infrastructure improvement, while much of Argentina's borrowings went for armament purchases and capital flight.

The lending nations are themselves differentiated, however much they might need to present a unified front in debt negotiations. Political factors and regional interests inevitably intervene in the debt management process. Thus, when Japanese banks first cut back precipitously on loans to Brazil, it was U.S. banks, at governmental prodding, that started to make new loans available there, reflecting the United States' special interest in Latin America. Similarly, Britain held up on some consortium loans to Argentina in an effort to force Buenos Aires to end sanctions imposed against British companies during the Falklands War.

The idea that the world is increasingly interdependent is an attractive one, and would seem to apply with special force to the international financial system. A default in one debtor country, however, need not create the chain reaction most feared in disaster scenarios. It is dangerously simplistic to consider only two possible outcomes, either a simultaneous default among all the biggest debtors or a smooth IMF-led renegotiation in which all parties repay on schedule. With the large number of countries in debt difficulty, it is probably too optimistic to expect the latter outcome. but interdependence does not mean that if one or two nations somehow fail to play their expected parts in the rescheduling game that other debtor nations will automatically join them.

If a serious default were to occur, it is most likely to begin with a single nation. It might also be directed at the banks of a single nation, as would be the case if Argentina refused to honor debts to Great Britain. Because of the differentiation among both borrowers and lenders, a great deal of room is left for strategic behavior directed at particular nations or coalitions in this process, in spite of cross-default clauses.

It is important to isolate any shocks that do occur so that they do not threaten the stability of the entire system. Over the past decade, individual shocks have in fact been quickly isolated and managed, protecting the system as a whole. While the world economy may be interdependent, it is also surprisingly resilient. In 1982, for example, the Kuwaiti stock exchange failed. An amount estimated at $94 billion was lost in a scheme involving postdated checks. Kuwait and the surrounding Middle Eastern governments were able to absorb this shock because the financial rules of the game were rewritten overnight by rulers who correctly foresaw the dangers of such a collapse getting out of control.[10] Bank failures, the change from fixed to floating exchange rates, and sudden oil price increases all seem to teach a similar lesson: that the world financial system is robust and capable of withstanding many shocks. Our concern is less with the rules of international finance than with the rulers, those actors who have the power to make rapid changes to avert a crisis that may threaten major parts of the system.

The resilience of the world economy offers new opportunities for strategic behavior without jeopardizing the stability of the entire system. One of the main arguments against national political use of the world financial system for its own strategic purposes is that any tampering in this area threatens the foundations of world economic stability. There is a parallel in this formulation in the rigid division of the world into two blocs, East and West. In its extreme form, this type of thinking interprets any event in world politics as a loss for the East or West. Almost everyone now understands that the world is pluralistic and complicated, but in international economic policy there is still a tendency to speak as if the smallest blunder will produce a world financial collapse. Such thinking paralyzes strategic analysis because it removes all freedom for integrating noneconomic strategic purpose into national economic actions. But whether one likes it or not, an important lesson of the debt crisis has been that governments do intervene in the world of private-sector international finance for broader political and strategic purposes.

SECRECY, TRANSPARENCY, AND RESPONSIBILITY

The debt crisis has focused attention on the fact that many debtor nations use parts of the world economy for strategic purposes, to stimulate economic growth, obtain funds for arms purchases, or increase their independence from more powerful nations upon which they choose not to rely. Creditor nations, on the other hand, have been dragged into policy issues involving influence and coordination of private-sector affairs, violating long-held preferences about the inviolability of the wall that supposedly separates the public from the private sector. Yet it is reasonable to ask if such complicated policy issues are limited to this particular debt crisis, so that once this problem is solved the world can safely return to a state in which business is left to business and government is left to government.

We believe that the debt crisis is not a unique problem and that the policy issues that it raised and the need to think about contingency plans must become an accepted part of strategic analysis. The problem of defining national purpose in economic policy will not go away.

The exact circumstances leading up to the debt crisis may not be repeated. The surplus of petrodollars and the use of private money-center banks to broker loans based on these funds was a function of the world energy situation of the 1970s. In the 1970s these loans were offered at negative interest rates, making them extremely attractive opportunities. The world economic situation has since changed, with high real interest rates and a drying up of the petrodollar funds. Indeed, the problem today is clearly that debtor nations are having difficulty obtaining loans of any sort, and are paying high interest on those they do obtain.

Nevertheless, when the current recession ends there will be a reversion to strong capital flows and economic ties between the developed and the developing nations. This may not necessarily take the form of activity coordinated through the international syndicated loan market, but may instead be channeled through different mechanisms. Already, many indebted nations are loosening their restrictions on direct foreign investment by reducing taxes or by making it easier to repatriate profits. More joint ventures in the developing world between home-based and foreign corporations could occur. An especially clear recent trend has been the increasing pace of acquisitions of foreign corporations by U.S., Japanese, and European firms. Banks and insurance companies in particular are being bought by newly emergent multinational financial services companies.[11]

The development of more extensive direct investment in developing countries, the emergence of true multinational financial services firms, the growing financial orientation of all multinationals, and the increased reliance on markets in a pluralistic world mean that questions of strategic purpose in the international community are likely to be permanent, even though there is a temporary drying up of the petrodollars that led to the burgeoning debt of recent years. Regardless of how strongly one feels about the desirability of a private sector unencumbered by government interference, there are many situations like the debt crisis where it is foolish to pretend that private economic action can be divorced from broader security and political concerns. It is more foolish still to believe that there is a necessary congruence of interest among the U.S. government, international banks, and multinational corporations.

By examining several distinctive features of the major actors in international economic affairs, it may be possible to understand the underlying tension between the public and private sectors. In the expansion of financial activity by international banks and multinationals, the emphasis has been on privacy and secrecy. President Eisenhower once said that "capital has no country." The strategy of private-sector actors in the world economy has been to search for mismatches and gaps in control systems between national and international legal and financial systems. They have invented Eurodollars, offshore trusts, and other new methods of economic arbitrage between legal and political systems.

Today, large European and U.S. multinationals are the biggest users of tax havens in the Caribbean, where they can book loans and currency transactions to avoid the taxation of West European or U.S. governments. This development is usually considered only in narrow economic terms; much revenue is lost to the Internal Revenue Service, for example. But there are broader implications. As an illustration, the Cayman Islands has become a major conduit for South American capital and a center for Euromarket bookings. In 1964 there were two banks in the Caymans; in 1982 there were 360, with over 8,000 registered companies and more telex machines per capita than any country on earth.[12] Brazil was able to book in excess of $1 billion in Euroloans in the Caymans in 1982 by exploiting the secrecy and availability of capital there.

The United States is by no means the only country with offshore tax and secrecy havens constraining its ability to monitor and control events. Switzerland has long played this role for the rest of Europe. In the Middle East, Bahrain has emerged as a major offshore financial center with $60 billion in banking assets in its branches in 1982.[13] Similar offshore facilities are now being developed in the Pacific and can be expected to grow as Tokyo becomes a great financial center in the 1980s. There is nothing inherently wrong in these trends. If these centers further reduce the transparency of international finance, however, problems could emerge that are far from purely economic. While the $94 billion Kuwait stock exchange failure gives evidence of the resilience of financial systems, who would like to test this resilience with a larger speculative collapse of the Saudi Arabian system?

The secrecy that shrouds a great part of international finance allows the system to be used strategically by a nation willing to coordinate its overall dealings with the many private corporations that make up the world financial system. Such has been the long-standing Soviet tactic in its relations with Western corporations. In like manner Brazil hid some of its large debt from concerned parties by running it through secret Caribbean havens. In fact, one of the reasons the magnitude of the debt crisis did not surface until late 1982 was that the information systems used to monitor debt were seriously flawed, depending on self-reporting and bank notifications that excluded much nonbank intermediation, loans to publicly controlled companies, and other major lending sources. It may be that insufficient data and information exist in a form that would allow swift intervention to forestall the financial disasters that are the nightmare of most central banks.

In 1982, Mexico seriously abused the interbank market to gain funds to meet its short-term debt needs. The interbank market is a $1-trillion network of loans extended from one bank to another for periods of time as short as overnight deposits to as long as one year. It is a vital lubricating system of international finance because it supplies liquidity to banks, preventing the system from freezing because of temporary deposit imbalances in one part of the world.[14] In the summer of 1982, Mexico nationalized its private banks, which then had an outstanding interbank position of $6 billion. At the same time, authorities declared that no hard-currency exchanges would be permitted, thus jeopardizing repayment to those banks that had lent short-term funds to Mexico. The abuse of the interbank market, which is ten times larger than the syndicated loan market, threatened to be the mechanism for a chain reaction of default.[15] At the time the loans were made, none of the international banks extending interbank loans to Mexican private banks knew that nationalization was coming, nor did they have any measure of knowing exactly how much money Mexico had been drawing in with this tactic. Although a bank has good information on its own worldwide interbank exposure, competitive pressures prevent banks from sharing this information with one another.

The international financial system is extremely complex and decentralized. The private-sector component of this system emphasizes secrecy and privacy as a matter of course. The result is a system that is opaque as to cause and effect, levels of activity, or ultimate responsibility. There is a fundamental and irreconcilable paradox at work here between money and credit, a paradox that lies at the heart of the international financial system. One of the basic purposes of currency or of coinage such as gold is that it is basically anonymous. Trust lies not in the relationship between individuals but in the object itself. One of the fundamental features of credit, on the other hand, is that it depends upon trust, and trust is not anonymous. But the inherent secrecy of the world financial system creates numerous ways to hide strategic purpose, whether the purpose is to maximize foreign capital flows or to damage the economic security of the state.

In a crisis, such as that of Iran in 1979, the connection among knowledge, responsibility, and authority to act needs to be clear if a nation is to defend its economic security. Yet the secrecy so necessary for operating in the international economy prevents any such clarity. Specifically, the U.S. government had only a crude estimate of Iran's holdings in U.S. banks, and even less information about the exposure of individual banks. Nor had any thought been given to a broader repercussions of freezing the assets of a major OPEC nation. When Iranian assets were frozen in response to the threat of sudden massive withdrawals from the U.S. financial system, it triggered a string of bank declared defaults on Iranian loans, which in turn caused considerable political strain between the United States and its allies. The government freeze included Iranian assets held in overseas branches of U.S. banks, thereby challenging the jurisdiction of national authorities. It also led to the invocation of cross-default clauses common to international loan agreements and to the freezing of the Iranians' stake in the West Germany Krupp complex.[16] When the initial freeze order was put into effect, few officials understood the full dimensions of their actions.

The sudden withdrawal of money from the U.S. financial system by an irrational Middle Eastern government is only one possible threat to economic security, and it is one that might be manageable. The issue is not the resilience of the world economy under most circumstances, but rather the responsibility to move quickly and boldly when the occasion arises. Under current conditions, the lack of transparency in international economic operations and the notion that the U.S. government has no business in private-sector concerns has the effect of reducing the importance of strategic considerations in economic security policy. Information is a necessary prerequisite for responsible action. The world is a closed financial system and the United States is, in essence, the best (that is, the safest) game in town. For these reasons, greater integration of economic factors into strategic policy would cost the United States little in terms of foregone business profits and would substantially improve our ability to take responsible, decisive action when necessary. Along with others who have examined the problem of ultimate responsibility for preservation of financial stability, we do not believe that private markets alone can enforce this stability under all of the pressures which could arise.[17]

IMPLICATIONS FOR STRATEGY

Changes in the economic structure of the world that have led to greatly expanded levels of trade, credit, and finance over the past 25 years have important implications for the way strategies are defined for both public- and private-sector organizations. Often the line between these two groups is blurred, either directly—as with state ownership of major commercial enterprises—or indirectly—through the interdependent control linkages that couple the actions of one to the other. Indeed, tied in with traditional control institutions such as the IMF, or the Paris Club of leading industrial nations are new interlinkages arising from the mushrooming growth in international markets and from multinational corporations themselves.

The possibility of using the larger and more complex economic structures found in today's world for security purposes has received surprisingly little attention. Studies of economic security have tended to concentrate on traditional kinds of economic warfare and sanctions that are strongly biased toward some form of commodity control. Food as a weapon, arms embargoes, and controls on high-technology exports have all received considerable attention. However, a recommended strategy in this area would be to use financial instruments and flows as a new source of leverage for security reasons.

Before we consider the financial aspects of security and economic warfare, another issue needs to be discussed: the widespread perception that no form of economic sanction can influence the behavior of a nation-state.[18] The United States would have great difficulty waging any sort of "food war" and has even found if difficult to block sales of components for the Soviet natural gas pipeline. The Carter administration's attempts to enforce its human rights policy through a set of economic and diplomatic sanctions were no more successful than the British action against Argentina mentioned earlier in this essay. What then can one expect of any new tools such as financial ones?

Most of the discussion about the utility of economic sanctions misses a key point with respect to the economic security of the American people. It is our assessment that acts of economic warfare, especially those involving financial actions, are poor offensive weapons but necessary defensive weapons. Clearly, economic and financial weapons are themselves influenced by political, societal, and legal considerations. When we consider blocking accounts, confiscating assets, or renegotiating financial instruments in our jurisdiction, we have considerable control. When the assets and instruments are overseas, even in Western Europe, our control diminishes quickly. Economic sanctions and financial warfare have important reactive or second-strike characteristics because such usage hinges on provocation, which better enables the United States to overcome preexisting political obstacles. Had the Iranians not seized U.S. hostages, it would have been far more difficult to obtain the needed European cooperation in blocking Iran's financial assets.

The second-strike aspects of financial warfare are the rule rather than the exception in the United States. It is not widely known, for example, that even during World War II Washington did not move to block the financial assets of the Axis until war had been officially declared. Even though the assets in the United States of both Norway and Denmark were blocked following their submission to German attack in 1940, the United States did not dare to seize German assets. The fear was that Danish and Norwegian overseas assets, both public and private, would be withdrawn to Nazi control, negating the rights of U.S. corporations to sue for them in German courts. More important, it was feared that the overseas assets of these two countries would be confiscated by the puppet governments and fed to the German war machine.[19]

Comparable second-strike financial asset seizures were employed against China in 1950, Cuba in 1960, and Iran in 1979. While details vary, in each case there was a desire to protect the rights of U.S. citizens and corporations with possible claims in these nations, but there was also a security dimension to the seizures in that the United States did not want to return billions of dollars to countries that were extremely hostile to us. It is useful to remember in this respect that the Soviet Union has been exceedingly careful not to have overseas exposure of assets that could be seized by the United States. In fact, it was the Soviet state bank that invented the Eurodollar market in the 1950s by placing dollars in their own banks set up in London and Zurich, where they would be safe from U.S. jurisdiction under most circumstances.[20]

The reactive nature of U.S. financial warfare suggests certain directions for the security dimensions of the world economy. Instead of asking whether an arms embargo can influence a Latin American dictatorship to forego its human rights abuse, it should be a far higher priority to explore the conditions under which the United States might react to a provocation that threatened the physical or economic security of its people.

Virtually all contingency plans for the world debt crisis have centered on ways out of the crisis. Higher economic growth rates, discounting of loans, involvement of the U.S. treasury, and involvement of international organizations to underwrite more debt have all defined the bounds of policy in managing the debt crisis. There is another side to the coin, however, one that should be considered if the economic security of the United States is to be safeguarded. While plans to forestall a crisis are important, they do nothing to protect the United States in the event of a collapse or a series of defaults in which other nations try to clean out the U.S. banks. The response to such action is as old as banking itself. Plans to freeze every relevant foreign asset must be thought through beforehand, in order to avoid the rapid flight of many "hostages" before any countermeasures can be taken. World financial collapses have occurred in the past and it would be naive to believe they cannot happen again.

If a collapse were to occur, or if one or two defaults were to take place, the government would have to act quickly and boldly to protect U.S. interests and to isolate the shock. It would be an understatement to say that the U.S. government is inadequately prepared; with the "let the free market rip" philosophy and flawed monitoring systems for determining what foreign assets are under U.S. jurisdiction, it is safe to say that better planning has been given to nuclear war survival than to economic security. The absence of attention to these issues is indicative of the exceedingly narrow scope of most analyses of economics and national security. Indeed, in our literature search the most recent book on methods of seizing foreign assets was written over 30 years ago, a remarkable fact, given the enormous growth in the world financial system over the past several decades.

A major default is not the only circumstance that could force the United States into second-strike financial warfare tactics. Presently, Arab oil producers have $80 billions invested in the United States. Saudi Arabia has some $160 billion invested overseas. Kuwait has unknown billions invested in the U.S. and West European industries. If a coup or invasion of the Middle East took place, would the United States stand idly by as such enormous assets were withdrawn, possibly to be put under the control of major enemies? Is it conceivable that the RDF could be sent to the Middle East without precipitating major attempts to pull assets out of the West? With the Iran-Iraq War continuing, it seems more than prudent to anticipate financial crisis dynamics. Just as in 1940 and 1950, when the United States was forced to act to prevent major assets from falling under the control of the Axis and China respectively, this concern over finances poses an immediate security problem in the fullest sense of the term.

Finally, financial warfare is even relevant in a Soviet-U.S. confrontation. While a nuclear showdown between the United States and the Soviet Union might be thought to dwarf any financial issues, there are cases where economic considerations become important. In a serious nonwar crisis, Moscow might intimidate European powers into acting against U.S. economic interests. The Soviet purpose might be less to destroy the dollar than to sow panic and chaos, reinforced by a precipitous Eastern-bloc default.[21] Another goal might be to force Washington into rigid exchange controls, thereby exposing the divergent interests of the government and multinational banks and corporations and further sowing dissension and disunity. If a prolonged political crisis took place involving a nuclear alert but not a nuclear detonation, issues of financial stability and public morale could become critical.

While the above examples of the direct connection between economics and security deal with extremely serious contingencies, there are daily manifestations of the coupling of security and economic issues that are often missed or given less importance than they deserve because of the overly narrow conception of economic security. The simple question of the location of "hostages" is very fruitful for understanding international political actions. By hostages we mean those physical and financial assets that are at risk of being blocked, confiscated, or lost. Given the large overseas investments in the modern international economy and the interlinked communication network that moves hundreds of billions of dollars around the globe daily, there are today more hostages than at any time in world history. Some of these would be easy to snatch in a crisis—one thinks of mines in South America or manufacturing plants in Asia. Others are far more elusive because of modern financial transfer technology. For example, multinational corporations can transfer enormous sums of money almost instantly through financial communication networks that can direct resources into safe havens. The point is that a complicated structure of overseas hostages exists with categories, distinctions, and implications that have received almost no attention in terms of economics and security.

Overseas exposure in physical and financial assets can shape political actions even if the threat of seizure or loss is only implicit. For example, British governmental actions in setting oil prices in 1982 must have been influenced by the potential damage to the enormous British stake in Nigeria. If oil prices had continued their slide, revenues to Nigeria would have shrunk even more than they did. The political situation there was, and is, dicey. Political turmoil would have put British assets at risk. An important feature of this example and most others is that it is not just governmental exposure that counts. British governmental loans in Nigeria may be less important than the exposure of British corporations and citizens. Since the privately controlled international economy so greatly outdistances government loans and assistance, it is this sector that offers the greatest risk of exposure. However, this exposure is most difficult to estimate because of the secrecy and opaque nature of private international economic activity described earlier. But it may be just such aggregate exposure that determines strategic actions at the national level, because domestic corporations and citizens have a powerful voice in shaping national policy.

It is not hard to think of examples in which overseas asset exposure, both public and private, is a major force in national strategy. The French exposure in Iraq consists of loans, direct investment, export credits, and probably much more that is not centrally recorded because of the secrecy and privacy surrounding international finance. If Iraq were to lose the war to Iran, it would be a financial catastrophe for the French, coming at a time when they are hard pressed economically for other reasons. This seems to be one of the reasons behind the "loan" of five French Super-Etendard fighters capable of carrying Exocet missiles to Iraq. French exposure in Iraq, in the form of billions of dollars of physical and financial assets controlled by both the public and private sectors, may now be so great that Paris may be committed to back Baghdad to the limit of French power.[22]

A clear implication for security strategy from this and other examples is that intelligent action may require estimates of the magnitude of foreign exposure among nations. It is hard to get such information, even about foreign exposure in the United States. Unless better information systems are established, it will be difficult to assess some of the fundamental forces driving security policy. At a deeper level, more attention should be given to the economic underpinnings of security in the world. Instead of concentrating attention exclusively on a small number of accepted economic security issues, such as food and oil or industrial mobilization capabilities, a broader conception of security and economics is needed, one which takes account of private capital flows and exposure, second-strike economic warfare tactics, and the decentralized interdependent nature of the international economy.

CONCLUDING POLICY ISSUES

Policy differs from strategy by including the full set of organizational and contextual issues necessary for determining particular courses of action. The changes in the world economy and the implications for strategy lead to many policy problems, two of which are raised here. First, there is no organizational focal point in the U.S. government that integrates economic issues with diplomatic and military considerations from a long-range national security perspective. Most outside observers have concluded that there is not even a coherent view taken of international economic policy. Adding problems associated with strategic purpose only compounds existing deficiencies. As argued earlier, these problems are not going to evaporate when the current world recession ends. Rather, the problems are embedded in the fact that the world political economy is growing more pluralistic, while the superpower security regime remains dominated by nuclear weapons. This mismatch—between world political economy and superpower military systems—is unlikely to change soon.

Since problems of economic security are unlikely to go away, it is time to take them more seriously. One way to do this is to establish suitable authority within the government for dealing with them in a coordinated manner. Realistically, the prospects are not promising. Authority for economic policy is highly fragmented within the government. There is no support for government intervention into areas considered to be the proper domain of private corporations. If one's philosophy is "to let the free market rip," then there is no reason to set up government control organizations to influence events. We are not enthusiastic about extensive government interference in private affairs, but if private affairs produce security problems, then it seems silly to cling to an outdated rhetoric. One of the ironic features of current reform proposals for the Joint Chiefs of Staff (JCS) is that they focus almost exclusively on the military dimensions of national security. Whether a reform of the JCS would lead to greater military efficiency is an open question, but it should not be viewed as the most important question. An improvement in military efficiency is welcome, but it is less important than the need for an integrated security organization that synthesizes military, diplomatic, and economic factors into a coherent action policy. Without this synthesis, concentration of greater power in the JCS may only lead to disproportionate emphasis on military factors at the expense of economic and political ones.

A second policy issue deals more with U.S. national style in business and economics than with questions of organization. While the United States did erect an enormous public-sector control system to administer an economy for security ends during World War II, it is neither possible nor desirable to duplicate this system today. That the Soviet Union has such a system is immaterial; in fact, it probably contributes so many economic inefficiences that it may actually work to our advantage. What all of this suggests for U.S. policy is that we should accept the basic private orientation of our economic affairs when designing control systems for managing the economic component of security; but where possible, the government should leverage the large private sector for security ends rather than trying to substitute for it. As an example, the imaginative use of insurance and reinsurance, especially political risk insurance, could be used to target private investments into areas that served a broader strategic purpose. Some of this is done today, but its scale is relatively small compared with what it could be. Privately offered political risk insurance is offered, but it is usually structured for profit rather than for strategic purpose.

Other government institutions could try to leverage the large private sector rather than remaining wedded to rhetoric of government-funded Marshall Plans, which are exceedingly unlikely to receive public or congressional support. In a larger sense, what is needed is a structure for a new partnership between the public and private sectors, where the broader responsibility of the former is backed up by the vitality of the latter. Such a partnership offers a better way to deal with questions of economics and security than recreating an enormous public-sector apparatus.

Finally, there is an issue that is too diffuse to be considered a policy question at all. That is, problems of economics and security need to be thought about, analyzed, and debated at a much broader level than has traditionally been the case in the United States. Security studies must not focus on an increasingly narrower set of problems that lose sight of the most important feature of the pluralistic and dangerous world we live in. Questions must be raised at the appropriate level of discussion before any definitive answers can be offered.

President Truman observed the need for one-handed economists. This chapter offers one-handed advice. The U.S. financial-economic control system is inadequate. We need not only discuss the inadequacies, as done here, but take steps to build an infrastructure for the 1980s and 1990s that will at least provide standby government control. Such a plan calls for coordinated action by Treasury, Defense, State, CIA, and White House and the development of intelligence capabilities. The time to undertake these steps is now.

NOTES

1. Overviews of the debt crisis and its origins can be found in Pedro-Pablo Kuczynski, "Latin American Debt," *Foreign Affairs*, Winter 1982-83, pp. 344-364; and in Susan Strange, "The Credit Crisis: A European View," *SAIS Review*, Summer-Fall 1983, pp. 171-181.

2. U.S. Treasury Department estimates, as reported in *New York Times*, February 28, 1983.

3. We have been aided in our thinking on this point by our colleague Sidney Winter, and also by discussions on economics and national security at the Yale Seminar on Security Policy.

4. For an extended discussion of related issues, see Charles E. Lindblom, *Politics and Markets* (New York: Basic Books, 1977).

5. U.S. foreign aid policies and their evolution are analyzed in Richard L. Hough, *Economic Assistance and Security* (Washington: National Defense University Press, 1982).

6. "Annual Report of the National Advisory Council on International Monetary and Financial Policies," 1981. This annual report is a very useful source of data on U.S. economic and security assistance efforts over many years.

7. Anthony Sampson, *The Money Lenders* (New York: Viking Press, 1981), pp. 123-128.

8. Specifically, we have in mind such works as Paul Kecskemeti, *Strategic-Surrender: The Politics of Victory and Defeat* (Stanford, Calif.: Stanford University Press, 1958); and Fred C. Iklé, *Every War Must End* (New York: Columbia University Press, 1971). For a useful statement about the politics of the debt crisis, see also, Henry Kissinger, "Saving the World Economy," *Newsweek*, January 24, 1983, pp. 46-49.

9. These differences are carefully expounded in Barbara Stallings, "Latin American Debt: What Kind of Crisis?" *SAIS Review*, Summer-Fall 1983, pp. 27-39.

10. This is a fascinating tale involving a Mr. Jassim Al-Mutawa, who has gone into personal bankruptcy to the tune of $10.5 billion before reaching his thirtieth birthday. See "Jassim, Jassim," *Financial Times*, February 1, 1983, p. 13; *Financial Times*, February 23, 1983. p. 8, and *New York Times*, February 18, 1983.

11. For a discussion of the business factors driving in this direction, see Theodore Levitt, "The Globalization of Markets," *Harvard Business Review*, May-June 1983, pp. 92-102; and Philip Wellons, "International Bankers: Size Up Your Competition," *Harvard Business Review*, November-December 1982, pp. 95-105.

12. U.S. Senate Committee on Governmental Affairs, *Crime and Secrecy: The Use of Offshore Banks and Companies*, 98th Cong., 1st sess., 1983, p. 25.

13. For a description of the offshore situation in the Middle East, see A.S. Gerakis and O. Roncesvalles, "Bahrain's Offshore Banking Center," *Economic Development and Cultural Change*, January 1983, pp. 271-293.

14. For descriptions of what is an especially obscure market to nonspecialists in international finance, see "A Job to be Remembered," *Financial Times*, March 1, 1983, p. 16; and "Eurobanks and the Interbank Market," *Bank of England Quarterly Bulletin*, September 1981, pp. 351-364.

15. "Chase Hits 'Misuse' of Interbank Market," *Financial Times*, March 1, 1983, p. 1.

16. Sampson, *The Money Lenders*, pp. 243-252.

17. Charles Kindleberger, "Dominance and Leadership in the International Economy," *International Studies Quarterly*, June 1981, pp. 242-254.

18. Different views are offered in the following works: Robin Renwick, *Economic Sanctions* (Cambridge: Center for International Affairs, Harvard University, 1981); Donald L. Losman, *International Economic Sanctions* (Albuquerque: University of New Mexico Press, 1979); and Shaheen Ayubi et al., *Economic Sanctions in U.S. Foreign Policy* (Philadelphia: Foreign Policy Research Institute, 1982).

19. Yuan-li Wu, *Economic Warfare* (New York: Prentice-Hall, 1952), pp. 95-96.

20. This began in 1954 when the Soviets sold gold for dollars and held these dollars in Soviet banks in Europe. These banks began to make dollar denominated loans to various businesses. See Martin Mayer, *The Fate of the Dollar* (New York: Signet, 1981), pp. 115-116. The legal jurisdiction over the Eurodollar market remains extremely complex and uncertain. See Gunter Dufey and Ian H. Giddy, "The Unique Risks of Eurodollars," *Journal of Commercial Bank Lending*, June 1978, pp. 50-61.

21. See Paul Bracken, "Mobilization Dynamics in the Nuclear Age," elsewhere in this volume.

22. "French-Iraqi Ties Get Closer," *Wall Street Journal*, August 19, 1983.

11

Mobilization Dynamics in the Nuclear Age

Paul Bracken

Economic mobilization for national security reasons was a much easier subject to deal with in past decades than it is today. By and large, the leadership of America's defense establishment did not really believe that mobilization *had* any role in the nuclear age. This attitude made planning easy. Attention of top officials was directed to acquisition and readiness of *standing* forces, and as so often happens in any organization, this attitude trickled down through the hierarchy so that it really took considerable nerve for anyone to even talk about mobilization in the nuclear era. To be sure, mobilization plans were maintained for the call-up of reservists and for production of some conventional forces and these plans will be reviewed later. But most of these plans did not seem to have much of a connection to America's real security needs as seen by the senior officials of the day.

What little emphasis there was given to mobilization planning in the 1950s, 1960s, and 1970s even seemed to prove the point that mobilization was all but irrelevant to national security. Nearly every study undertaken talked in terms of a three-year buildup, and this seemed ludicrous to strategists and defense officials who were concerned about the ten-minute warning of missile attack or the ten-day war in Europe. The idea of large-scale mobilization became almost an object of ridicule, of "refighting World War II with thermonuclear weapons."

By the late 1970s, however, a (very) few students of strategy began to develop some different ideas. The gist of their argument was that mobilization might be a useful tool of national security *before* a shooting war started, or as a response to a limited strategic reverse for the United States. What is so surprising is that this idea was not appreciated earlier. After all, the United States mobilized, in a limited sense, as a response to the Berlin crisis of 1961, where forces were built up in the preceding months. It proved an effective way to manage that crisis. And in Korea in 1950, the United States mobilized as a response to initial reverses, and as preparation for a worldwide war that had not yet begun, but appeared imminent. In both of these examples ample time *was* available to bring mobilization to bear on the problem, giving the lie to the "common sense" view of the irrelevance of mobilization in the nuclear age. What is ironic is that the United States has used mobilization repeatedly since 1950, yet the planning mentality of this era has never grasped this fact, and has instead devoted overwhelming attention to alert standing forces.

This chapter will take a hard look at the idea of mobilization in the nuclear age. Our discussion will be descriptive rather than directive, meaning that the flaws in a mobilization strategy as we see them will be examined explicitly. There is a tendency in the analysis of national security policy to give only one side of the picture, with the downside risks attendant to a position being withheld. In the course of examining the pitfalls of using a mobilization strategy, we will discover problems that are by no means unique to this particular strategy.

The chapter first defines what a mobilization in the nuclear age is, and how it might functionally be used. Following this, some of the dislocations and difficulties associated with mobilization are discussed. These deal with some interesting, and very neglected issues: the economic, and especially financial impact of a major nuclear crisis wherein a mobilization might be involved, and the operation of America's nuclear forces during a protracted crisis. This latter issue is not the usual one of "protracted nuclear war," but rather the operation of the forces under the highest alert conditions whilst a mobilization is underway. Here, there is an analogy with the "cover forces" of World War I that protected frontiers while major mobilizations were occurring on the home front.

Following this the question of national will is raised. More than in any other area this may be a key vulnerability if for no other reason than that the public reaction to these total emergency situations may cause a shock reaction that swamps any political direction. It is just this type of problem that suggested the term "mobilization dynamics" for the chapter title.

Finally, the problem of institutionalizing a mobilization strategy into American defense policy is discussed. The difficulty of establishing a mobilization base suitable for meeting the needs outlined earlier, with a defense industrial base designed for producing standing forces only is addressed and offered as a key planning problem. More worrisome even than this are the absence of administrative and training mechanisms for thinking through the problems of mobilization. Conclusions for the entire chapter are then presented.

MOBILIZATION IN THE NUCLEAR AGE

As used here, a *mobilization* is defined as the rapid assembly, production, or deployment of a superior force of military arms. The mobilization of American industry in World War II is in some ways typical, but the efforts during the Korean War are far more interesting for our purposes. During the Korean War both nuclear and conventional armaments were produced on a major scale. Mobilizations of current interest could last months and even years, not just the days and weeks it would take for a manpower call-up of reserve forces to reinforce a war in the Middle East or in Europe. While short-term crises employing stockpiled armaments are not precluded from examination, they are mainly examined in comparison with options requiring a much greater length of time.

Broadly speaking, most studies of mobilization undertaken by the Pentagon during the 1960s and 1970s focused on just this kind of question, that is, to what extent the production potential of America's defense industry could substitute for weapons deployed in the field. The subject of interest here, however, is broader, for it includes the political and arms control effects of relying on mobilization, as well as more narrow questions of substitutability. Sometimes the terms "strategic mobilization" or "mobilization war" are employed to convey the more expansive use of mobilization intended here. Definitions are always problematic, but the crucial features of a mobilization in the nuclear age which must be accounted for are its deterrent and threat value, and not merely its capability-enhancing characteristics. It is thus not exclusively concerned with aircraft and tank production rates, but with the broader political and military consequences of invoking rapid build-ups and production increases.

There is an interesting contrast between a mobilization and the nuclear forces. Basically, a mobilization relates to a slow motion war while the nuclear forces relate to conflict that will be over in hours. Despite the attention recently given to the topic of protracted nuclear wars, there is little doubt that mainstream thinking about nuclear war has centered on campaigns that are measured by the flight times of nuclear missiles and bombers. In sharp contrast, even the mobilization of reserve military manpower would require much greater time than this. Should new weapons be produced, the time required would increase greatly, perhaps to several years. It is ironic that the development times for new nuclear weapons systems have been growing considerably, so that it often now takes well over a decade before a new system can be deployed. At the same time, the duration of a war where such weapons could be used is shrinking as the nuclear forces become more quick-reacting and as they become vertically integrated with warning and assessment sensors. An odd situation is reached wherein systems needing in excess of a decade for development are to be used in a period of a few hours or less.

As both superpowers move into an era where, for all practical purposes, there will be a de facto dependence on "launch on warning" nuclear strategies for protection of land-based missile forces we should stop and ask ourselves about the general reliance, not to mention safety, of depending on such quick-reacting strategies. Slow-motion strategies could be of more value in many situations. Our concern is thus directed not only to mobilization in itself, but equally important, as an alternative to the precipitous employment of nuclear weapons. In this view the very thing most critics of mobilization see as its chief drawback, its slowness, is offered as a positive advantage. The extent to which Soviet and American nuclear forces depend on ultra-fast decision making for their survival is not generally appreciated, and the greatest need of American national security is the development of some means for breaking the rapid momentum leading to the nuclear decision point.[1] This is a critical consideration in our interest in mobilization. For it is not whether tanks can be produced at 3000 copies per month, but rather, whether a series of interlocking nuclear alerts during some political crisis might lead both the United States and the Soviet Union into a move-countermove sequence of actions ultimately ending in catastrophe. The parallel with the now familiar way in which the interlocking mobilization of World War I led to war is not with the use of industrial and economic mobilization today. Instead, World War I style mobilizations are more analogous to the ratcheting up of the American and Soviet DEFCON systems in a crisis, as each nation takes protective actions which threaten instant nuclear attack on the other. While it took the Kaiser's Army 17 days to mobilize in 1914, it now takes only about 17 minutes to produce the analogous reinforcing alerts in the nuclear forces. Mobilization in the nuclear age is therefore best viewed as an alternative to the use of even worse options involving nuclear weapons.

SOME SCENARIOS

The most common objection to a mobilization strategy in the nuclear age rests upon the seemingly common sense observation that a nuclear war, or even a large conventional war, between the superpowers would be so intense and devastating that the American industrial base which proved decisive in World War II would be of no use whatsoever. For this reason America's defense industrial base has been organized to produce weapons in peacetime for use in wartime. Very little high level attention has been given to the role of American industry in a transwar period. For a few years, in the early 1950s, the U.S. Army advanced the different idea that American industry would be used *after* an atomic war. In this scenario, a war would see mutual atomic strikes by long-range bombers on the urban-industrial areas of each nation. This would be followed by a month-long, or even a year-long, mobilization of whatever survived the atomic attack, or whatever could be reconstituted after the attack, to again produce a large army to regain lost territory in Europe. Whether or not this idea ever made any sense is something we will not go into now. With small arsenals of atomic weapons it may not have been completely implausible. However, the advent of the hydrogen bomb, and the expansion in size of the nuclear arsenals put this argument to rest as a practical matter. We say "as a practical matter" because since the early 1950s (until *quite* recently), there has been an increasing aura of unreality about mobilization planning. It has been disconnected from the central themes of American national security policy.

However, mobilization planning did continue throughout the 1960s and 1970s, and it is distressing to see how much of this "planning" has been wasted by looking at problems of industrial hardening to nuclear attack, post-attack construction of naval and army forces, or mobilization for some narrow purpose such as supplying the needs or victory in a particular theater. If mobilization is to make any contribution to America's security, some hard facts must be faced. Realistically, no one is going to take seriously calls for hardening America's factories against the effects of Russian missiles, or for acting as if a major American mobilization to meet the needs of a war in the Middle East against Soviet forces will not produce a completely changed political and strategic world. While it may be necessary to assign these problems to some obscure bureaucratic agencies inhabited by retired colonels, these are not the kinds of issues that will attract the attention of the best minds, or that will produce actions to make mobilization as relevant as nuclear deterrence is to our security.

But rationales exist for mobilization planning other than that of a thermonuclear version of World War II. Let us ask ourselves precisely what it is that has prevented the Soviet Union from seizing Berlin or overrunning Iran at any time since 1945. Many people would respond that the Strategic Air Command (SAC) is what stops Moscow from such major provocations. This is almost surely wrong. What restrains Soviet leaders from such actions is far more likely the fear of initiating an overwhelming American reaction that would cause a search for many ways to respond to the Soviets. Chiefly, on any given day the Soviets do not "take Berlin" because they do not want to produce a concentration of America's political and economic energies focused against Moscow's interests. This sets the stage for mobilization, for such a provocative Soviet action would create the conviction in the United States that major war was likely, or even imminent. And if a major conflict with the Soviet Union suddenly appeared likely the American government would be prepared to spend immense sums of money on defense. This scenario is similar to that which took place during the Korean War. At that time Congress was debating whether to spend \$14 or \$16 billion for defense. Following the North Korean invasion of the South, and after American involvement, Congress was catalyzed into voting for \$50 billion for defense in the first year, and \$62 billion in the second.

The most important consequence of this fourfold increase in defense spending was its effect on the Soviet Union, and not on North Korea. Soviet losses of weapons in Korea were insignificant compared to the shift in world military power that resulted from the American commitment of $60 billion for defense. For these immense defense budgets were not devoted exclusively to the ground campaign in Korea. Large shares were devoted to research and development, and to an expansion of America's nuclear arsenal. The jump in defense spending ultimately made possible the development over the next decade of the nuclear stockpile, the modernization of SAC, the Atlas, Polaris, and Minuteman missiles, several intermediate range ballistic and cruise missiles, three major early warning systems, and a score of other programs which directly threatened Soviet security. Just as important, the increase helped create the American military-industrial complex with its technological prowess in the field of defense armaments. In effect, then, the large defense expenditures of the early 1950s sowed the seeds for a rapid shift in the world balance of military power. It bought an American military superiority which lasted by all accounts until the mid-1970s.

Mobilization could be a useful policy for meeting situations involving a long period of worsening relations, minor and major provocations, and hostile actions short of general war. Naturally, there can be no guarantee that a long preparatory period will be available. But strategic planning must consider situations other than short intense wars. The attention given to a short war in Europe, and to the one-hour, Single Integrated Operational Plan (SIOP) exchange scenario make it even more important to consider slow-motion options such as mobilization. The basic scenario for using the mobilization option is then a peacetime series of confrontations, analogous to a return to the cold war, but on a more intense level of competition. This could involve a sequence of minor acts which culminate in some crisis involving actual Soviet military force which necessitates an American response, for example, a limited territorial conquest in an area where the United States possessed little conventional military capability.

Specific scenarios for mobilization are now easy to imagine. Suppose that following a long period of worsening relations between the United States and the Soviet Union, Berlin was militarily seized by Russian or East German forces, producing thousands of casualties within the city. As the Soviets maintain 20 divisions in East Germany, and they could easily reinforce these, there is little point in mounting a counterattack with the four and a half American divisions to free Berlin. An escalation and threat manipulation response could be exercised, whereby a small column of American forces would attempt to reach Berlin. Yet if the Soviets had enough initiative to seize Berlin, it is hard to imagine that they would back down before a small American probing force. Moreover, a small probe force could not do very much even if it did get through. What would likely happen in this scenario is that the Pentagon would dust off some old war plans calling for the probing action described above, to be followed in the event of a rebuff by a launching of the NATO general strike plan. Although such a plan may sound like a good one in peacetime, its flaws would become fatally apparent in a crisis. No president of the United States is going to launch a nuclear attack on the Soviet Union, or even on Soviet forces in East Germany, as a response to a Soviet seizure of Berlin, no matter how bloody and ruthless that seizure might have been. What, then, could be done?

Following the lines of the mobilization strategy the president could declare a state of national emergency, and could then order a full alert of America's strategic and conventional forces. He could then request Congress to authorize an immense increase in the defense budget. If the Korean scenario were paralleled, this would mean a fivefold increase in authorization, or in terms of the early 1980s, about a $1 trillion defense budget. Given the symbolic and long-standing importance of Berlin, this is surely a low estimate, and a $2 trillion defense budget may be more likely.

It is important to recognize that in this scenario no nuclear bombs are landing on the United States. A "phony war" period might ensue, as the Soviets stayed in Berlin and as the United States mobilized. Each side might be too scared to initiate wholesale attack, or each might be desperately searching for some kind of negotiated face-saving settlement to the crisis. Of course, the military and political situation would be extremely tense, and might explode into all-out war at any moment. Yet the rationale of the mobilization strategy is that it is a slow-motion option which does not force the other side into major nuclear retaliation as would an American limited nuclear strike against, for example, the Soviet oil industry or army units in Eastern Europe. The escalatory effects of even a small limited nuclear option do not need to be elaborated upon.

Other scenarios for mobilization easily come to mind. A Soviet invasion of Iran is something about which the United States could do relatively little. Even if we committed a few divisions, there is the possibility that they could be defeated by superior Soviet ground forces, at which point nuclear weapons would again be the only means capable of inflicting prompt damage on Russian forces. But the dangers of uncontrollable escalation would be confronted again, because any nuclear strike could start a chain reaction of "small" nuclear exchanges. In a world where there were only a few thousand nuclear weapons available to each side such escalation ladder bargaining games might be played, but I don't think so. In a world where each side possesses tens of thousands of nuclear weapons, as is the case today, and where we are just beginning to comprehend how real command and control systems function, beginning to climb the escalation ladder of nuclear conflict looks more like an obscene joke than a serious strategy.

In the above scenarios the main functions of a mobilization strategy were to serve as an alternative to all-out war. Other functions could also be well served by mobilization. Some mobilizations might be directed at winning a theater battle, either with American forces or surrogate forces. In this case there could be an additional need to mobilize nuclear or conventional supporting forces so as to enhance deterrence in other theaters. Mobilization might thus be used to make sure that a shooting war be confined to a single theater.

Special kinds of narrowly focused or limited mobilizations also seem plausible. For example, if an intense confrontation led to direct threats to seize or neutralize oil flows from the Middle East, or to other supplies of critical raw materials, a concentrated effort to deploy conventional forces necessary for protecting these supply lines would be called for. A major expansion of the Marine Corps, including air and sea projection forces, might be the appropriate response. Instead of taking the eight years adjudged necessary to organize an effective Rapid Deployment Force, this time might be compressed into six months to one year. Whereas in a business-as-usual environment, money is scarce but time is available, in a mobilization environment, time would be scarce and money readily available.

Another form of specialized mobilization might arise from a technology race, much as the race to launch an earth satellite in 1957 and 1958 had strong national security overtones. Today, some analysts are already convinced that the United States ought to begin a crash program to acquire space-based laser weapons, and even exotic particle beam weapons.

Mobilization for political influence is another function of great importance. An example was President Kennedy's decision to mobilize reserve forces and to take other military preparations during the 1961 Berlin crisis.[2] This, of course, was not an all-out industrial mobilization, for it only amounted to bolstering U.S. troops in Europe over a period of a few months. To some people it would not even qualify as a mobilization, but to the president it *was* a functionally useful buildup of military force. Reserves were called up, emergency preparedness measures were undertaken, and war reserve material stocks were increased.

So far, little has been said about what a mobilization might look like in the nuclear age. Broadly speaking, a mobilization in the 1980s would look quite different from the mass production industrial mobilization of World War II. A far more capital-intensive mobilization would generally be needed today. Beyond short term needs, such as the calling up and arming of reservists, it could conceivably be oriented toward an overwhelming buildup of long-range nuclear forces, thick ballistic missile defense systems, or massive antisubmarine warfare barrier systems. The assembly line production of thousands of nuclear cruise missiles and development of a dominant capability for a war in space are other options which could exploit special talents. The shock value alone of an American Congress authorizing a multitrillion dollar defense budget would have an important effect upon an opponent's willingness to negotiate a settlement to a crisis. The threat value of this type of mobilization to deter an enemy from engaging in provocative acts in the first place is itself a crucial issue.

One objection frequently raised is the escalatory and dangerous character of exercising the kind of mobilization described here. But this is precisely the purpose of mobilization—to be escalatory and dangerous. Large mobilizations would only be employed in the most extreme crises, such as when resorting to nuclear strikes was also under consideration. One of its main advantages is that it temporizes, rather than speeding up the pace of the crisis. Accompanied by a declaration of national emergency, it could provide extended time for negotiations while communicating American resolve, while preventing a total deescalation. Because precise settlement terms of the crisis would not be detailed at the outset, American options would be preserved for a relatively long time. This might allow for more limited demands involving achievable aims. Alternatively, following the initiation of a mobilization, the Soviets might feel compelled to "buy us off." In other words, Moscow might wish to end the crisis well short of a completed American mobilization in order to prevent attainment of American superiority. Termination of a mobilization could be based upon negotiation or ultimatum. The main point is that a mobilization could be employed to slow down a crisis, averting the possibility of a twenty-minute showdown conducted over the hot line.

The other most frequently mentioned objection to the kind of mobilization described here is the ability of a nuclear-armed opponent to preempt before it could get underway. This is a possibility that must be taken seriously, for there are no guarantees in this business. However, if no nuclear weapons had yet been launched, there would be strong inhibitions against crossing this threshold, especially because each side would preserve its own retaliatory force. Even if limited or battlefield nuclear weapons had been employed, and strikes on homelands somehow avoided, a mobilization could be implemented as an excuse to deescalate. If theories of victory, or even escape from annihilation were beginning to be doubted, both sides might be eager, even desperate, for a way to instigate an ad hoc cease-fire. But as already mentioned, there can be no guarantees in these new and bizarre situations. One feature of a major mobilization would then be the alerting of nuclear forces, or even the development of emergency cover forces that bolster deterrence against nuclear attack. Some implications of this are described later.

In summary, a mobilization could prove useful in a multitude of political-military situations. Rapid armament buildup induced by provocation, treaty abrogation, or some other stimulus would offer definite advantages not found with the most often considered alternatives, such as limited use of nuclear weapons. Little or no large-scale combat might take place; rather there would be a maneuvering for position based upon the respective armament buildups. This could involve the dispatch of massive conventional forces to Europe during a future Berlin crisis or the construction of strategic forces to alter the world balance of military power. The mobilization strategy would not, of course, be useful for bolt-from-the-blue surprise attacks. For deterring such attacks, competent standing forces are required. But this is an issue that is well understood, and one that has been studied at great length in all of its many manifestations. Our belief is that such surprise attacks are among the least likely of any kind of conflict, and that provocations where mobilization could play a key role are among the more interesting and overlooked of any in the nuclear age.

DISLOCATION AND STRESSES

The discussion of mobilization and scenarios where it could be employed are intended to convey what seems like a truly bizarre idea, that mobilization war, and the "nation in arms" are concepts not made obsolete by the nuclear age. The long history of harnessing a nation's economic and industrial power that began with the Napoleonic Wars and continued with two world wars in this century is a history that is still very much with us. While the types of weapons produced in a mobilization would be very different today, and the functions for which a mobilization was intended would change from the past, there are surely other major differences as well. The temporizing effect of a mobilization raises the question of just what such a world would be like, and indeed of the tremendous shocks that would be inflicted on the economies of the nations involved.

The hypothesis we advance is that it is myopic to consider the economic consequences of mobilization solely in terms of fractions of gross national product allocated to defense, increased aircraft production, and tradeoffs, between the civilian labor force and military manpower. None of these captures the magnitude of the crisis faced when a large mobilization is undertaken. The core question is really: What are the problems of national cohesion during a protracted mobilization and nuclear crisis, and how do particular defense actions (such as alerts) affect this? The Cuban Missile Crisis lasted for little more than a week in its public manifestations, and the 1973 nuclear alert during the Yom Kippur War lasted but a day. But what if a nuclear showdown lasted six months? And what if it involved going to the highest nuclear alert levels in the United States and Western Europe, something that has never even remotely come close to happening?

At the highest levels of alert, all commercial air traffic in the United States and Europe would probably have to be grounded. The National Guard and Reserve units would be called up with hundreds of thousands of soldiers airlifted to Western Europe. Special demolition plans around the borders of the Soviet Union might be effected to close down or flood invasion corridors. Nuclear bombers might be kept on continuous airborne alert, as they were during the Cuban Crisis of 1962, or dispersed to secondary civilian airfields.

Since the Soviet Union has never gone on even as much an alert as the United States, it is difficult to know what to expect. Would going on alert be interpreted as going to war? Would they reinforce their European or Chinese fronts? Would they release thousands of tactical nuclear weapons to forward military units, just in case they were needed for prompt use? The fact that we have so little experience in knowing what to expect during a Soviet nuclear alert makes it extremely difficult to interpret the evidence when they actually do go on alert.

What will happen to the world economy during the protracted confrontations visualized in the mobilization scenarios? As of today, there average about $270 billion a day in world foreign exchange flows, mainly between the United States and Western Europe. In a crisis, this could fluctuate enormously if Western Europe seemed threatened. Scores of banks in Western Europe would find themselves unable to meet depositors' or foreign debt demands and might find continued existence precarious. Central banks could, and undoubtedly would intervene. But how successful could this be, given the scale of the capital flight and the magnitude of the potential disaster?

Insurance policies for everything from North Sea oil rigs to Persian Gulf oil tankers would probably be terminated, and this might seriously influence the world economy. The $40 billion world reinsurance market might vanish overnight, because "everything" would be vulnerable to destruction in this environment. When Lloyd's refused to underwrite war insurance in 1936 against German attack it set in motion a sense of panic about the consequences of war. A critical question is the extent to which global financial mechanisms would instantly transmit a nuclear crisis throughout the world. How could Brazil pay its massive debt to the major New York money centers if it were denied access to borrowing in Euromarkets? How could Argentina export its grain if world shipping halted for lack of insurance and reinsurance?

The intriguing economic question is the extent to which the growing scale of military preparations would interact with internationalization of the world economy to feed upon itself, increasing the tempo and pace of a crisis. Especially if there were no lender, or insurer, of last resort, and the mobilization crisis lasted several months, a world depression could result simply as a consequence of both superpowers going on alert. It seems clear that national cohesion, especially in Western Europe, could be strained to the breaking point if these events occurred at the same time as fears of imminent nuclear or biochemical destruction were being whipped up by Soviet propaganda. The relative autarky of the Soviet Union (but not Eastern Europe) would seem to insulate it more from these forces than Western Europe or the United States.

The problems of protracted crisis and mobilization are deeply intertwined. To treat them only as problems of going on alert to enhance nuclear deterrence and of spending a larger fraction of GNP on defense is myopic in the extreme. Thus, econometric or input-output models of mobilized economies may fail to convey the seemingly simple fact that going on alert may set off a chain of consequences ranging from tens of millions of refugees on the German autobahns to a world depression. We know of not a single study of this issue.[3]

Another aspect of mobilization that causes great stress is the need to operate nuclear forces in a way that is very different from the way they were designed to be employed. They would be needed to guarantee that the American mobilization was not preempted by a Soviet attack. Usually a worst case test for the nuclear forces consists of its ability to survive a large nuclear attack. But here, a very different requirement is being placed on them—the ability to implement political direction for prolonged periods under stressful conditions short of massive attack. From the perspective of American political leaders, it might well be that the nuclear forces would be used for war avoidance rather than prosecution. This would involve exploiting the entire American strategic system in a controlled manner to prevent dangerous enemy actions, protect allies, and cover attacks on the homeland.

Although the exact nature of any mobilization scenario is difficult to specify in advance, a very plausible Soviet action would be to demonstrate its seriousness about the level of danger faced. A distinct possibility is Soviet reinforcement of its garrisons in Eastern Europe. Suppose a major crisis evolved in the Middle East. It would be a useful educational exercise for American political leaders to ask themselves what their response would be if the Soviets moved 50 divisions from western Russia to Eastern Europe. A slow-motion reinforcement might take months and indeed the Soviet Union itself might not want to surge such a force to forward positions for fear of triggering a completely uncontrollable situation. The United States would be under enormous pressure to respond with caution, but it also would be essential to honor its NATO commitment.

American political leaders might well undergo more strategic education in such a period than during the entire postwar era. And military commanders might have many unusual constraints placed on their actions. SAC bombers would likely be ordered to implement airborne alert procedures for what could turn out to be months in duration. Launch control crews would be under great stress because of canceled leaves and double and triple shifts. Fleet ballistic missile submarines would be flushed from port and placed on station for periods lasting well beyond their normal 60-day crew rotations.

This kind of super alert strategic posture would demonstrate American nerve. It would also be used to protect the mobilization and to maneuver a favorable termination to the extended crisis. But to accomplish this goal the U.S. alert must be more enduring than a competitive Soviet alert. The Red Army could probably maintain a reinforced striking posture in Eastern Europe for a considerable time. Three, four, six, and even ten months could conceivably go by with tremendous demands placed on SAC and the U.S. Navy, as well as on their Soviet counterparts. Which nation would break first under the strain? This may be the ultimate question concerning the effectiveness of the mobilization option.

MOBILIZATION AND NATIONAL WILL

A tendency exists to consider national will as the ultimate means by which mobilization problems can be surmounted. But the preceding discussion should suggest that national will to support mobilization is a more complicated and subtle issue than first perceived.

National will to support American mobilization is certainly important and indeed it is often used as a test of the seriousness of a nation's commitment, there can be no doubt that in many scenarios, national resolve will be present, and will sweep away many of the constraints against getting things done. The classic example is American mobilization after December 7, 1941, where the executive was given a free hand in setting prices, determining allocations, and in silencing troublemakers.

However, even with the many positive advantages of having national will behind a presidental decision to mobilize, *it is probably a mistake to base planning on this assumption*. It is an even bigger mistake to take national will as an indicator of whether or not any mobilization program is "serious." The reason for this is that it is so easy to find examples of cases where there was a great deal of national will, but where nothing very much came as a result of it.

American mobilization in World War I had almost total popular backing, but it started too late, was plagued by too many delays and bad management. As a result, almost none of America's industrial output reached the troops until after the war was over. One of the reasons that mint-condition World War I tanks are found on display in many small New England towns today is that they were completed too late to be sent to the front. America's World War I industrial mobilization disaster was so great, despite popular support, that it led to the founding of the Industrial College of the Armed Forces in Washington, D.C., as an institution whose reason for existence was to prevent another mobilization debacle.

The "Great Leap Forward" of 1957-1958 in China was another attempt to substitute leadership, morale, and will for knowing anything about economic development. And the "wars" in the United States every few years waged on cancer and crime are undertaken with great popular support, but, unfortunately, with few results.

Each of these examples is very different but they all point to the need to think through a complicated policy problem. Broad popular support alone is often not a substitute for this knowledge.

Another point worth emphasizing is the tendency for a chief executive not to even *want* a mobilization of national will. During the Berlin crisis of 1961, President Kennedy wanted a military buildup, but was decidedly opposed to a declaration of national emergency.[4] He was afraid of starting an uncontrollable process of expectations and demands that would back him into a corner. Similarly, Lyndon Johnson hardly wanted a national mobilization of will to back his Vietnam policies because this might have forced him to take actions in the war he was just unwilling to take. Many persons will disagree with these presidental decisions, but this is hardly the point we are making. Whether anybody likes it or not, future presidents are going to be concerned about limitations in mobilization, for the very same reason that limitation in Korea and Vietnam proved necessary. This all suggests that national will of the kind that existed for mobilization in 1941 may be especially unlikely in the nuclear age. Mobilization would then not be impossible, but might have to be conducted as the wars in Korea and Vietnam were, with years of eroding public support.

MOBILIZATION PLANNING

Throughout its history the United States has always held a distinct military advantage by its economic vitality. Admittedly, the advantage has often taken considerable time to convert into tangible military strength. Yet even when this great resource was not used in combat, such as during the cold war, it has had a tremendous impact upon friend and foe alike. This is an influence and source of power that ought still to have great advantage if properly managed. While it can have little effect for bolt-from-the-blue deterrence, it can be a very threatening response that any adversary must incorporate into his defense planning. Indeed, for the more likely forms of superpower confrontations, it is a resource that offers special advantages not possessed by other options.

For these reasons, it is imperative to identify ways to turn the promise of mobilization into an *institutionalized* reality that will endure into the future, much as the past emphasis on standing alert forces had endured. Getting an administrative handle on this problem is then a necessary step, for without effective management, there is the likelihood that any increased support for mobilization will be funneled through old management mechanisms, which have been set up for maximizing standing forces in quantity and readiness.

The existing American defense industrial base is, to put it mildly, poorly designed for mobilization. Its output is characterized by a long term trend toward ever greater unit costs for missiles, tanks, planes, ships, and nearly every other piece of hardware. Not only is this real unit cost curve increasing, but it seems to be doing so at an exponential rate. This translates into the acquisition of ever smaller lot sizes as total budgets cannot expand at the pace of inflation in unit weapons costs. Recent experience with peacetime increases in defense spending seem to lead to greater unit price inflation rather than more hardware. Clearly, this is the very reverse of what is needed for mobilization. The long term effect of this trend is that the United States fields far fewer weapons today than it did for comparable expenditures in previous periods.

The decreased buys of hardware, measured in output rather than input terms, produces a smaller defense industry. With its shrunk capacity it is less able to meet demand surges for more weapons. Slack capacity does exist, often caused by cancellation of projects or cutbacks in acquisition levels, but this capacity is not in general in the areas needed for surge production. The slack that exists is spread around at random, and is dependent on year to year funding decisions in the Congress.

Finally, the American defense industry is today a highly specialized handtooled business. It is optimally structured to turn out a very few number of extremely complex weapons systems at a very high unit price. As such, it not only lacks a capability for surge production in the short term, but has an even greater inability to mobilize in a major way. For the larger mobilizations discussed in this chapter, or for a really serious national security emergency, its production potential would be all but irrelevant. This has induced many analysts who have studied the matter to conclude that we cannot really look to America's defense industry for mobilization.

If this conclusion is even partially correct it means that the way to administer planning for mobilization is in need of serious reevaluation. It is an especially opportune time to think about this because the Reagan administration is committed to enhancing America's mobilization capabilities. Some $500 million has been earmarked for this task, and the president has created an Emergency Mobilization Preparedness Board to coordinate programs and activities. At present, mobilization planning in the United States is decentralized among several departments and agencies. The individual services bear a great deal of responsibility for weapons, spare parts, and supplies acquisition. In this environment, an increased emphasis on mobilization would lead to the following kind of planning.

Existing mobilization programs would be reviewed and their funding levels evaluated. This includes everything from the Army's ammunition production base and the Navy's "Mobilization Deficiency List" to the Air Force's selection criteria for industrial planning. Typically these programs are drastically underfunded, either directly or through authorization cutbacks reflected in Program Objectives Memoranda and Program Decision Memoranda. One can then either fund these service programs up to their authorized level, or reset their authorizations based upon studies done by the services or by an agency of the Defense Department. Since these programs are already in place, it is plausible that someone in the services has at least thought about them, and considered how they affect the mobilization of at least, their own service. Familiarity with an existing mobilization program would suggest that objectives had been set, production tradeoffs determined, and that an internal service balance had been struck about mobilization versus standing forces.

Because these mobilization plans exist, it is an easy and seductive step to conclude that an administrative control on mobilization would be obtained by making allocation decisions about the funding levels for them. But several adverse consequences can be anticipated from this approach. First, each of the services, and groups within the services, will apply their own standards of what to concentrate attention on. This is the situation today, and examples of its pathological effects are widely available. For example, recent studies indicate that items selected for industrial preparedness planning by the Army, Navy, and Air Force are not coordinated, so that demands on industry cannot be reliably predicted, and that the forces produced upon mobilization are not necessarily balanced with each other. To take an example, each of the Navy's five subordinate commands having mobilization authority interpreted recent guidance on industrial preparedness differently.[5] Here we have individual commands interpreting the *same* guidance in fundamentally different ways. One command selected items for preparedness planning based on high dollar value and essentially, another from reparable parts lists, while another command chose not to select any items for planning because of time and resource constraints. All were operating under the same guidance.

Why does this happen? One reason is that mobilization policy is currently defined in such broad terms as to encompass almost any activity. Another reason is that mobilization is today inadequately defined as the business that mobilization planners are in. Considering that there are literally thousands upon thousands of possible mobilization planning activities, it could be expected that without a well-defined direction, the system would run off on its own in many directions at the same time. The 1980 Defense Science Board summer study on *industrial responsiveness* listed hundreds of actions that could be taken to improve our mobilization performance, ranging from the need to expand tank turret production to setting quotas on the consumption of foreign produced semiconductors.[6] The recommendations each have merit on their own, but in totality they constitute an enormous collection of unorganized and uncoordinated activities that would require a superhuman management ability to implement them as they stand, far transcending any ability found in America's largest corporations.

In such an environment of unorganized complexity several things can be expected to occur. Since no single mind, or committee, could possibly cope with the thousands and thousands of actions called for, there would be an inevitable delegation and decentralization of decision making. Without an institutionalized management framework that imposes order on the problem, laser BAMBI, M-16 ammunition, semiconductors, ships, F-15s, and helicopter rotor blades will all be mixed together with bureaucratic interests and "scenarios" to produce a disconnect between policy and outcome. A *stuck-in-the-middle* strategy will evolve, whereby increased mobilization budgets will produce limited incremental changes to the current system, but organizational and management barriers will block major change. Mobilization planning will be stuck in the middle between near total emphasis on standing forces, and an ability to mobilize superior military power in short order. Such a compromise may be an improvement over past planning, but the difficulty with stuck-in-the-middle strategies is that they are unlikely to endure. If mobilization programs are not built on a firm foundation, they will be milked at the first opportunity to get more resources for acquisition of standing forces. The lesson from this is that mobilization planning must be *institutionalized*. And the way to do this must necessarily face up to the question of why the United States would ever want to mobilize. In short, mobilization must be defined in such a way that it truly meets the needs of American security.

What does this suggest for strategic planning and mobilization? First, to decide how much mobilization money to give the armed services, how much to fill up the war reserve material stocks, which items to select for industrial preparedness planning, whether to fund a warm production base for F-15s, and so on, is to put the cart before the horse. Allocation of either dollars or management attention to these decisions begs the question if the definition of mobilization has not been made explicit. Mobilization planners must "define their business" just as major corporations define theirs.

Based on our research we would argue that the mobilization business is not uniquely defined, but that it is largely understood in terms of *producing military equipment*. Mobilization planning is supposed to help produce tanks, airplanes, ships, and ammunition. This is why so many studies concentrate on methods and procedures for speeding up tank production, addressing what we can do about bottlenecks in ship construction, and attending to the thousands upon thousands of other items needed for war. When we ask what is mobilization for, the answer is that it is for the production of armaments. With this definition, national will is viewed in terms of whether we can squeeze out public support for more production, emergency preparedness issues are ignored (because they are *not* armaments), and the Soviet threat is interpreted as to whether or not it would trump our tank production schedules with a preemptive nuclear strike. We believe that in almost any plausible mobilization, public support, emergency preparedness, and Soviet reactions are going to be far more complex and subtle than described by these characterizations, and furthermore, that such a one-dimensional view arises because of the belief that mobilization is defined exclusively in terms of weapons production. Defined in such narrow terms, it is hardly any surprise that standing forces have received so much emphasis compared with mobilization. Once the policy question is defined in terms of choosing either a "real" tank versus a "potential" tank, what would any rational individual select?

The possibilities for improving America's defense mobilization potential must grapple with both the narrow definition of this concept, and with the simple fact that the existing defense industry is not designed with mobilization in mind. The first of these may be easier to deal with than the second, but both are interrelated. A broader definition of mobilization can extend the reach of this important notion beyond the concerns about armament production rates. It can, for example, include the *functions* for which mobilization is useful. These may range from establishing military superiority to finding a temporizing alternative to the employment of nuclear weapons. By emphasizing functional aspects of mobilization in addition to narrow technical questions of productivity, it will be easier to integrate mobilization thinking into overall national security policy and process. With a functional definition, mobilization can better take its place in the spectrum of deterrence, and can more easily be exploited for its threat utility. Moreover, only when functional purposes are settled can weapons production planning make any sense. The current tendency in mobilization is to first address problems in production bottlenecks, without a clear specification of the rationale driving the assumptions about selection of the infinite variety of alternative, but possible, production schedules. This puts the cart before the horse.

The second need for improving America's mobilization capability is to recognize the limitations in the defense industry as it is now organized, and to understand that many proposals for enhancing its ability to mobilize are extremely expensive. Proposals to intentionally support excess production capacity for major weapon systems so that a surge capability would exist may sound like good ideas at first, but when they are costed out, it is nearly certain that they will prove to be prohibitively expensive. Similarly, proposals to stockpile long production lead-time items means that large resources will be devoted to potentially obsolete weapons, and it is hard to imagine anyone making such a decision. The principal reason that America's National Strategic Stockpile is made up of raw materials or only partly processed goods is to preserve flexibility about what actually is built. This avoids locking the stockpiled resources into what may prove to be ineffective, unusable, or even irrelevant military products.

Despite the limitation in mobilization potential inherent in the defense industry as it now exists, we are left with the fact that this is the only defense industry we have, and that like any industry it can be reshaped in different ways. We cannot expect to acquire a large ability to mobilize overnight, but must instead think through the problem of building additional mobilization capability into the American defense industry over a period of many years. The increases in real defense spending which began in the mid-1970s, and which have more recently increased further, provide a lever to reshape the defense industry in a way more suitable for mobilization. A redefinition of mobilization to include its functional as well as its production characteristics should also help, because it will cause people to start thinking about mobilization, and cause planners to take the concept more seriously. In summary then, a more expansive definition of mobilization, and a long-term industrial policy to reshape America's defense business along lines more compatible with mobilization are the cornerstones of strategic planning in this area.

CONCLUSIONS

The main conclusion developed in the earlier part of this chapter was that mobilization remains an important strategy relevant to America's security needs in the nuclear age. Once intitial reactions are overcome about the unthinkability of mobilization when both superpowers are armed with tens of thousands of nuclear weapons it is seen that this particular strategy offers unique advantages over other more commonly considered strategies.

Mobilization is a slow motion strategy that is less likely to intensify a crisis than are the use of nuclear strikes. Furthermore, it is an option which exploits advantages peculiar to the United States. Not only is the American economy some 70 percent larger than the Soviets, but equally important, American economic strength is respected and feared in Moscow. This ought to make mobilization a powerful deterrent against many, but not all, provocations.

All of this said, there are still some serious obstacles to depending on mobilization as a core element in America's overall national security policy. Usually these are noted to be the ability of a nuclear armed Soviet Union to trump the American mobilization schedule. The not inconsiderable list of situations where in-being forces are essential are also put forth as flaws in the mobilization response. In our view, neither of these counters to mobilization nullify the importance of this strategy, because they both leave open a large number of situations where mobilization can be a productive and relatively safe response. To dismiss the mobilization option as irrelevant in the nuclear age simply because there are situations where it does not apply is not very wise.

The more important problems of a mobilization strategy lie not with the situations to which it does not apply, but to those where it does. Three distinct kinds of problems were identified in this regard. First, the stresses and dislocations of major mobilization could produce vast unintended consequences. The pace of a crisis could be magnified, and transmitted instantly through financial and economic institutions which are today far more central to an orderly world than has ever been the case before. During a mobilization nuclear forces would likely be operated on the highest alert levels for a prolonged period. Because these forces have not really been designed with this in mind a real danger exists that major breakdowns in performance would occur. This possibility means that a mobilization may possess a near inevitable dynamic to turn into nuclear conflict, not through premeditated preemption, but rather through the inherent uncontrollability of super alerted forces interacting against a context of acute political crisis.

A second problem of a mobilization strategy is that severe political limitations may make it difficult, or even undesirable, to exploit national will during such intense crises. Instead of public support rallying behind a president, a shock reaction may swamp political considerations. Alternatively, and equally plausible, massive public support may bind a president to a risky course of action he would not otherwise wish to pursue.

Finally, the American defense industry is not designed with mobilization in mind. Its products are complex, and very hard to produce in a timely manner.

There is little reason to believe that this is something which can be easily changed, despite recent emphasis given to the problem. Of course, the problems of complexity and very long weapon development times are not unique to mobilization but afflict the entire defense acquisition process.

Despite these defects, mobilization in our view still retains importance as a recommended strategy. It does so because of the dearth of alternatives to it, in addition to the unique features outlined earlier. Unless an unforeseen breakthrough occurs in other areas of national security policy, mobilization promises to be among the more prudent strategies for the nuclear age.

NOTES

1. For a thorough discussion of this problem see Paul Bracken, *The Command and Control of Nuclear Forces* (New Haven: Yale University Press, 1983).
2. See Theodore C. Sorensen, *Kennedy* (New York: Harper & Row, 1965), pp. 657-678.
3. But see Paul Bracken and Martin Shubik, "Strategic Warfare: What Are the Questions and Who Should Ask Them?" *Technology in Society*, Winter 1982, pp. 155-179.
4. Theodore C. Sorensen, *Decision-Making in the White House* (New York: Columbia University Press, 1963), pp. 45-47.
5. U.S. General Accounting Office, *DoD's Industrial Preparedness Program Needs National Policy to Effectively Meet Emergency Needs* (Washington, D.C.: Comptroller General of the United States, 1981), p. 22.
6. U.S. Defense Science Board, *Report of the Defense Science Board 1980 Summer Study Panel on Industrial Responsiveness* (Washington, D.C.: Under Secretary of Defense for Research and Engineering, 1980).

12

Economic Targeting in Modern Warfare

Benjamin S. Lambeth and Kevin N. Lewis

The public's contemplation of strategic issues is often dominated by the fear that the United States or the Soviet Union may launch an all-out attack against the other's economic target system, even though this scenario is probably the least likely military contingency for which either country prepares. Such strikes, generically termed countervalue attacks, would direct thousands of nuclear weapons against cities and other facilities so as to destroy the adversary nation as an organized entity. Because both sides maintain enough survivable warheads to inflict what would seem to be mortal damage upon the other, the mutual ability to unleash such a blow is presumed, at least by many analysts in the West, to shape all other aspects of strategy. Thus, the relationship of this capability to other possible roles for nuclear forces is a central policy issue. Some commentators, fearful that even a limited use of nuclear weapons would lead inexorably to catastrophe, maintain that any consideration of nuclear use is madness. Others contend that a strategic concept that postulates *only* the alternatives of total or no nuclear war is improvident. Despite years of debate, however, we seem no closer to answering the basic question of how, if at all, massive attacks relate to other kinds of nuclear employment.

Much of the confusion about this question stems from a widespread misunderstanding about the nature and purpose of economic attack planning. In particular, the popular "hail of doom" image is a poor representation of the economic targeting problem. The usual lurid imagery aside, a general attack would, like any other use of nuclear force, be designed to satisfy specific requirements. Current U.S. planning remains tied to the tradition of strategic economic bombing that originated before the nuclear age, when planners tried to design precise theoretical rationales for the application of air power. Thus, while some view an economic attack as an indiscriminate brute-force blow, a full-scale nuclear strike must serve specific goals, at least in principle.

It is worth thinking through economic targeting issues to understand the nature and purpose of such attacks and more important, to determine how attacks aimed against an enemy's economy relate to other possible applications of military force. This chapter treats both questions from the perspective of U.S. and Soviet strategy. The goals of an economic attack may be stated in many ways, although in practice technical constraints and other factors may obscure some of the distinctions between attacks based on different theories. Further, there exists in the popular forum a tendency to oversimplify, as though there were just one sort of economic attack with only one purpose at any given time. In fact, economic targeting, like other war planning, has undergone intensive efforts to rationalize the underlying strategy. Moreover, each superpower maintains its own distinctive image of its security predicament. Since there have been considerable differences in each side's deterrence concepts over time, U.S. and Soviet approaches to economic targeting remain very dissimilar.

ECONOMIC TARGETING IN U.S. STRATEGY

Since 1945, the declaratory and theoretical bases of U.S. economic targeting policy have undergone many revisions. In practice, however, the technical nature of this attack problem has remained stable, as most Soviet economic resources have been concentrated in only a few locations. It has long been fairly easy to damage the enemy's economy severely with relatively few properly delivered weapons. Since the Soviet Urban/Industrial (U/I) target base changes at a glacial pace, the raw requirements for destruction of a given percentage of Soviet economic capability remain roughly the same, even over decades. (By contrast, Soviet *military* target systems tend to change at a faster pace, necessitating a constant offensive response.)

We can—and do—sandpaper our fingertips and run economic damage models to many decimal places. But despite doctrinal gyrations, technical innovation, threat evolution, and so on, the essential economic attack problem has not changed much over time. Accordingly, this section tracks two subordinate kinds of change in U.S. economic targeting policy over three decades. The first concerns the role of economic attacks within the body of U.S. nuclear strategy. The second involves the analytic means we use to weigh and plan economic attacks.

Economic Attacks as a Component of the Total U.S. Nuclear Plan

Between 1945 and 1950, U.S. planning for nuclear war was casual, to say the least. Neither force structure nor employment planning was done in a systematic way.[1] Similarly, only marginal provisions were made to acquire effective bombing forces. From a targeting policy perspective, nuclear operations were simply cast in the image of the attempted precision-bombing campaigns of World War II. But awesome operational and technical deficiencies virtually ensured that the U.S. Air Force could not accomplish the ambitious goal of "knocking out the USSR" in this way.[2] Despite the problems that bedeviled the design of a decisive precision countereconomic campaign, that strategy was retained, at least as a basis for force sizing.

An important milestone in the evolution of economic targeting came in 1949-50. At that time, a bureaucratic struggle to determine which service would be the "first line of national defense" was resolved in favor of the air force, or more precisely, strategic air power. Strategic bombing advocates won the debate by convincing political leaders that precision nuclear bombing could promptly and single-handedly defeat any major instance of communist aggression. The key point to recall here relates to the timing of the onset of bombing effects. Prompt results would not be terribly relevant if a future U.S.-Soviet war were to be a replay of World War II, featuring an eventual invasion of Europe. No one was very enthusiastic about another protracted conventional war. Accordingly, preventing the Soviet Union from overrunning the continent in the first place was a top priority. The alternative to quick atomic results was the maintenance of a large and expensive conventional posture first to check and then to defeat Soviet armies, in conjunction with more slowly maturing bombing effects. Given other budgetary priorities, the appeal of fast bombing payoffs proved decisive in our strategy debate.

As nuclear weapons entered the U.S. inventory in increasing numbers, they were assigned to targets other than economic ones.[3] Economic objectives, however, remained the highest targeting priority, and the precision strategy was retained. The development of high-yield thermonuclear weapons obviously undercut the need for very careful targeting. Yet relaxed targeting criteria (and a corresponding reduction in force requirements) did not appear. Rather, as new weapons became available, they were simply applied to longer and longer target lists.

Operational doctrine emphasizing prompt and total force commitment, historical targeting practices, technological shortcomings, and high bomb yields combined to assure that any U.S. nuclear attack would include an indiscriminate blow against Soviet cities. Indeed, "the mass killing of noncombatants came to be viewed as a 'bonus' effect . . . . Our knock-out blow would paralyze the Red Army not only by demolishing railroad yards, factories and party headquarters, but also by decimating the urban population and thus (perhaps) crushing Russia's morale."[4]

Although the Eisenhower administration saw the Strategic Air Command (SAC) as a relatively inexpensive counterbalance to seemingly invincible "Red hordes," some analysts began in the mid 1950s to question the wisdom of committing all U.S. forces against the full range of Soviet targets immediately upon the initiation of hostilities. The Soviets were slowly but surely accumulating nuclear forces capable of striking back. The decaying credibility of the "massive retaliation" strategy gave rise to a search for new concepts. In particular, some analysts cited the benefits of separating military from economic targets in U.S. plans by creating separate employment options.

To resolve simmering arguments about strategy, targeting priorities, and force levels, President Eisenhower ordered a National Security Council panel (known as the Hickey Panel) to weigh the relative importance of Soviet economic and military targets. The panel maintained that attacks on military targets alone would not defeat the Soviet Union because an undamaged Soviet economy could eventually make good those losses. But a purely economic attack would also be inadequate, since the Soviet Union could not only retaliate against the United States but could also use its military power to seize the resources necessary for quick recovery. The Hickey study concluded that an "optimum mix" of both target types was best. As a result, a single shot, massive war plan continued in force, first as the "mix" and then, in 1961, as the first single integrated operational plan (SIOP). Had those plans been executed, as one commentator has alleged, the results would have included 325 million immediate Communist bloc fatalities.[5]

The picture changed dramatically, however, after 1961 as the Kennedy administration's strategic reforms were implemented. This second strategic epoch witnessed two departures from previous custom that continue to shape planning to this day. The first change was a redesign of war plans to incorporate multiple options. Provision for such options—along with force changes to support them—was motivated by the maturation of Soviet capabilities, by the recognition that massive threats were not credible in many scenarios, and by changing alliance requirements. Because the fundamental purpose of options was to provide an opportunity to stop a war before catastrophe resulted, economic attacks were accorded a new status, that of a withheld "reserve" force that would not be executed unless deemed necessary *in extremis*. The second change was occasioned by the development of new technologies that not only made withholding feasible, but also made possible comparatively discriminating nuclear attacks. With lower yield, more accurate weapons, new intelligence, and better command-and-control systems, one could begin to think about a separate "campaign" against military targets.

Thus, the role of economic attacks in U.S. nuclear doctrine has not changed appreciably over the past 20 years. A countervalue attack has been, and remains, a "final sanction" designed to deter Soviet escalation if a nuclear war starts (and implicitly to back up, by posing that ultimate escalatory threat, less destructive U.S. options). The key U.S. strategy developments of the past two decades have concerned military options. By contrast, the economic targeting problem has not been so interesting.

Evolution of U.S. Economic Attack Planning Concepts

The second major trend in U.S. targeting policy has concerned the concepts used to plan economic attacks. Very little information has been made publicly available about U.S. attack options in the 1950s, except that many World War II conventions were retained. Since the early 1960s, on the other hand, two frameworks for evaluating U.S. attack effectiveness have been widely aired. First, through the early 1970s, the U.S. aim in an all-out economic retaliatory attack would be, as Secretary McNamara said, to "destroy the attacker as a viable 20th century nation." This capability to inflict "assured destruction" on the Soviet Union was to be guaranteed under all scenarios. What did this doctrine require in an operational sense? For a nation's economy to be "viable" essentially means that sufficient production can be restored before essential stockpiles are exhausted. If viability has been destroyed, according to the theory, one cannot get started on the road to recovery, and total collapse ensues. This in turn raises the questions of how to compute force requirements for achieving this aim and how damage should be measured. Though improved means for making such calculations have been devised, they remain less than ideal.

A more difficult question is: Within the context of any measuring system, how much overall damage must be done to destroy viability? Although we are obliged to devise rationales to define "sufficient" damage, such determinations ultimately revert to fiat. The well known rationalization for "assured destruction" given by Secretary McNamara was said to be based on rapidly diminishing marginal returns in both fatalities inflicted and economic destruction caused after 400 "equivalent megatons" (EMT) had been exploded over Soviet cities.[6] It was not McNamara's purpose, however, to specify the size of the force required for the destruction of the Soviet Union as a viable nation, at least in this way. Rather, his statement of an assured-destruction criterion was intended to suppress what seemed to him at the time to be excessive service requests for strategic systems. Actual operational planning and force requirements probably were based on other standards.[7]

No available reference indicates that such broad criteria have been amended over time. But in public statements, the declared aims of retaliatory attacks have often seemed to change for reasons having little to do with economic targeting requirements. In particular, by pointing to increasing threats, Soviet civil defenses, a more diverse target base, and so on, some critics contested the adequacy of the alleged 400 EMT force size. Rather than give in on the point and acknowledge a case for new procurement, McNamara modified the apparent requirements of assured destruction. (McNamara also qualified the manner in which the attack was to be evaluated.) This step, duplicated in successive years, was undertaken solely as an extension of assured destruction's intended constraint on procurement.

Similarly, official commentators have often articulated new aims (and, in particular, abandoned nearly all quantitative references to the requirements of an economic attack) for a number of reasons, usually relating to procurement pressures. For example, Clark Clifford said that the effectiveness of the strategic forces was gauged by "their ability . . . to inflict unacceptable damage."[8] Melvin Laird suggested that U.S. forces should threaten potential aggressors with "unacceptable risks,"[9] and James Schlesinger said that deterrence demanded the ability to inflict "irreparable damage" on the Soviet Union.[10] But despite such declaratory peregrinations, no significant change in basic economic targeting policy was implemented in the 1960s and early 1970s. One author cites an official who said in 1971 that "the SIOP has remained essentially unchanged since (1962). The targeting philosophy, the options, and the order of choice remain unchanged from the early 1960s."[11]

Only recently, it seems, have some aspects of U.S. economic targeting policy changed. The early and mid-1970s saw two major shifts. These were made possible by new technologies, chiefly the multiple independent targeted reentry vehicle, (MIRV) and were also encouraged by the steady trend toward U.S.-Soviet strategic parity. The first shift featured more employment options. The idea was to tailor U.S. nuclear use to specific wartime requirements and to provide a greater opportunity for stopping a war at a relatively low level of fighting. The second shift, beginning in about 1974, was from "assured destruction" to "assured retaliation." The new policy differed from the earlier one in not requiring that the Soviet Union's viability be destroyed. Rather, said Secretary Rumsfeld, the new strategy sought to retard "the ability of the USSR to recover from a nuclear exhange and regain the status of a 20th century military and industrial power."[12]

This antirecovery targeting objective supposedly marked a significant departure from previous theory.[13] Despite much debate, however, the reasons for the change were less significant than most explanations suggested. Among other things, the new aims owed their creation to the steady equalization of the strategic balance, to a desire by Presidents Nixon and Ford to depart, at least in appearance, from the strategy of Presidents Kennedy and Johnson, and to U.S. concern about the Soviet interest in civil and strategic defense.[14] In any case, the test of the new strategy was as follows: "If the Soviet Union could emerge from (general war) with superior military power, and could recuperate from the effects more rapidly than the United States, the U.S. capability for assured retaliation would be considered inadequate."[15]

Excluding political twists, the strategies of the 1960s and 1970s did not differ to any appreciable degree. Both sought to deprive some Soviet economic sectors of necessary inputs to cause bottlenecks in the economy and prevent surviving resources from being used effectively. In effect, an attack to destroy viability simply ensures that the enemy nation is unable to reconstitute far enough to worry about recovery in the first place.[16]

Methodological Problems

A key planning task is to design an adequate offensive posture for the economic attack mission. Several difficulties, however, are involved in determining how much is enough. First, the data problems are staggering. Furthermore, the methodologies used to assess the consequences of economic attacks pose serious problems. Because of the historic emphasis on "bottlenecking," input/output (I/O) analysis has been a popular approach. According to theory, destruction of an input into an I/O tableau (analogous to the annihilation of a particular sector of the economy) will undercut associated sectors and the economy will be "brought down." However, the difficulties inherent in assessing the effects of attacks (even given excellent target intelligence) are obvious.

Given the corollary assumption that the United States will be unable to destroy the viability of the Soviet economy, we are left with the problem of computing recovery paths and times, a task for which I/O analysis—in the absence of assumptions about the enemy's postattack policy choices, among other things—is not particularly applicable. Analysis of the postwar utilization of surviving resources also relies on usually dubious assumptions about the surviving government's ability to coordinate residual capacity, the ability of transportation systems to move people and supplies between imbalanced regions, the dedication of workers and others to postattack reconstitution, and so on.

Treatment of specific capabilities also becomes vitally important, because unless these can be introduced directly into the damage model, we cannot assess the consequences of destroying supposedly pivotal targets. But in an I/O model, inputs may be infinitely substitutable within sectors, and there may be no substitution between sectors. Failure to take into account substitution and the changed nature of demand can lead to absurd results.[17] The usual solution proposed for such problems is to increase the number of sectors modeled in the economy. But data requirements can quickly get out of hand as more sectors are added.[18]

Thus, it is hard to translate destroyed capability into estimates about recovery times. Recently, some studies of Soviet civil defense have referred to its ability to reduce recovery times,[19] but those findings enjoy less than universal acceptance. Although some recovery-pathway analysis has been undertaken, most work has focused on estimating the time it would take to eliminate bottlenecks in critical sectors. Yet as Sobin and Bull observe, "It is not easy to conclude (from a survey of the literature) that any particular kinds of capacities are the critical ones in the sense of providing absolute limits to objective achievement."[20] In other words, some economic activities are more essential than others but it is hard to say which are truly critical.

New Possibilities For Economic Targeting?

Related to political and other rationalizations for "assured retaliation" was the U.S. MIRV program begun in 1970. In particular, the net sea-based deterrent force grew from a total of about 650 warheads in 1969 to approximately 5,000 by 1975. With MIRV, many opportunities for increasingly articulated U.S. economic targeting emerged. In addition, more sophisticated targeting systems, improved accuracy, the lower yields of Poseidon, and better target intelligence have created new possibilities for discriminating economic attacks.

Such attacks might be designed to intimidate the Soviet leadership by threatening further damage, or they might seek to exploit specific vulnerabilities in the Soviet economy in order to gain some advantage in an ongoing theater war.[21] Much attention has also been paid to the ostensible advantages of confining U.S. economic targeting to the specific elements of Soviet power that pose the most immediate threat to U.S. interests. It has been pointed out that the United States has no quarrel with a Soviet civilian population that, for the most part, cares little for its own leadership. Accordingly, some commentators have begun to speak in terms of such objectives as enemy leadership, "ethnic fracture points," and the like. Naturally, a precise data base and very sophisticated damage models are necessary for such targeting—as are techniques for holding down collateral damage.

Finally, many analysts have become increasingly aware of the fact that a blanket targeting doctrine may not adequately take into account outside aid, whether coerced, purchased, or volunteered. Historical experience suggests the importance of resources available outside of war zones. Target planners might be mindful of the fact that such aid may be obtainable from territory the Soviets might capture.

In short, although the context of overall U.S. strategic targeting and the U.S.-Soviet balance have shifted dramatically since the early postwar years, the current economic targeting problem does not differ fundamentally from the one we faced in the 1950s, although some refinements have been effected and others are under way. This is true despite the occasional gyrations that mark apparently new strategic rationales. Changes relating to the role of economic attacks within overall U.S. nuclear planning, however, have been very important. While it will be interesting to see how new weapons technologies—more accurate sea-based systems, cruise missiles, and improved command, control, and reconnaissance capabilities—will influence the evolution of economic targeting policy, it is likely that major changes in U.S. nuclear policy over the near term, if there are any, will relate to military options.

Patterns in the Evolution of U.S. Economic Targeting

In light of the preceding review, we can discern a few consistent threads in the evolution of U.S. economic targeting policy. First, U.S. target planning has been strongly influenced by the U.S. independent strategic-bombing tradition. Initially, this meant that a massive blow against a wide range of targets was supposed to thwart a Soviet invasion. As the Soviet ability to return this favor came to be widely recognized, economic attack was transformed into a withholdable option. Yet while U.S. strategy has been tending toward increased flexibility, the basic dogma of an "assured destruction" blow continues to influence U.S. strategic deliberations in other areas and continues to shape force and employment planning generally.

Second, in many respects we seem to have become prisoners of our economic targeting methodologies. It is clearly essential to be very specific about the technical aims of an economic attack, if for no other reason than that explicit guidance must be given to our target staff. Excessive adjustments of attack criteria, however, as well as expansion and complication of damage models and data bases, seem to have made our planning more sensitive to the perturbations and uncertainties that pervade all calculations about nuclear war, although they may not be very important. Since nuclear planners are very conservative, apparent shifts in capabilities give rise to large and unnecessary compensatory responses. This may lead to the artificial inflation of U.S. economic targeting requirements, possibly to the detriment of other needs.

Third, the economic targeting problem has been strongly influenced by technological developments. Ideally, we should expect our nuclear policy to identify prospective requirements to be served by available and evolving technology. In many cases—the development of the hydrogen bomb and the fractionation of U.S. missile payloads come to mind—targeting adjustments have instead conformed to fit the new force capabilities. In turn, our national wartime strategy has been affected by new technologies.

Fourth, the relegation of economic sanctions in the U.S. war plan to a "reserve" status has important force-structure and employment ramifications and may require refinements in technical capabilities and operational procedures. Although it is conceivable that we may develop some relatively limited economic options, the heavy co-location of leadership, population, and industrial and transportation targets will probably militate against too much emphasis on these kinds of attacks. An interesting development may result from an apparently inevitable conflict between the reserve status of economic options and the traditional U.S. concept of escalation linkage. Even when we have developed limited options, we have generally tried to deter Soviet nuclear employment of all types by maintaining a full spectrum of U.S. response options. Moreover, we have disavowed reliable control over escalation once a nuclear war begins. The greater emphasis on reserve capabilities, therefore, forces a new look at these old issues.

Fifth, whatever else is decided in the economic targeting policy debate, we can expect continued complication in the design of these attacks. Considering current popular discussion, more attention may be paid to specialized components of the Soviet urban-industrial target base, primarily political leadership and administration, internal security capabilities, energy production, and communications. Despite continuing rhetorical emphasis on "policy shifts," the major options will probably not differ significantly in their aggregate effect from massive economic options based on more simple guidance. Indeed, even if some salient new guidance were devised, such attacks, like any others could be subject to Soviet counteraction.

SOVIET PERSPECTIVES ON TARGETING

Two explanations account for the dissimilarity in U.S. and Soviet approaches to economic targeting. One lies in the Soviet Union's lack of a strategic bombing tradition comparable to that developed by the United States during World War II. The other is the long-standing preference of Soviet leaders for basing key elements of their nuclear strategy on premises different from the assured-destruction model that has so heavily influenced U.S. strategic planning.

To some degree, Soviet disdain for the urban-industrial bombing policies of the Western allies against Nazi Germany has been a classic case of making a virtue of necessity, since the Soviet air force almost completely lacked the strategic reach needed to carry the air war to the German heartland.[22] Soviet military writings openly concede that, of all the wartime bombing sorties of long-range aviation, only about 4 percent were targeted against the Nazi economic and military-industrial base.[23] Instead, Soviet planners were driven by military-technical and operational necessity to concentrate their combat efforts almost exclusively against the German military formations that were directly threatening the Soviet heartland.[24] In Marshal Sokolovskii's words, the principle criteria that governed the Stavka's deliberations prior to mounting an offensive were "the composition of Soviet forces, the configuration of the front lines, the composition of enemy forces, weak and strong points in the enemy's defenses, and the character of the theater of military operations."[25]

Conspicuously absent from this formulation was anything like the Western notion that the defeat of the enemy could be brought about by attacking his rear-area infrastructure. The Soviet tendency was to argue that economic attacks could not, short of near-total devastation, guarantee crippling the enemy's key industrial vulnerabilities. For example, one Soviet writer singled out the case of the German chemical industry:

> During the past war, the U.S. staff section for the study of strategic bombing calculated that the Allied Air Command made a serious error by not selecting as a first-priority target the sole and very vulnerable plant for the production of diboromethane. This plant produced the ethyl compound required for high-grade gasoline, and which is so necessary that not one modern airplane can fly without it. Specialists maintain that the bombing of this single target could have caused greater damage to the German air forces than was caused by all the saturation bombings against aircraft plants throughout the war.[26]

Given the unavailability of high-confidence intelligence regarding where critical vulnerabilities lay, the preferred Soviet approach was to concentrate available military resources directly on the most tangible instruments of enemy military capability. To the extent that economic-strategic aims entered their war planning, the Soviets seemed less interested in destroying the nonmilitary assets of the adversary than in "liberating economically and politically important areas" that might, in turn, be exploited to support the Soviet war effort and subsequent postwar reconstruction.[27]

All in all, the Soviets maintain—with considerable justification—that they prevailed on the Eastern Front primarily by engaging German forces in a head-on confrontation of countervailing firepower, and that the Wehrmacht was ultimately ground down by the superior weight of Soviet numbers and their capacity for sustained operation. By the same token, Soviet commentators hold that the countereconomic bombing by the U.S. Eighth and Fifteenth Air Forces and by the RAF Bomber Command contributed only marginally to the defeat of Germany and thus entailed an expenditure of manpower and material far out of proportion to their combat significance. Not surprisingly, these painful antecedents have carried over into Soviet thinking on rear-area attacks in the postwar period.

Transition to the Nuclear Age

With the introduction of nuclear weapons into the Soviet arsenal, the formerly derided strategy of comprehensive rear-area targeting quickly attained a level of major importance. During the prenuclear era, the standard Soviet formula held that victory could only come at the end of a lengthy process of cumulative successes at the operational and tactical levels. In light of the destructiveness of nuclear weaponry, however, this traditonal view became replaced by one which held that, under the right circumstances, effective employment of intercontinental strikes could achieve fundamental strategic objectives at the very outset of a war, eliminating the need for the painstaking and methodical sequence of steady force application over time. As Marshal Sokolovskii described the change, the emergence of nuclear weapons had rendered war aims achievable "not only by the defeat of the enemy's armed forces, but also by the complete disruption of the enemy economy and demoralization of his population."[28]

This new refrain was echoed in subsequent years by the Chief of the General Staff, Marshal Zakharov, who reaffirmed that "whereas in past wars the armed forces as a whole were . . . a target, now one should add the economy of the warring countries."[29] A similar formulation was put forward by Major General M. I. Cherednichenko: "In light of the revolutionary changes that have taken place in the weapons used, the economy has now become a target for . . . nuclear missiles."[30] The point of all this was to underscore that the difficulties that once attended effective economic targeting through precision conventional bombing had been virtually eliminated by the comprehensive destructive coverage of nuclear warheads. Given this new-found capability to bring major sectors of the adversary's rear area under attack, a Soviet writer was able to proclaim by 1961 that the "necessity to weaken the economic potential of an aggressor" had become "one of the most important rules governing modern warfare." Accordingly, he went on to note, it had become important for Soviet planners to study carefully the enemy's economic and military-industrial nexus so as "to discover strong and weak points" that might help inform purposeful target planning.[31]

Despite these dramatic changes, however, Soviet military doctrine in its conceptual fundamentals remained sharply divergent from the premises regarding the value of economic targeting that came to dominate U.S. strategic thinking and planning during the same period. Although through the early 1960s the Soviet armed forces possessed meager intercontinental attack forces that offered few options besides destroying selected U.S. urban-industrial centers, Soviet doctrine retained the counter-military orientation that was forged and case hardened during the trials of World War II. Even in the earliest years of the nuclear era, a major distinction between Soviet and U.S. approaches to deterrence began to crystallize, and, despite the increasing technical comparability of Soviet and U.S. strategic forces, it has persisted to this day. This distinction, in the now-familiar idiom of Western strategic theory, was between a growing U.S. intellectual preference for deterrence by the threat of punishment and a persistent Soviet commitment to the more classical notion of deterrence by denial.

The Current Soviet Image of Nuclear War

Aside from periodic refinements in allowed mission support and a gradual shift in Soviet thinking during the mid-1960s regarding whether a conventional war in Europe would "inevitably" escalate to the nuclear level, Soviet strategic doctrine has remained remarkably constant over the past two decades, particularly in its characterization of a future global war.[32] In this conception of warfare, there seems to be no place for the sort of incremental and measured application of nuclear firepower aimed at intrawar bargaining and "crisis management" that has for so long figured prominently in U.S. strategic theory. Instead, as Sokolovskii has asserted, the imperatives of such a war will call for a "strategy of missile and nuclear strikes in depth, along with the simultaneous use of all branches of the armed forces, in order to achieve complete defeat of the enemy and the destruction of his economic potential and armed forces throughout his entire territory.[33]

Despite the surface bravado of their doctrine, Soviet planners do not approach the specter of nuclear war with equanimity or indicate a lack of appreciation for the profound uncertainties that would attend the Soviet Union's prospect of emerging from such a war with a victory worthy of the name. As one senior Soviet officer noted, "There is too great a risk of the destruction of one's own government, and the responsibility to humanity for fatal consequences of nuclear war is too heavy, for an aggressor to make an easy decision on the immediate employment of nuclear weapons from the very beginning of a war without having used all other means for the attainment of its objectives.[34] The pervasive tendency toward risk aversion that has long characterized Soviet crisis comportment would be likely to disincline Soviet planners strongly from any course of escalatory action that did not promise fairly certain prospects of success.[35]

At the same time, Soviet leaders have powerful countervailing urges to nip undesirable trains of events in the bud, before they have a chance to burgeon and become totally uncontrollable. This blend of caution and impulsiveness in Soviet style would probably exert a major restraining influence on their nuclear employment in most crisis conditions. Yet it could also place irresistible pressures on the leadership to pre-empt massively in circumstances where it seemed apparent that war was definitely coming sooner or later and that continued Soviet inaction would carry greater risks than proceeding with forceful military initiatives. As one Soviet commentator has observed in this regard, "The principle to attack the enemy only when one is sure of success does not exclude but presupposes the need of taking risks, even big risks, when this is required by the situation."[36]

In view of the destructive power of nuclear weapons and the unbearable costs that could attend a failure to land the first punch, Soviet doctrine strongly endorses the notion of "striking first in the last resort," in Malcolm Mackintosh's apt formulation. It further maintains that the initial strike will determine the subsequent course and outcome of the war:

> The decisive act of a nuclear war in all conditions is the infliction of a strike by strategic nuclear means, in the course of which both sides will obviously use the main portion of the most powerful nuclear ammunition. The moment of infliction of this strike will be the culminating point of the strategic effort, which can virtually be combined with the beginning of a war. This was not the case in any of the past wars.[37]

Soviet rhetoric only rarely gives express endorsement to pre-emption as a preferred strategy. Its frequent usage of suggestive euphemisms for the idea, however, provides good reason to believe that Soviet planners appreciate the operational advantages that could accrue from timely exploitation of a surprise attack at the brink of major war.[38] Whether the Soviet warning capability, alert posture, command-and-control network, and decision-making system possess the combined responsiveness needed to support a pre-emptive attack under the actual stresses of a crisis remains a separate question. But there seems little doubt that Soviet commanders attach great importance to beating the enemy to the draw—at least as an ideal goal to be striven for in peacetime contingency planning.

In the characteristic Soviet hierarchy of strategic attack missions, the first priority is to destroy the enemy's strategic nuclear forces. In this primary target set, as a Soviet general has noted, "strategic rockets are regarded as the most important strategic objectives."[39] Also included are enemy alert bomber bases, ballistic-missile submarines (SSBNs), both at sea and in their home ports, nuclear weapons storage facilities, and strategic command-and-control nodes. Second-priority Soviet targets in general war encompass theater-based nuclear forces and their associated support and command-and-control networks. In the third priority are other military targets, such as major troop formations and marshaling areas, aerial ports of debarkation in the forward land theater, reserve forces, conventional weapons stocks, and the like. The fourth category includes political leadership and administrative centers that the enemy would require to maintain social cohesion during a war. *Only last* in this array of target priorities is the broad category of economic-industrial facilities, such as power stations, refineries, production plants, and so on.[40]

Economic Targeting in Soviet Strategy

Beyond the absence of "assured destruction" inclinations in mainstream Soviet strategic thought, the subordinate status assigned to economic targeting stems from the stress Soviet planners place on attending first to those enemy assets that would most directly serve his ability to damage the Soviet Union and permit him to continue fighting in regional theaters afterwards. It is also affected by the general Soviet tendency to dismiss the utility of either side's defense-industrial base as a reliable source of support to its war effort during the cataclysmic throes of a nuclear exchange. As Marshal Sokolovskii and Major General Cherednichenko once expressed this point, a future nuclear war will most likely be conducted "only with those means existing at its beginning, since it will not be possible to count on the mobilizational development of the economy in these conditions. The possibilities of production continuing to function in a period when nuclear strikes are being exchanged and during a lengthy period thereafter are wholly problematic."[41]

The most basic explanation for the subordinate status economic targeting commands in Soviet strategy, however, lies in the fundamentally counter-military orientation of Soviet doctrine and operational planning. This emphasis calls for concentrating Soviet nuclear strikes primarily against the U.S. military posture and command-and-control infrastructure. Of course, in the process of attempting to eradicate the U.S. leadership's "will to resist," Soviet planners will not exclude from their target list the major U.S. urban-industrial centers. These targets, however, will probably be attacked with a studied economy of force, since there will always be more theoretically interesting aim points than the Soviet Union will have forces to use against them.[42] One repeatedly finds comments throughout the Soviet military literature to the effect that nuclear strikes should only be made against the "most important" targets affecting the enemy's war-making potential. As Colonel Sidorenko has remarked, from a cost-effectiveness viewpoint, "nuclear strikes are best delivered (only) against the most important objectives and the main enemy grouping. The use of nuclear weapons against insignificant, secondary objectives contradicts the very nature of this weapon."[43] In a similar vein, Colonel Shirokov noted in a recent article that "the quantity of objectives, especially military-economic, located on the territory of warring states . . . is very great. Therefore, the belligerents will strive to select from the objectives those which have the greatest influence on the course and outcome of the armed struggle."[44] In other words, those economic and industrial targets will be included in Soviet operational plans not so much because of whatever postwar significance they might have for the adversary as because of their tangible relevance to more immediate Soviet combat objectives.

In working toward victory, the Soviet high command will not flinch from employing all force deemed necessary to break the enemy's combat capability. This could involve collateral damage to enemy economic assets on a very large scale. Although there is ample evidence of tendencies toward selectivity in Soviet war planning, nothing in Soviet thinking remotely approximates the Western idea of sparing enemy cities for "intrawar bargaining" or purposely avoiding attacks on the enemy National Command Authority. By the same token, while Soviet writings reveal many indications of target discrimination motivated by a desire to maximize economy of force, the Soviet conception of the initial period of war envisages rapid, intense, and simultaneous nuclear strikes against very large numbers of countermilitary and countervalue aim points in combination.

In short, the operational objective of any economic damage that might be inflicted on the adversary is, in Soviet thinking, quite different from that which has hitherto informed U.S. planning. Rather than merely assure the comprehensive wrecking of the enemy's economic base to prolong his postwar recuperation, Soviet targeting is principally intended to serve the more proximate wartime goal of disrupting the enemy's capability to fight. Soviet planners apparently have little interest in striving to influence the geopolitical contours of a postnuclear world in any circumstances in which their own military victory cannot be satisfactorily vouchsafed. Undoubtedly, there is a place in Soviet planning for destroying elements of the enemy's economic system that might enhance his strategic stature in postwar global affairs (the war is, after all, plainly envisaged by Soviet doctrine as being decisive). Yet the most immediate and paramount Soviet operational concern is targeting that will bring about a favorable military resolution to the conflict in the shortest possible time.

The Enduring Countermilitary Emphasis of Soviet Doctrine

Since the beginnings of the Soviet build-up inaugurated by the Brezhnev regime in 1965, almost every feature of Soviet strategic force deployment has been aimed at providing a high-confidence attack capability against the strategic offensive posture of the United States. There is a strong presumptive argument that the Soviet SS-9 inventory was expressly targeted against the U.S. Minuteman launch-control network.[45] In addition, periodic Soviet SSBN patrolling patterns have indicated a possible Soviet interest in attacking with surprise from close-in launch points so as to bring SAC's bomber bases and command, control, and communications facilities under prompt fire. With the advent of their fourth-generation SS-18s and SS-19s, the Soviets have now acquired both the warhead numbers and accuracy needed to engage all U.S. fixed land-based forces and other hardened capabilities directly.

To be sure, with their submarine-launched ballistic missile force and the ICBMs that would be withheld from any initial hard-target counterforce attack, the Soviets would have more than enough remaining offensive assets to cover all interesting U.S. economic, administrative, and urban-industrial targets comfortably, whether in simultaneous laydowns or in sequential strikes. The point, however, is that neither Soviet doctrine nor Soviet force development has ever reflected any special concern over meeting the requirements of countervalue targeting. While the importance of enemy economic power is duly recognized in Soviet strategic policy, the overwhelming impression radiated by the Soviet military literature is that acquiring and maintaining the wherewithal for that mission constitutes among the least demanding tasks of Soviet force development. One Soviet officer almost casually dismissed the economic targeting problem by noting that although enemy economic assets would certainly constitute a "primary objective" of Soviet operations in a nuclear war, these can be attended to "literally in a matter of hours and days" through the appropriate application of nuclear firepower.[46]

Far more pressing, in the view of Soviet doctrine is the timely reduction of the enemy's capacity to wage war, an objective which in no way requires either comprehensive economic targeting for its own sake or the retardation of enemy economic "recovery potential" to any prespecified level. As Colonel Shirokov expressed this point in 1966,

> The objective is not to turn large economic and industrial regions into a heap of rubble (although great destruction apparently will be unavoidable), but to deliver strikes that will destroy strategic combat means, paralyze enemy production, making it incapable of satisfying the priority needs of the front and rear lines, and sharply reduce the enemy capability to conduct strikes.[47]

This observation, one might add, was ventured well over a decade before

Soviet forces acquired a plausible capacity to underwrite such an objective. Aside from accentuating the counterforce emphasis of Soviet military thought, it dramatically underscores the crucial role of doctrine in shaping Soviet strategic developments more generally.

CONCLUSIONS

There is no doubt that a nuclear war fought according to any strategy would be destructive beyond previous human experience. The differing views of nuclear strategy held by the United States and the Soviet Union, however, have important implications for U.S. defense planners.

The two sides' view of the role of economic targeting in nuclear war are so deeply embedded in their respective planning traditions that they reflect what are essentially two very different strategic cultures. The origins of this divergence considerably predate the advent of nuclear weapons and can be traced back to the earliest years of World War II. The United States, by virtue of its pioneering efforts in strategic air power, became attracted to the idea that the most vulnerable dimension of enemy power was his comparatively "soft" rear-echelon infrastructure and that the enemy's war effort could be most effectively crippled by destroying the economic and industrial assets required to support it—particularly at critical "choke points." The Soviet Union, with different defense requirements and lacking comparable air-power capabilities, adhered to a wartime strategy of engaging enemy military potential directly on a battlefield. With due allowance for the subsequent impact of nuclear weapons and long-range delivery systems on the strategic policies of the superpowers, this divergence in the targeting orientations of the two countries has persisted to the present day. It is thus appropriate to consider the effect of this divergence on current U.S. security interests and its implications for future U.S. nuclear planning.

Whatever merits it may command as a fairly certain means of destroying any adversary as a functioning social entity, economic targeting should not become the focus of all strategic employment planning. Although the United States has developed a variety of selective employment options over the years, the principal deterrent effect intended remains the threat of escalation to overarching general war. In light of this, development of selective options has not removed a number of difficulties with a strategy based on a final massive economic attack.

Foremost among these is the questionable relevance of such a strategy to the determination of immediate war outcomes. Comprehensive destruction of an enemy's economic infrastructure and industrial base would profoundly affect the complexion of the postwar world and the enemy's place in it, but it cannot by itself resolve the strategic issues at stake. For this, the enemy's forces and supporting battle-management instruments must be neutralized. It is highly unlikely that any country's economic and industrial infrastructure could weather the stresses of general nuclear war and continue functioning with even a modicum of effectiveness. It is hard to see how efforts to impair that capability, however successful, would contribute significantly to the outcome of a war that would necessarily be fought almost entirely by weapons and forces already deployed.

Such efforts could prove suicidal, furthermore, in the absence of accompanying capabilities for massive countermilitary and counterpolitical targeting intended to eliminate the enemy's ability to continue the campaign in the first place. It would do little to support our basic national survival interests to obliterate an enemy (even in flawless conformity with the most recondite economic targeting criteria) if, in the process, he were allowed to retain sufficient elements of counteroffensive nuclear power to inflict comparable damage in punitive reprisal.[48] The Soviets, unfortunately to their credit, appear to appreciate this far more than we do.

To be sure, *threatening* to demolish an enemy's economic livelihood may be highly appropriate as a peacetime deterrent. Yet however impressive general attack capabilities may be in the abstract, reliance on them after deterrence has failed begs the question of insurance. Even if neither side sees any advantage in nuclear use, the possibilities of accident, miscalculation, and madness exist. The question thus remains: Would we deliberately execute our final deterrent threat, knowing that retaliation in kind would certainly follow?

For such a threat to prevent enemy initiatives that might otherwise appear attractive, it must be capable of being invoked with relative impunity to enemy countermeasures. This, in turn, requires either comprehensive counterforce capabilities linked to a surprise first-strike strategy or reliable active and passive damage-limitation capabilities, neither of which the United States possesses. It is more than a little ironic that despite its vocal disdain for "assured destruction" notions and related economic targeting concepts, the Soviet Union either now has or is vigorously striving to acquire precisely the wherewithal to lend credible support to such concepts. The United States, by contrast, has at best registered only the most desultory progress toward acquiring significant hard-target capabilities and other damage-limiting assets during the past decade, when it has also been so fervently adjusting the sort of economic targeting strategies for whose support such capabilities would be absolutely essential.

In light of these considerations, the idea of making the use of nuclear weapons against economic targets, the principal focus of strategic planning warrants skepticism, particularly since the United States lacks the capabilities that would be required both to enforce the deterrent credibility of these strategies in peacetime and to contribute to a successful outcome in the event of war. Certainly, more narrow efforts to destroy an enemy's military-industrial and other war-support infrastructure would make operational sense in a general war, especially one that appeared likely to take on protracted dimensions of a sort that would allow those assets to be exploited to the enemy's advantage. But more undifferentiated economic targeting aimed at creating intrawar bottlenecks, imposing "unacceptable damage," shattering the "will to continue fighting," or impeding enemy postwar recovery is unlikely to be a sound basis for U.S strategic planning in the decade ahead. Not only would continued emphasis on economic targeting be of questionable utility on either deterrent or war-fighting grounds in the absence of effective damage-limiting capabilities, it could actually be counterproductive were it allowed to divert attention from systematic development of those forces and concepts that would be needed to fight to a favorable settlement should deterrence fail and events leave no better alternative.

NOTES

1. It has been noted that "early target lists and intelligence estimates were tentative and the military role of the atomic bomb was not yet clear." See David Rosenberg, "American Atomic Strategy and the Hydrogen Bomb Decision," *The Journal of American History*, June 1979, p. 66.

2. For a more detailed discussion of early U.S. offensive nuclear deficiencies, see Kevin N. Lewis, *Strategic Bombing and the Thermonuclear Breakthrough: An Example of Disconnected Defense Planning* (Santa Monica, California: The Rand Corporation, April 1981).

3. The target base in 1949 was broken into three distinct classes: DELTA (essentially countervalue); BRAVO (counterforce); and ROMLO (targets to be destroyed to retard the advance of the Red Army into territory along the periphery of the Soviet bloc). Taking into account all target sets, General Vandenberg speculated that as many as 6,000 Soviet targets of all types would have to be hit to destroy the Soviet Union. See "Memo for the President," from General H.S. Vandenberg, January 17, 1952, p. 3 (National Archives).

4. Fred C. Iklé, *Can Nuclear Deterrence Last Out the Century?* (Santa Monica: California Arms Control and Foreign Policy Seminar, June 1974), p. 12.

5. Ellsberg's "A-Weapons Plant Vigil Recalls One 1958 Option: Holocaust," *Indianapolis Star*, July 9, 1978.

6. McNamara's analysts produced a chart which showed that 400 delivered EMT would destroy about half of the Soviet Union's population and about two-thirds of its industrial capacity.

7. For example, destruction of 70 percent of Soviet manufacturing is said to have been the U.S. economic damage objective since 1961, according to a statement in *Hearings of the House Appropriations Committee on DoD Appropriations for 1978* (Washington, GPO, 1977), part II, p. 212.

8. Clark Clifford, *Annual Defense Report for FY 1969* (Washington: GPO, 1968).

9. Melvin Laird, *Annual Defense Report for FY 1971* (Washington: GPO, 1970).

10. James Schlesinger, *Annual Defense Report for FY 1975*. In his FY 1979 defense report, Harold Brown referred to a "200 city" standard, but this figure was deleted from subsequent reports.

11. Desmond Ball, *Deja Vu: The Return to Counterforce in the Nixon Adminstration* (Santa Monica: California Seminar on Arms Control and Foreign Policy, December 1974), pp. 16-17. That account goes on to report that "an Air Force planner was quite emphatic (in 1973) that the SIOP was never reworked under (President) Johnson. It is still basically the same as 1962."

12. Donald Rumsfeld, *Annual Defense Report for FY 1977* (Washington: GPO, 1976).

13. See, for instance, Richard Burt, "Pentagon Reviewing War Plans," *New York Times*, December 16, 1977.

14. The specific statement of the goal of delaying recovery was thus made in part to warn the Soviets that they should not expect to emerge from all-out war on the better side of some postattack "chaos gap."

15. Rumsfeld, *Annual Defense Report for FY 1977.1*

16. It is worth noting that the Carter administration's PD-59 strategy revision apparently did not change the economic targeting components of U.S. war plans. See "Slocombe Clarifies PD-59 Policy: Industrial Targets Still Important," *Defense Week*, November 17, 1980, and *Secretary of Defense's Annual Report for FY 1983*, submitted by C. Weinberger (Washington: GPO, February 1982).

17. The classic case in point is the apparent significance of the Soviet paint industry in an I/O tableau. Most finished products in the Soviet economy are painted, and it is said that there are few paint plants in the Soviet Union. Paint plants are difficult to harden and they take a long time to rebuild. Hence, a small attack on the Soviet paint industry should bring the entire Soviet economy grinding to a halt. Obviously that result is nonsense, because destruction of paint plants simply would mean that Soviet finished goods would not be painted.

18. R.U. Ayers has pointed out several additional faults with I/O research. See his *Models of the Post-Attack Economy*, report HI-648-RR (Croton-on-Hudson, N.Y.: Hudson Institute, August 1966).

19. For some leading examples, see T.K. Jones and W. Scott Thompson, "Central War and Civil Defense," *Orbis*, Fall 1978, and J. Pettee, et. al. PONAST briefing charts (no date). For a critique of these models, see Michael Kennedy and Kevin Lewis, "On Keeping Them Down, or Why Do Recovery Models Recover So Fast?" in Desmond Ball, ed., *Strategic Nuclear Targeting*, (Canberra: Australian National University, 1983).

20. Bernard Sobin and B. Bull, *Measurement of Critical Production Capacities for Models for the Post-Attack Economy*, (McLean, Va.: Research Analysis Corporation, February 1970), and also Sobin, *Post-Attack Recovery*, (McLean, Va.: Research Analysis Corporation, June 1970).

21. A number of obvious Soviet economic vulnerabilities come to mind. Recent Soviet industrial layout has stressed economies of scale, and so some Soviet industries are heavily concentrated in a few very high value clusters. It would be possible, under the circumstances, to knock out significant segments of certain kinds of production with relatively few weapons. An example of such a limited economic attack is the counterrefinery one presented in the Office of Technology Assessment report, *The Effects of Nuclear War* (Washington: GPO, May 1979).

22. Interestingly, the Soviet Union built the world's first full strategic bombing force in the early 1920s. In the 1930s, however, it reversed course and redesigned its air forces around tactical missions.

23. Marshal V.D. Sokolovskii, *Soviet Military Strategy*, trans., The Rand Corporation, (Englewood Cliffs, NJ: Prentice-Hall, 1963), p. 260.

24. As Marshal Sokolovskii observed years later, the principal goal of Soviet military operations was "to destroy the main enemy forces in one or two most important sectors," with particular concentration on "the largest enemy formations threatening Moscow." (Ibid., pp. 235, 241.)

25. Ibid., p. 239.

26. Colonel M. Shirokov, "The Question of Influences on the Military and Economic Potential of Warring States," *Voennaia mysl*, no. 4, April 1968, translated in *Selected Readings in Soviet "Military Thought,"* SPC report 584, (Arlington, Va.: System Planning Corporation, April 1980), p. 321.

27. Sokolovskii, *Soviet Military Strategy*, p. 235.

28. Ibid., p. 235.

29. Marshall M.V. Zakharov, "Leninism and Soviet Military Science," *Krasnaia zvezda*, April 5, 1970.

30. Major General M.I. Cherednichenko, "Modern War and the Economy," *Kommunist vooruzhenykh sil*, no. 9, September 1971, p. 20.

31. Colonel A. Lagovskii, *Strategiia i ekonomika* (Moscow: Voenizdat, 1961), p. 32.

32. Soviet commentators routinely stress that any major superpower confrontation would constitute a "decisive clash between the two opposing world socioeconomic systems," in which Soviet combat operations would be uncompromisingly directed toward achieving total victory in the shortest possible time. See Colonel General N. Lomov, ed., *Scientific-Technical Progress and the Revolution in Military Affairs* (Moscow: Voenizdat, 1973), translated by the U.S. Air Force, Soviet Military Thought Series no. 3, p. 137.

33. Sokolovskii, *Soviet Military Strategy*, p. 93.

34. General S. Ivanov, "Soviet Military Doctrine and Strategy," *Voennaia mysl*, no. 5, May 1969, in *Selected Readings*, p. 412.

35. For elaboration on this point, see Benjamin S. Lambeth, "Uncertainties for the Soviet War Planner," *International Security*, Winter 1982-83, pp. 139–66.

36. Cited in Jacquelyn K. Davis et. al., *The Soviet Union and Ballistic Missile Defense* (Cambridge, Mass.: Institute for Foreign Policy Analysis, 1979), p. 26.

37. Major General V. Zemskov, "Characteristic Features of Modern Wars and Possible Methods of Conducting Them," *Voennaia mysl*, no. 7, July 1969, in *Selected Readings*, p. 438.

38. Consider, for example, the assertion that "a correct estimate of the elements of supremacy over the opponent and the ability to use them before the opponent does are the key to victory." (Emphasis in original.) Colonel B. Byely, ed., *Marxism-Leninism on War and the Army* (Moscow: Progress Publishers, 1972), p. 217.

39. Major General Kh. Dzhelaukov, cited in Joseph D. Douglass, Jr. and Amoretta M. Hoeber, *Soviet Strategy for Nuclear War* (Stanford, California: Hoover Institution Press, 1979), p. 75.

40. This hierarchy of target priorities has been extracted from pertinent Soviet military writings and developed by Desmond Ball, *Can Nuclear War Be Controlled?*, Adelphi Paper no. 169 (London: International Institute for Strategic Studies, 1981), pp. 31-32.

41. Marshal V.D. Sokolovskii and Major General M. Cherednichenko, "Military Strategy and Its Problems," *Voennaia mysl*, no. 10, 1968, in *Selected Readings*, p. 388.

42. This is not to suggest that the Soviet National Command Authority would feel constrained from attacking any and all enemy U/I targets deemed important by Soviet war planners. It is only to note that the Soviets will probably not be much inclined to waste re-entry vehicles needed for critical countermilitary tasks by reflexively using them against large numbers of highly exotic U/I targets in a pointless effort to destroy some arbitrary percentage of U.S. economic capacity.

43. Colonel A. A. Sidorenko, *The Offensive* (Moscow: Voenizdat, 1970), translated by the U.S. Air Force, Soviet Military Thought Series no. 2, pp. 88.

44. Cited in Leon Gouré and Michael J. Deane, "The Soviet Strategic View," *Strategic Review*, Winter 1980, p. 81.

45. In this regard, former Defense Secretary Harold Brown expressed the view that "more than 200 SS-9 ICBMs were almost surely targeted against the 100 Minuteman launch control complexes, two missiles to a complex." Text of address to the U.S. Naval Academy, May 31, 1979, pp. 6-7.

46. Major General V. Zemskov, "Wars of the Modern Era," *Voennaia mysl*, no. 5, May 1969, in *Selected Readings*, p. 420.

47. Cited in Ball, *Can Nuclear War Be Controlled?*, p. 39.

48. This argument is developed in considerable further detail in Colin S. Gray, "Targeting Problems for Central War," *Naval War College Review*, January-February 1980, pp. 3-21.

Index

About the Editors and Contributors

RICHARD E. BISSELL is a Professorial Lecturer at The Johns Hopkins School of Advanced International Studies and former Coordinator of Economic Security Studies at the Foreign Policy Research Institute. He is the author of *The U.S. and South Africa: The Erosion of an Influence Relationship* (Praeger, 1983) and is the co-author of *Economic Sanctions in U.S. Foreign Policy* (Philadelphia Policy Papers, 1983).

PAUL BRACKEN is an Assistant Professor in the Department of Political Science and the School of Organization and Management at Yale University. He was formerly with the Hudson Institute and is the author of the *The Command and Control of Nuclear Forces* (Yale University Press, 1983).

DAVID DEESE is an Assistant Professor of Political Science at Boston College and a Research Associate at Harvard University and MIT. Formerly Director at Harvard's Energy and Security Research Project, Dr. Deese has recently published *Energy and Security* (Ballinger, 1981), edited with Joseph Nye.

ROBERT GILPIN is the Eisenhower Professor of International Affairs at Princeton University. Among his books are *U.S. Power and the Multinational Corporation: The Political Economy of Direct Foreign Investment* (Basic Books, 1975) and *War and Change in World Politics* (Cambridge, 1981).

KLAUS KNORR is Professor Emeritus of, Princeton University, where he taught economics and international affairs. Among his many books are *The War Potential of Nations* (Greenwood, 1978), *On the Uses of Military Power in the Nuclear Age* (Princeton, 1966) and, with Frank Trager, *Economic Issues and National Security* (Kansas, 1976).

BENJAMIN LAMBETH is a senior staff member of the Rand Corporation and has published widely on Soviet strategic affairs. He has also served in the Office of National Estimates and Office of Political Research, Central Intelligence Agency.

HERBERT S. LEVINE is Professor of Economics at the University of Pennsylvania. He has taught at Princeton, Harvard and Columbia and is a consultant for several U.S. government agencies. He is the author of *Mathematics and Computers in Soviet Economic Planning* (Yale, 1967).

KEVIN LEWIS is a staff member of the Rand Corporation, concentrating on strategic affairs. He has degrees in operations research and defense policy from Yale University and MIT.

JOHN H. MAURER is a Research Fellow at the Foreign Policy Research Institute, specializing in military history. He has contributed to numerous professional journals and is the co-editor of *Military Intervention in the Third World: Threats, Limits and Options* (Praeger, 1984).

GORDON H. McCORMICK is the Managing Editor of ORBIS and Coordinator of Military Studies at the Foreign Policy Research Institute. He has advanced degrees in economics and international politics and has taught courses on the relationship between economics and national security at The Johns Hopkins School of Advanced International Studies and the University of Pennsylvania.

ALAN S. MILWARD is Professor of European Studies at the University of Manchester Institute of Science and Technology. He was previously an Associate Professor of Economics at Stanford University. His books include *War, Economy and Society 1939–1945*, (University of California, 1977), *The Fascist Economy of Norway*, (Clarendon Press, 1972) and *The German Economy at War*, (Athlone Press, 1965).

MARTIN SHUBIK is the Seymour H. Knox Professor of Mathematical Institutional Economics at Yale University. He is the author of *The Uses and Methods of Gaming* (Elsevier, 1975), *Games for Society, Business and War: Towards a Theory of Gaming* (Elsevier, 1975) and co-author of *The War Game: A Critique of Military Problem Solving* (Harvard, 1979).

MARTIN VAN CREVELD is a Professor of History at the University of Jerusalem. His recent books include *Supplying War: Logistics from Wallenstein to Patton* (Cambridge University Press, 1977) and *Fighting Power: German and U.S. Army Performance, 1939–1945* (Greenwood Press, 1982).